Where Do I Belong?
The Journey of a Country Girl

Astrida Straumanis Ramrath

A Crewel Embroidery Sampler I made with
symbols of my childhood home, Plikeni

DEDICATION

I dedicate this book, in thanksgiving and love, to my family, for their selfless giving and caring – to my father, Karlis, my mother, Anna, and my two sisters, Skaidrite and Ruta.

TABLE OF CONTENTS

ACKNOWLEDGMENTS

I would like to recognize all of the people who, in the course of writing my life's memories, have given me suggestions or have helped me in some way. The list is long. In my heart and mind I am silently thanking them all.

Here, I will mention, in deep gratitude, two contributors, without whom my story could not have developed in the way it has or have reached a point ready to be published.

Sophia Nibi was an instructor for the Needham Adult Education program. I joined her course on Writing an Autobiography. She was a marvelous teacher. As I listened to her lectures, I learned how to write more effectively, to know what was important to say, and how to say it. Even though I had always loved to write, Ms. Nibi gave me wisdom that changed my skills.

My daughter-in-law, Debi Ramrath gave me the biggest gift possible: under her initiative, wisdom, and long hours of editorial work, she gave my story shape and fluency; created a book. Debi has been an angel of unselfish giving and love.

My gratitude goes also to my writing companions, Cindy Helwig, Phyllis Brandt, Eiblis Goldings, Alda Kirsis, among others, who gave me ideas and constructive suggestions at our regular group meetings.

INTRODUCTION

Why do I wish to write my life's story? Why is it important? Two main reasons come to mind.

First, life is a collection of events, places, experiences, meetings, and partings. When one attempts to organize and reflect on one's life, there is potential to gain insight, and to find meaning in it all. How did I begin this journey? Where did it lead me? How did I change? What did I learn? Where am I planning to go? Who were the people who have influenced me, taught me lessons, helped me grow and survive? How did I touch the people around me? How did I influence them? What were the crucial turning points in my life?

The second of the two reasons is, to acknowledge and give thanks to all the people who at one time or another touched my life and were my companions in this journey: my family, my friends, my teachers, or, at times, just a casual acquaintance.

My hope is that I can write with insight and sensitivity, that it will be an enlightening and learning experience for me. I also hope that the reader will come to know me in an intimate way, and hopefully, find my story interesting.

When I was young, very reflective and idealistic, I was determined to make a positive difference in this world. Was I successful and to what degree? I expect to find some answers to these important questions. Since I was born in Latvia, a small country in Northeast Europe, and was forced to leave it at the end of World War II, my past holds many unusual events.

I will try to show the reader what happens when lives are disrupted, and torn apart by a senseless and cruel war. I hope that by writing my story, by reliving the most significant experiences and events, by revisiting the places where I lived or have just visited at some time or another, and by meeting again the people who contributed to my journey in some meaningful way, I will come to see with some clarity what my life was all about.

The contents of this book are arranged in a loosely chronological manner, the essays woven together by time, place, and people who have been significant at those specific periods. No book can fully tell the story of a person's life. This does not attempt that. There are many I love and have loved that receive little or no mention here. I simply have not the ability to do so. Still, they are all close to my heart.

The title of this book, "Where do I belong? The Journey of a Country Girl", is significant. Even though I feel deeply rooted in the soil of my family's farm, fed by the values and strength of my origins, the events of my life have taken me away from my native land and taught me to accept a new country, the United States of America, as my home. Deep in my heart, though, I also belong to Latvia. My soul is Latvian.

A SHORT HISTORY OF LATVIA

"Where are you from?" is a question I often hear when people detect traces of another language in my speech. It seems that many people are unaware about my native country of Latvia.

Latvia is located in the Northeastern region of Europe and is directly bordering the Baltic Sea. Latvia's closest neighbors are Lithuania and Estonia, the other two Baltic countries. Historically, this territory has been inhabited since 9000 B.C.

The early Baltic people, the ancestors of today's Latvians, originally settled the area in approximately 2000 B.C. At that time, the region was famous, as Europe's trading crossroads and the Balts actively participated in this activity. Amber, which was plentiful in the Baltic Sea, was a popular and valuable object of trade all over Europe.

The land bordering the Baltic Sea was fertile, and agriculture became an important source of income and subsistence for the people living in the area. Eventually these Balts formed four individual stable communities, and for many centuries lived a relatively peaceful and productive life.

This charmed life ended in the early 12th century, when the Christian missionaries joined the German traders/crusaders in an attempt to convert the local people to the Christian faith. Out of loyalty to their ancient pantheistic beliefs, the Balts resisted this attempt to have a foreign religion and its rules imposed on them. Eventually, however, they were forced to comply, were overcome, and converted to Christianity.

German crusaders founded the city of Riga in 1201, which eventually became the most powerful city in the region. This period was also significant with the start of the feudal system in the Baltics. Thus, the development of separate Baltic regions of ancient Latvia came to an end. For approximately 700 years, the original people of today's Latvia were ruled by various foreign forces and feudal landlords, mostly of German ethnicity.

But the Latvian people survived, the language survived, and the dream and wish for an independent Latvia prospered. On November 18, 1918, Latvia was proclaimed an independent democratic republic for the first time, and a new era had begun.

This new independence brought freedom of choice, freedom to develop those choices, and the freedom to grow in whatever direction that was important to the country and its people. Latvia grew and developed in many areas: education, research and culture. Learning about past history was of great importance. Economical development, primarily based on agriculture, was strong. Life was good for most people. They enjoyed the political freedom and took pride in their country and its achievements. These good years, however, were relatively short-lived. Outside forces and their politics brought major changes to Latvia. In 1939 a Pact was formed by two governments led by Hitler and Stalin which decided the destiny of Latvia and other Eastern European countries. Based on this agreement, on June 17, 1940, Latvia was invaded by the Russian Red Army, and independence was replaced by a year of severe and brutal Soviet dictatorship. No one was safe. In July of 1941, Germany invaded Latvia and it became a fighting ground for both Russian and German forces, until the end of the war in May, 1945. During the last months of the war, many Latvians left their homeland and escaped to the West in fear of Soviet reinvasion. These fears were justified. Eastern Europe, including Latvia, remained in Soviet control and influence. As the English statesman, Winston Churchill, remarked, "An iron curtain descended between East and West Europe".

In 1991 Latvia regained its independence, and today is a free democratic republic, and a member of the European Union and NATO.

My personal story is also the story of my native country Latvia.

PROLOGUE

It is a sunny and bright morning, June 14, 1941. A new spring day is starting on our farm, Plikeni. I am sitting at the kitchen table with the rest of our farm family having breakfast when Father walks in. His face is very serious and he looks troubled. His eyes are fixed on us as he says: "The Kula family was taken away last night". We all look at him. What does he mean? Where has the Kula family been taken? "I do not know", father's voice trails off. A heavy pick-up truck had come, had loaded the family in and taken them away. Nothing else is known. The Kula's are our neighbors, and also our family's friends. Their twin children, Velta and Zigurds, are our playmates. They are an important part of our community. Only later do we learn what really happened that night. It had been a night filled with terror and pain. It had been the culminating event of a year of Soviet occupation. In June of the previous year, the three Baltic States had been invaded by the Soviet Union, destroying their independence and democratic governments, and imposing a brutal and extremely ruthless and bloody rule over the Baltic people. A year of extreme terror had followed.

During the night of June 14, 1941, 34,000 people were rounded up and deported to the Soviet Gulags, among them more than 4,000 Latvian children, ages infancy to 16. Later, I learn that my dear school friend, Aija Ziedina, and her family, were also part of this tragic group. Aijina, as we all called her, my blond, sensitive friend who was paralyzed as a result of poliomyelitis - how can she survive? My heart aches. To this day, I have a talisman, a tiny porcelain piglet, that Aija gave me at our last parting. What has been her fate?

The story of these deported children was filmed and recorded by a young Latvian film producer Dzintra Geka who strongly felt that the tragedy should never be forgotten and that the children's stories should be heard. After the collapse of Soviet Union, Dzintra Geka traveled to Siberia in search of the still-living victims of this deportation. She located about 400 survivors. Still being afraid of the Soviet system, many of them were reluctant to talk. The terror they had experienced had left permanent imprints within their psyche. Some did not even realize that the Soviet Union had collapsed. Their isolation from the rest of the world was almost absolute. Among the many she visited, however, Dzintra found several who were willing to share their experiences. With a camera and microphone ready to document their stories, the "Children of Siberia" was filmed. The following are the survivor narratives.

A loud banging at the door awakens the family. It is dark, the middle of the night. Strangers, hostile men with shotguns burst into the house. Loud voices urge: "Get ready! Hurry! Why? Where?" Questions never answered. There is total confusion as families try to gather some items of food and clothing to take along. There is no time to think or understand. What is happening to them is beyond all comprehension. It feels like, and is, a nightmare. Outside, a big truck is waiting for them to climb in. A bewildered group of people, huddling together for warmth and comfort. On the way, stops are made at other houses where the frightening scene is repeated and new groups of people join them. The final stop is a railroad station where a long line of cattle cars are positioned, waiting for their human cargo. Truck after truck arrive, carrying people, men and women, young and old. All are unloaded and ordered into the waiting cattle cars.

In Stalin's rain of terror, anyone could be accused of being the enemy of the Soviet system, enemy of the Communist ideology. It was wrong to be educated, to own property, to have some political association with the previous regime, to be part of what was considered a bourgeois class. This group of people needed to be eradicated so that the new world of the proletariat could be born.

At the station, the men are separated from their families. "When will we see you again?" At that moment nobody realizes that for most, this is their very final good-bye. Only much later do families hear that the majority of the men have died within the first year of their deportation. The incomprehensibly brutal conditions in the slave labor camps kill even the strongest of them.

Mothers, grandmothers, infants, teenagers, holding onto their few belongings, chosen in haste, huddle together through hours of uncertain waiting. "What is happening to us? Where are we going?" they ask of each other in confusion and fear. The wagon doors are locked. It is dark inside. The only light comes through one small barred window. The only toilet is a hole in the floor. After a long wait, the train starts to move, slowly, persistently, on and on. People are hungry and terribly thirsty. At times the train stops. At times, they are handed bottles of water. Never sufficient. They all share the food that has been taken along by some. The journey is long. After days and days, after an eternity of moving on, the train reaches its destination. There are many trains and many destinations, all of them in the far away Siberia, beyond the Ural Mountains. There, often in open fields, or next to a river or forest, small groups are removed from the trains and left to wait in uncertain expectation. Eventually the waiting groups are picked up by local functionaries, slave traders, as they are called by the victims, and taken along to do hard labor digging ditches, cutting forests, working in the fields. Older children join their mothers and grandmothers in the long hours of work; the young ones are left alone to fend for themselves.

As I watch the film, and listen and look at the old, lined faces, the pain that is written there, the tears that escape their sad eyes, my heart is filled with grief and compassion. And anger. A child's photo is flashed next to a time-lined, aging face. It emphasizes the terrible waste, the cruel injustice done to these human beings. Sixty years ago, they were children, living among loving people, in a normal home, with father and mother taking care of them. Sixty years ago, their lives held the promise of a good future.

An old, bent woman standing next to a shack that is her home says in a tired voice: "My childhood was taken away. I did not have youth and I don't have old age. Is this how one spends one's final years? I have nothing."

I hear and see her destitution, her total submission to hopelessness.

Another woman in another house brings out a small box. "This is my life," she says. She opens the box, takes out a small piece of fabric with a rose pattern. She tenderly smoothes the faded piece. "It is a part of my robe that my mother took along from Latvia. It is still the same as it was when I left home. This is Latvia to me." Next she removes an item wrapped in an old newspaper. "This is part of my hair", she says.
"My mother had to shave my head because I had lice." She folds open the paper and takes out a golden braid. She wipes away tears from her lined face. "Yes, this is it. My treasures. My life."

My heart fills with compassion and I would like to touch her, wrap my arms around her bent shoulders, and hold her close.

A man stands next to a cross that marks a gravesite. "My mother is buried here. It was a hard life. She did not survive long. I was left alone." He takes a drink from a bottle he holds in his hand. "To wash away the pain", he says. What else can one do when there is not much to look forward to? And there is nothing!

A woman sits at a table in her humble house. She looks up, a gentle smile lights up her face, and she says: "You know, I am glad that I have no hate in my heart. The past is gone. Much has happened. Nothing can be changed."

As story after story is told, I see how they are all similar yet different. The screen shows many old, lined, tragic faces. Then, as a burst of sunlight, a child's happy face smiles at us. Present and past. A story of a promise not fulfilled.

A criminal injury has been done to many lives that can never be erased, never forgotten, and very likely never forgiven. There is no future to any of these lives. No light at the end of the long dark tunnel. There is no road back. The humble buildings far away from their native country are their homes. The gates to their true home, their native country Latvia, are locked. They have no income, no pension. They are old and tired; too old and too tired to begin another journey, even if the journey would take them back to their native land.

"The Children of Siberia" tells only a part of the tragic events of the Soviet Occupation and rule over the Baltic Countries. At the end of the Second World War, Soviet forces reoccupied these countries, forcing many to leave their homeland and to seek refuge in the West. The one-year of terror could never be forgotten. It was hoped, however, that the road home would soon open up, that the Western powers would never leave the once independent countries under Soviet occupation. It was a false hope. The peace treaty signed to end World War II allowed the communist regime to continue its occupation. A trust was betrayed. As a result, many refugees, among them my family, were forced into exile. I will never forget the day, July 28, 1944, when my family had no choice but to leave behind our beloved home and embark on that dark and long journey, our future a vast unknown.

Part One:
The Early Years

"Much of what we experience is not of our choice. We are placed in a certain place in time, with certain travel companions. What shapes and molds us are the moments in history that we are made to face and the people we come in contact and interact with. Much depends, also, on our biological makeup, our psyche. Each life holds an interesting story. The story has to be told to give it visibility."

Astrida

CHILDHOOD

The process of recapturing fragments of the very early years of my life is like looking through a kaleidoscope. I see tiny colorful pieces; visions, intertwining and moving, coming together, then separating as in a dance.

The very first house that I remember as our family's home is a one-story building, called Mezmales. It is a lonely house, and not a very friendly one. There is no greenery around it, and no flowers blooming in the garden. It is unusual for my mother not to plant flowers. To the left and right of Mezmales, stand a few neighborhood houses. In these houses live my parents' best friends.

Another glimpse back. It is a sunny and warm day, probably spring or summer. I am sitting on the front steps of our house feeling content and comfortable. The warm sun lovingly embraces my small body and the world is a safe and happy place. A long, straight road stretches in front of me and vanishes in the distance. At the end of this road is my father's country store. He is there, and all is well with my world.

As I continue looking into my kaleidoscope, in focus comes a cold and calm midwinter day. I am sitting on top of a sled, well-bundled up, feeling warm, safe, and cozy, and enjoying a ride through the woods. My two older sisters, Skaidrite and Arija, are happily pulling the sled, talking, laughing, and frolicking. At times, they look back to check how I am doing, to be sure that I am safely holding on. They should not worry! I am sitting tightly, knowing that nothing really can happen to me while my big sisters are in charge. Tall trees are lining the narrow, snow-covered path. The forest is mysteriously silent, a bit scary, and completely magical. It must be late afternoon because the trees are dark, and the shadows are long.

Suddenly, the sled stops. The talking and laughing also stop. I look up. There, on the path in the silence of the forest stands a deer, so very beautiful and so unexpectedly present. I look at him with the wonder of a two-year-old. Is he real? Or is he a mysterious part of the magical forest surrounding me? My heart jumps in excitement. The deer stands frozen, looking at us. Then, suddenly, it is gone. Was he really there? We resume our journey.

Not all days of my early life hold only lightness. Some have shades of disappointment, like the one when Mother visits her friend Mrs. Bumburs. Mrs. Bumburs lives across the road to the right of our house. Her home, an old farmhouse, seems to have grown out of the earth. It's roof almost touches the ground. It looks ancient and mysterious. Tall trees and pretty flowers surround it. I follow my mother through the door into Mrs. Bumburs's living room. It is a rather dark room with lots of fancy furniture. I am keeping close to Mother, sharing the excitement of the visit, observing the two women as they sit down at a table to share coffee and begin their visit. The conversation is apparently about something that my young ears should not be overhearing, because my mother turns to me and says, "Children should not be listening when adults talk. Go out and play".

I feel rejected and saddened as I leave the room. Across the yard facing me is a long building, possibly an animal barn, and chained there is a big brown dog that angrily barks, jumping and pulling at his leash, trying to run towards me. I am scared and keep a safe distance from the angry animal. I walk around and inspect the yard, enjoy the beautiful flower garden behind the house, and wait for my mother to finish her visit.

A very special moment in my memory is the day of my visit to Father's country store. It is not far from our house, and I can walk there on my own. The store occupies one end of a long building that had once been an inn, serving as a resting place for travelers and their horses. As I enter the store from the bright outside light, the room feels dark. Gradually, people and objects emerge from the shadows. Behind a long counter stands my dad. The wall behind him is lined with shelves that are stacked with a great variety of goods, all the useful and necessary items for household needs of his customers. I walk around the store, observe the people, listen to their talk, and watch how Father helps his clients. As he fills their orders, he writes them down on a piece of paper. On the counter is an ancient adding tool called an abacus, and I watch with amazement as his fingers quickly move the wooden discs up and down the board. I feel very proud of my dad and proud and glad to be his daughter! I enjoy being in the store. It is friendly and lively, and never empty. People come and go, and conversations are always going on. It is a fun place, a busy place.

Later, during the Great Depression, my father loses the store. Times are hard for many people. Many of Father's customers have no money to pay for the goods that they purchase, and Dad fills their orders on credit. Eventually, Father is forced to sell his store because, as Mother remarks, his kind heart could not refuse people in need.

I turn the kaleidoscope and see myself when we first arrive to Plikeni. I am three years old. At first we live in a tiny three-room house, until Father builds our new home; a much bigger house with lots of room for everybody. But it is the small house that holds several early memories. To this day I remember very clearly an episode in the kitchen. The household cat has stolen my dinner, a chicken leg. I try to get it back from him, but he snaps at my finger and holds it tightly between his teeth. I cry out in pain and bewilderment until someone comes to my rescue. A scar on my index finger is a reminder of this painful incident.

My mother's brother, Uncle Edis, has left me with another memory. He is a joker and teaser. One day he asks me: "Do you want to see Riga?" Naturally, I want to see Riga! It is a city with high church towers and big buildings. "Come, I will show you," he invites me. He puts his big palms around my ears and lifts me up. "Did you see Riga?" It hurts. I feel humiliated, angry and disappointed.

It is early morning in late September. The house is wrapped in an intangible air of mystery. Adults are rushing around and I am asked to stay in the kitchen and to be out of their way. I have a feeling that something important is about to happen. Then, a sound of a baby's cry is heard from the next room. "A baby in our house? How can that be?" I wonder.

The door opens, a smiling face appears and a voice says, "A baby sister just arrived for you." A vision of a stork flashes by my eyes. I know that storks bring babies, and certainly must have also brought the new sister. It is a total mystery to me how the big bird got into our house to place a baby into my mother's arms! Later in the day I am invited to visit Mother and the new baby-sister. She is so tiny! Thick black hair covers her small head. She is the smallest person I had ever seen and I view her with tender interest and admiration.

In 1934, our new house is finished and we can move in. It is big, spacious, and beautiful. It smells of fresh wood and newness. In future years it will welcome family and friends in the loving generosity and hospitality of its owners.

From these very early years of my life I have been grounded in the soul of Plikeni. It is my living water, the rock on which I am standing. Plikeni is and will always be part of me.

PLIKENI

Plikeni is the place that will always symbolize Latvia to me. My fondest and happiest memories are tied to the years spent on the family farm.

The name of our farm had some historical significance, but, as far as I remember, no one actually knew where this very unusual name had its origin. Plikeni is located in the region of Zemgale, in the southern part of Latvia. It is considered to be Latvia's "bread basket", the most fertile area of the country. The surrounding countryside is relatively flat with a scattering of farms as far as one's eye can see.

The easiest way to visit our farm would be to take a train to the Berstele railroad station. Then, by following the railroad tracks east for a very short distance, the visitor would come to an unpaved country road. A left turn leads one to a road sign, "Plikeni", on the right. Here begins a long narrow driveway that welcomes the visitor to the very heart of our tree and garden-embraced farm.

In the following pages I will guide the reader through the farm, the home of our family, as it was when we lived there many years ago and as I remember it.

The farm's buildings are clustered together on a small hill, called Plikeni hill. A gravel courtyard is the central point of the farm and its three principal buildings - the animal barn, the harvest barn, and the main house - are easily reached from this courtyard.

My very favorite building is the animal barn. It is the oldest building on the farm, a long field stone structure, probably built a century or so ago. It is divided into three sections that are separated by walls. Each section could stand on its own, similar to a row house.

In the first part of the building, closest to the main house, is the hay barn. The middle section is the largest of the three, and houses the farm animals. At the other end of this long building is the grain storage area.

Each of these three parts has its very own character, its own smells and sounds; its own soul. The hay barn is always in a friendly semidarkness, the only light entering through the open double door. The fragrance of the summer meadows, memories of freshly cut grass drying under the warm midday sun, sounds of a cricket's happy chirps greet all who enter. The hay is harvested in late June and brought here for storage. During the warm summer nights, we bring our sheets and blankets to the barn, spread them over the fresh hay, and fall asleep embraced by its fragrant softness.

From the hay barn, a door leads into the animal barn. One has to step over a high threshold to enter a distinctly different world. The sense of safety and welcome is the first greeting. I love the feeling of warmth and coziness that surrounds me here. The cows, the horses, the pigs - they all are my friends. There is a mutual bond of trust and affection among us. The most exciting times are when a new calf is born or a pig has a litter. The newborn calf's first home is a small cage. The piglets are not separated from their mother since they depend on their mother's milk for sustenance. The animal babies are adorable. They love human contact and love to be patted and held. Just like little children, they enjoy closeness and affection.

A door at the far end of the animal barn leads into the grain storage area. The area is divided into several chambers for storage of the individual crops. A scent of fertility saturates the air here. The room is kept very clean. I only go there when I am sent to fetch things; never to linger around unnecessarily.

A small distance up the road from the main house and the animal barn is a large wooden building where the harvest is stored after being gathered from the fields and before the autumn threshing takes place. In the winter, the barn is used to store farm machinery and tools. For me, this building holds a close association with my father. It personifies his efforts, his successes, his plans; the fruits of his labor.

The main house where we all live has been recently built and is still to be completed. The foundation has been laid for a veranda and the outside walls need finishing. The house has two stories with rough, medium brown walls and a tin roof that shimmers with a silvery light. The rooms still hold the fragrances of fresh wood and paint. On the first floor are the dining and living rooms, our parent's bedroom, the kitchen and the maid's room. Upstairs are our bedrooms. Later on, our father converts the largest upstairs room into a small apartment that is rented out most of the time to anyone who needs a place to live.

Plikeni is not a large farm. To make it profitable, my father grows unusual crops and gradually converts the fields into orchards. Apple trees, pear trees, plum trees, cherry trees, and all kinds of berry bushes have taken over, and at the same time, beautify the land. Spring looks, and feels, like a Garden of Eden; the pinks and whites of the blossoming trees, the fragrances that saturate the warm air embrace our world in a spirit of magic. During the summer months, we can observe the ripening of the fruits and berries until the day comes when they are ready for picking. Every member of the household, including the children, take part in the harvesting. We, the children, similar to the adult workers, receive pay for our labor. I am sure, it is not much, but it feels very rewarding to receive wages for my day's efforts. It gives us an incentive to help out on the farm, even though the work is neither easy nor much fun!

My mother has a love for flowers, and she expresses this love by planting a beautiful garden. Our house is surrounded by colorful plants. The flowerbeds are neatly organized, and during every season, something new and different is blooming there. Father also takes part in the garden project. He grows unusual dahlias and a variety of hybrid roses. Every evening they have to be watered, and it falls to me to do this job. I remember, as I, watering can in hand, walk from plant to plant giving each a refreshing gift of moisture. Facing the animal barn is a group of tall, yellow perennials that bloom all summer long and into the late fall. They are hardy plants and look like yellow daisies and are my favorite; they look happy and seem to reflect the brightness of sun. Behind the yellow flowers grow wild rose bushes, hydrangeas and peonies. This part of the garden is a bit wild, plants growing whichever way without a definite plan or order, but it has a special magic. I love to wander through the garden, imagining and creating my own stories, living in a wonderful world of fantasy.

My two sisters and I have our own garden patches to plant and take care of. Skaidrite, the oldest of us three, is the most creative and imaginative one. Her garden looks like a piece from a miniature Greek classic. My part of the garden is quite ordinary, but I feel joy and pride in my ability to plant and to see my plantings grow and flower.

A large vegetable garden with neat rows of lettuce, cabbage, radishes, cucumbers, tomatoes, all green and healthy looking, slopes down the hill on the east side of the farm. I remember being sent by my mother to pick the first radishes or lettuce in the spring for our dinner salad. What a delicious taste a freshly picked radish has!

A narrow road by the vegetable garden leads down the hill to the cow pasture and to a meadow that extends to a narrow river called "Svitenis". In the spring, when the ice and snow melt, the river overflows, and the meadow becomes a garden of marsh-marigolds, a magic carpet of yellow!

In the early summer, the meadow is covered by an abundance of colorful field flowers that grow among the grass. The grass is almost as tall as I am, and my small body can safely hide in this magical maze. I love to lie down on the soft earth, feeling completely secure and protected, and to look up into the sky above. I remember one very special warm, sunny and peaceful day, when high above me in the blue, completely cloudless sky, I notice a lark flying up to the sun, singing its happy song. To this day, when something is troubling me and I need to relax, I return to that summer day in the meadow and hear again the tiny lark's song of joy.

The river marks the end of our property on the east side. It continues to snake through the countryside, marking the borders of the neighboring farms. Not far from our house, the river becomes wider and deeper. During the summer months, we spend many happy hours wading through its waters. This is where I first learn to swim.

To the north and south away from the main buildings are rows of fruit trees that cover the fields; most are apple. To the west, the orchards continue on both sides of the road and end at a small brook. A narrow wooden bridge crosses the brook, and the road continues on, separating the wheat and rye fields on the right from the cow pasture on the left side. This road leads to the end of the farm's land, meeting up with the unpaved country road and the sign "Plikeni" where the visit began.

On the magic carpet of memories, I return quite often to "Plikeni", walk through the time spent there, revisit the buildings, wander through the orchards, the gardens, the meadows, meet the people who lived there, and the animals they took care of. I am a child again, carefree and innocently happy.

OUR FAMILY

I remember our family as a stable unit, as something permanent and indivisible. Our parents, Father and Mother, and we, three sisters - Skaidrite, Astrida, and Ruta - are joined together in a very special, binding relationship. I never question its stability and never doubt its continuity.

My parents had lost two daughters, Dzidra and Arija, in the early years of their marriage. Dzidra had died in her very first year of life, before I was born. She would have been about a year older than me, had she lived. As a child, I often thought about her and wished that she had not died. We would have been good friends. We were so close in age. Our mother remembered her as a very beautiful baby with big blue eyes. "Dzidra looked like an angel", she often said. I was born shortly after her death. My eyes were small, I had freckles, and I felt rather ugly; a very poor replacement for Dzidra!

Arija, the older of the two girls, became ill and died when she was only seven or, maybe, eight years old. I was then between two and three years of age, and my memories of Arija are very scant and vague. My first memory of her is of a sled ride through the woods. I am sitting on a sled which she and Skaidrite, our older sister, are pulling. It is a very joyful memory. My other recollection is of the day when she became ill. I am with her as she is climbing into her bed. She complains of a tummy ache and asks me to call Mother. Next, I remember a white coffin with Arija lying in it. What had happened to Arija is not real to me. I do not understand death. Arija is just gone. Later on I am told that she had died very suddenly from a ruptured appendix. Our mother would often say that Father's hair had turned white overnight from the shock and pain of losing his child.

Ruta, the youngest of the three girls, is born soon after Arija's death. She completes our family. Our parents give us stability and support, and a strong foundation. To me, father is the ultimate source of strength. I like to compare him to the biblical person of Peter, on whom Jesus built His Church. Nothing bad could happen to me, or to any of us, as long as our father is around and is in charge. I believe that my concept of him is shared by all of us, including our mother. Even though she independently runs the household and is our family's cook and caretaker, Father bears the ultimate responsibility for the family. He is a tall man, not only in stature but also in character. Father very seldom wastes words, but his kind authority is felt by all of us. Where our mother finds it hard to share affection or give praise, Father welcomes our hugs and acknowledges our accomplishments. I enjoy sitting on his lap, feeling safe and loved. I remember his big hand stroking my head and his voice saying, "Well, daughter..." At those moments, my young heart, always longing for affection and signs of love, melts in a warm glow of love and appreciation.

Father is a wise person and a natural leader. Many of our neighbors come to him for advice and help. He is always willing to assist. He is a good administrator and very ably manages our farm with imagination and foresight. Our father, the first-born in a family of three sons, grew up on a large well-run farm. Very likely, our grandfather's influence guided and helped him to become an achiever and a good manager.

Since our father's ancestral farm is not far from our homestead "Plikeni", we visit our grandparents regularly. I am always impressed by the grand house, the fine furniture, and, most importantly, the colored glass windows in the veranda. To me, the colored glass is the most admirable feature in the house, never to be forgotten.

Both of our parents came from families of farmers. Mother,

the oldest of nine children, was born in Vidzeme, which is in the northeast region of Latvia. They met when Father served in the military as a border guard and was stationed near Mother's family farm.

I have a photograph of Mother on her Confirmation day. She stands there in a long, white, high collared dress, her hand holding a Bible; a very pretty girl, her black hair tied back with a white bow. She looks very young, very innocent, and very serious. It must have been easy for Father to fall in love with such a pretty woman!

My mother came from a family with a puritanical Lutheran background, where obedience, humility, and charity were foremost in a person's life. Her upbringing and the values taught her in early childhood color her personality and the way she treats her family and everybody else. She always seems very serious; seldom do I hear her laugh. Mother's generosity defines her; she is a natural giver. Nobody who enters her house goes away without being treated to a meal or at least being offered a chair to sit on and a cup of tea. I recall a gypsy woman who regularly visited our house for handouts. She never went away empty handed.

Our home is always welcoming to anyone who wishes to stay for a few days, weeks, or even months. In summer, our household grows by leaps and bounds as our city relatives and friends spend their vacations on our farm. The front door of our house should have had a sign: "All, who are weary, tired and hungry, please come in, rest, relax, and partake!" It would have been very appropriate.

Although, my mother's acts of charity set a wonderful example for her children and others, her teachings of humility do not always have a positive impact, at least, not on me. Mother teaches us, her "golden rule" to never be pushy, let others go first, "enter through the back door rather than the front", always give others the "bigger half". Humility is good up to a certain point. My mother's "golden rule" does not help me to overcome my natural shyness, meekness, and lack of self-confidence. It takes years and much work on my part to conquer these personal stumbling blocks and learn to value and respect myself.

The positives of our mother's example and teachings, however, far outweigh the negatives, and I have tried to follow her model in my relationships with others. Our mother is an ethical and a good person. "Loving her neighbor" is a natural part of her personality. Even though she very seldom shows physical affection to her children (which I strongly suspect is influenced by her early upbringing), there is no doubt in my mind that she cares for us and loves us, and would give her life for us if that were necessary. I feel Mother's love and caring the most when I am ill or am disabled in some way. Then, she watches over me with great tenderness and concern. It almost makes me wish to be sick more often so I could thrive under her tender attention.

We three sisters are called the "Plikeni girls" (Plikenu meitenes). I do not remember details about our personalities or what we looked like in our early childhood, but a photograph of us as children shows us dressed in similar outfits, standing next to each other. It is a formal picture. Ruta, the youngest, her pretty, gentle face framed by a crown of black hair, looks at me with an almost startled expression in her dark eyes. I stand next to her. I am four years her senior, and a middle child. My hair is much lighter than Ruta's, cut in the same pageboy style. My cute face has a bit of a peeved look. Skaidrite, the oldest, completes the group. She is almost six years older than me and is a tall twelve-year old in this photograph. Her dark hair is parted on the side and pinned back; her pretty face looks seriously at me.

Skaidrite, being the first-born, has the privileges, but also the responsibilities of that special position. I remember her as a "mother hen", always watching over her two younger siblings. She is kind and considerate, and I like to be around her. Even though she is older and her interests are different from Ruta's and mine, she tries to include us in her activities.

My relationship with Ruta has many ups and downs. I remember our frequent fights where I tease her and she responds by hitting me. Ruta tells me now that she felt excluded and neglected by us, the older children, especially during the summer months, when our cousins and friends from the city were staying with us on the farm. It is possible that jealousy causes our frequent battles. When Ruta was just eight years old, a ruptured appendix interrupted her schooling and almost took her life. She spent long, difficult months in a hospital recuperating, and when she finally came home, she was under the very protective and watchful care of our parents. I am sure that the loss of Arija and Dzidra many years earlier moved them to do everything in their power to prevent the same fate from visiting our family again.

I feel very fortunate that I was born into a strong and loving family. Through good and through very difficult and trying times, my family has always been my strength, my support, and my home. My two sisters are my very best friends. We are bound together by our common upbringing, our common values, our strong love for each other and our unchanging loyalty to each other. The moral heritage that our parents left us with is, and has always been, the binding glue that holds us together.

FAMILY GATHERINGS

To this day, my heart fills with a warm glow as I walk back through the many years of my life to the home of my childhood where I meet the people who have helped me to develop and grow, who gave me a sense of security and stability. My early childhood laid a firm foundation on which I would build my life. I am sure that our family gatherings, the days and evenings when we all came together to share, to talk, to read, to solve puzzles or play games in an easy atmosphere of companionship, were important building blocks for this foundation.

I remember our family gathering at the kitchen table for breakfast. The day starts early on the farm. There is not much time for idleness, especially at the beginning of the day. When our father and the farm help come in from their early morning chores, we, the children, are already seated and eagerly wait for the meal to start. Mother is at the stove preparing a hearty breakfast. She very seldom joins us, as she is preoccupied with cooking and serving. I sense that this habit of never having time to share the meal with the rest of the family is a tradition that she has brought along from her childhood home, Jaunzemes. I miss her, and wish that she would leave the stove, sit down at the table, and eat with the rest of us.

There is a warm and safe feeling at these breakfast gatherings. The conversation usually centers on the planning of the day and assignment of tasks. The adults as well as the children have to help with the farm work. Dad assigns chores for the jobs in the fields; Mother is in charge of the household duties and the farm animals. The children are not always eager and willing workers, but we know our place and feel important that we are considered a part of the household and can be useful. Our father, the very center of the farm's unit, is a source of strength and wisdom. He knows what needs to be done, where we all fit in and can be helpful. Our small hands are appreciated and necessary.

Mornings allow no time for leisure and idleness, but evenings are different. In the evenings, our family, including all the members of the household, gathers around the dining room table for supper. Our dining room table is long, stretching from one end of the room to the other. We all comfortably fit around it. After supper is finished, the table is cleaned and the dishes washed, we come back to the dining room table to enjoy our evening activities. We read, talk, or play games. Father always reads the daily newspaper. When there is an especially interesting or important news item, he usually shares it with the rest of us. One such news item I remember very clearly. "Italy has just invaded Ethiopia", Father reads, raising his eyes from the newspaper and looking at us. I think to myself: invasion means war, and war is something dreadful and menacing. War is a horrifying event. A feeling of disquiet enters my heart; I hope that war never, never, comes to our country! Little did I realize on that safe and peaceful evening that the world would soon be turned upside down and our lives totally disrupted by such a destructive war.

After reading his paper, Father likes to join the children in games. One of our favorites is BINGO. It is a good game, because everybody who wishes can participate. All evenings are not alike. Our activities change, however reading is almost always included. At times, we tell stories or solve riddles. Father likes to give us challenging puzzles, such as: "How can you write the number ONE using four ciphers?" When no one can come up with the correct answer, he usually helps us out. I believe that my love for books had its beginning in the quiet evening hours at the long dining room table.

SATURDAY EVENINGS IN PLIKENI

Saturdays on our farm differ from all the other days of the week. The tone of this day is set by our Mother, who, after her marriage and move to her husband's home in Zemgale, brought along many of the traditions from her childhood homestead. With great affection and admiration, she remembers her mother and sets her as an example.

Saturdays in our house involve certain rituals, certain rules, and certain activities. The house gets a thorough cleaning, and the children are required to take responsibility for most of these tasks. The courtyard also undergoes a "facelift". Mother often remarks about how tidy and well kept the yard had been in "Jaunzemes", on her parent's farm, and she likes her own place to look just as nice. Therefore, after we have finished the house cleaning, we take rakes and brooms and rid the courtyard from the week's accumulation of litter and dirt. All misplaced tools and farm equipment left around during the busy workweek are put away in their proper places. From the yard, attention is turned to the farm animals. The cows and horses are cleaned and brushed. This task I enjoy the most. I love to feel the softness of the animals' fur and see the beautiful shine after brushing. Everything and everyone has to be ready for Sabbath evening. In Latvian, Saturday evening is called "svetvakars", which in direct translation would be "the holy evening".

Another one of Mother's wonderful Saturday traditions is to bake bread. Generally, it is a whole wheat bread, very possibly from a recipe that she has brought along from her mother. The most delicious aroma of fresh baked bread spreads throughout the house. That alone is sufficient to make our Saturdays very special and unforgettable. It is an aroma that has followed me along my life's journey and brings me back to the wonderful Saturday evenings in Plikeni.

After all the necessary chores have been completed, usually by late afternoon, Mother sends the children to the garden to cut flowers to bring to the cemetery. It is our family's tradition every Saturday evening to visit the cemetery where our two sisters and my godfather are buried. The cemetery is not very far and we usually walk there, but sometimes Father harnesses one of our horses to make the trip faster.

The cemetery is old with greenery, many trees and many ancient headstones. I like to visit the headstones, pausing, to read the names and inscriptions on them. A narrow path leads up an embankment, where, hidden behind a green hedge are our family's gravesites. It is a very peaceful and quiet place. We observe a moment of silence in honor of the departed. After that, we set to work. The previous Saturday's flowers are removed and replaced by fresh ones. We remove all weeds and rake the golden sand around the graves. Everything has to look neat and cared for. Usually around that time, we hear the cemetery's bell ring. We continue to linger a bit, and sitting on the white wooden bench next to the gravesites, we reflect in silence and enjoy the evening's tranquility. Loud voices are not allowed - it would show lack of respect to the deceased, as Mother says. At times, my thoughts try to penetrate the hard and heavy earth, to imagine my sisters lying there in their small coffins. I never succeeded in unraveling the mystery of death, or to reach my sisters. The cemetery is silent. We feel immersed in its peace, stillness, and tranquility. Then we say "Our Father", touch the tiny white crosses in the final farewell, and depart for home.

Work on the farm ends at five o'clock on Saturdays. Except for the necessary chores of taking care of the animals and attending to their needs. All other work is put aside until Monday morning.

Supper is set in the dining room. Our meal is usually simple: fresh milk, Mother's freshly baked bread, butter, cottage cheese, some cold cuts and tea. Often, the meal includes porridge or a milk-based soup. Around six o'clock, everybody arrives, having taken a quick swim in the river if the weather permitted. All have changed into clean garments and are ready to enjoy Mother's good food and an evening of relaxed and friendly togetherness. Tomorrow is Sunday, a day of rest. After a week of hard physical work, it is a most welcome gift to everyone on the farm.

MY FAVORITE HOLIDAY

Christmas. It is a holiday that stands separate and superior to all the other special days in the year. It has a glow, a warmth, that ties together people in a loving family of humankind. The most wonderful memories of Christmas come from my childhood years. Their light transcends time, and continues to live through the traditions I carry on in my home today.

My Christmas of yesteryear starts with the ending of the school semester. During the school year, I live in Riga with my aunt's family. Therefore, celebrating Christmas also means rejoining my family in Plikeni. A double joy! I say good-bye to my friends and my city family, and with a happy heart, board the train in Riga's main railroad station to travel home. The train is usually overcrowded, mostly filled with students, just like me, who are leaving the city to spend Christmas vacation with family or friends.

It takes about three hours to reach Berstele, the railroad station closest to Plikeni. Cold wind greets me as I step out from the warm train. My legs feel a bit shaky after the long ride. My dad stands waiting next to the station. A warm joy floods my heart. I have come home! Dad takes the small suitcase from my hand and we both walk to the waiting sled behind the building. Smaida, our faithful horse, stands patiently and raises her head as we approach. I stroke her brown, soft face. The twilight of the approaching evening has softened the familiar landscape. Dad helps me into the sled and wraps me up in a warm blanket. "Now, Smaida, let's go", he says getting into the sled next to me and picking up the reins. She obediently starts her trot. Smaida knows the road home. I feel safe and warm, and listen to the soft sound of snow against the sled's runners. We approach Plikeni. The buildings step out from the gathering dusk, as if by magic. The lighted windows beckon a warm welcome. Smaida stops in the middle of the courtyard. I untwist myself from the warm blanket, jump out, and my eyes say "hello" to the familiar sights. "It is so good to be home"! I say, more to myself than anyone else. "Home is the place where the heart is", I remember from somewhere. I know for sure my heart is in Plikeni.

Pre-Christmas time is a busy time for our household. We are all joined together by the invisible ties of special tasks and responsibilities. Our mother puts a lot of effort into preparation for the Holidays: cleaning, baking and other small and large chores are taking up her days. A day is set aside to make a special Christmas cookie - piparkukas. In the morning the long dining room table is cleaned and becomes a work station for us, the cookie-makers. Previously prepared spice cookie dough is rolled into thin sheets, and with cookie cutters, our busy hands carefully cut out stars, bells, angels, hearts and other seasonal shapes. The next step is to arrange them on cookie sheets. When they are full, mother places the pans in the hot oven. Soon the whole house is wrapped in the most delicious aroma!

One of the special tasks for us children is to memorize seasonal poems to be recited on Christmas Eve. We try to pick out poems that can be easily learned and recited with some artistic flare. Ruta's and my special poem is a conversation between two sisters titled: "Little Sister, Do You Know What?" (masina, vai zini ko?). Today, so many years after, I still remember the poem.

The morning of Christmas Eve is filled with busy comings and goings, with happy talks and activities. We all have responsibilities - adults, as well as children. The kitchen is our mother's domain. Wonderful fragrance fills the house from the freshly baked bread, the stove is covered with pots and pans; the evening meal is being prepared. We manage to sneak in now and then to sample some of the delicacies our mother is creating. The air of excitement and expectation surrounds the house and the people.

"Dad, when are we going to get our Christmas tree?" we ask. "What Christmas tree?" he says with a twinkle in his eyes. Soon, we see him walking across the snow with an axe over his shoulder in the direction of the nearby woods. He will bring home our Christmas tree, and we hope that it will be big and tall and beautiful.

To decorate the tree is the children's responsibility, and we settle in the living room to prepare the decorations. Apples and Christmas cookies will be hung on the branches. We use special apples for this purpose. They are small in size and bright pink in color. Our grandfather, our mother's dad, always spends Christmas with us and brings these special apples from his farm in Vidzeme. We attach a piece of thread to their stems and make a loop. With a very fine needle, we carefully pull a thread through the Christmas cookies. The most colorful of all the decorations are the Christmas tree decorative chocolate candies. They are specially wrapped in brightly colored papers with long fringes at both ends and are only available during the Christmas season. Then, we place Christmas candles in small holders that will be carefully and securely placed on the branches for Christmas Eve lighting.

"Here comes the tree!" It is tall with thick branches, and fills the room with the fragrance of woods. "It is beautiful!" we happily approve. Father secures the tree in a stand and we are now ready to transform it into the magical symbol of the Holy Season. First, we attach the candles very carefully to the branches. They have to stand straight and be away from other branches. Then, all the rest of the decorations follow. Eventually, our plain tree becomes a festive messenger of Christmas.

Work on the farm is finished early. The baking and cooking has been completed; the table has been set and displays the end results of our mother's long hours of preparation. It justifies every bit of her efforts. Peace and joy permeates the entire house; good will extends to all people. "Go and invite Mr.

Stengelis to join us", mother sends me upstairs to his small apartment. Mr. Stengelis works at the local post office and lives in the two-room apartment that our father specially built for him when he arrived to work here several years ago and had no place to live. All the members of our household have gathered in the living room around the colorfully decorated Christmas tree. Father lights the candles. As if by magic, the tree becomes a messenger of the heavenly light, the symbol of Christ's arrival on earth. Grandfather reads the Christmas gospel. We sing Christmas carols, ending with the most beautiful of all, "Silent Night". Then follows the children's presentations and giving of gifts. There is a gift for everyone under the tree. The children usually get a book or something to wear. One can almost touch the excitement and happiness that surround everyone present. We wait until the last candle's light flickers out before sitting down to enjoy the dinner.

In Latvia, three days of Christmas are celebrated. The Holiday is spent with the family at home, just relaxing and enjoying the free time, doing only the necessary chores, playing games and reading, or visiting friends and neighbors. The week between Christmas and New Years is practically a long holiday for everybody on the farm.

There are some memories of different Christmas holidays, some of which we spend on our grandfather's farm with much more pomp and circumstance. On those occasions, the family is warmly wrapped into a sled, and our father, holding the reins, leads the horses over the snow covered fields to the house where he was born and grew up in. We have a great time, and spend the whole Christmas holiday there. The adults play cards and talk; the children play games, run around the farm, go sledding.

In my childhood days, I was an avid reader. It still is one of my favorite pastimes. Mr. Stengelis, our upstairs renter, had an extensive library of Scandinavian authors, and he allowed me to read his collection of books, which I did, each and everyone of them. That was a gift that has always remained with me. "Thank you, Mr. Stengelis!"

Swedish author, Selma Lagerlof, wrote a Christmas story

called "The Holy Night". To conclude this journey into my childhood Christmas, I would like to summarize the message of her legend, which, in my view, well expresses the meaning of Christmas:

On a dark and cold night a lonely man walks from house to house asking for a log of fire to bring warmth to his wife who had just given birth to a baby boy. Nobody lets him in. He continues to walk over the empty fields when he notices a bonfire burning in a distance. As he approaches, he sees a shepherd sitting by the fire guarding his sheep. Three vicious dogs lay at his feet. They jump at the man when he comes near but freeze in their attack and can do no harm. The shepherd is a mean person who never has helped anyone, and when he notices the stranger, he throws his sharp cane at the man. The cane stops in its flight and does not harm. The shepherd is bewildered after what he has seen, and when the stranger asks for fire to warm his wife and child, he says: "Take what you need!" The man gathers the hot coal in his bare hands and walks back to the place where he had left his family. The shepherd follows him to find out who is this strange person whom nobody could harm, not even a burning fire. They arrive at an open cave. There, on a bare floor, sleeps a mother and her baby. The shepherd feels sorry for the child, and he pulls a sheepskin from his sack and hands it to the father for the baby to sleep on. This act of compassion opens the shepherd's eyes. He sees angels surrounding the cave; the baby, the parents, all singing in chorus about a Savior who was born this night to redeem the world from sin and darkness, to teach people to love. The shepherd feels great joy, happiness and light. The anger, greed, and selfishness have vanished from his heart. The Christmas miracle has entered his soul and transformed him.

MY GODFATHER, AUGUSTS

I think of my life and the people I have met during my time on earth. Some of the encounters are deep and very meaningful, some are casual, some are sad and troubling, and some are filled with light and happiness.

I wish to meet them again, acknowledge their gifts and say "thank you".

Outside my immediate family, there are many whom I recall as being significant. My Godfather August comes first in mind. I remember him as someone very special in my life. He was my paternal grandmother's brother, a bachelor who, according to my mother, was a rather lonesome person.

To give him somebody of importance in his rather solitary life, they gave me to him as his goddaughter. And I was special to him. This I knew. The feeling was mutual! I eagerly waited for his visits. One of these visits stands especially clearly in my memory. Godfather is coming through the garden. He wears a gray suit and a top hat. This is how I remember him, always formally dressed. I run to meet him. He is carrying three boxes of chocolate. He smiles in greeting and hands me the largest of the three with a beautiful, colorful picture on its cover. He keeps the two smaller ones with no pictures on them to give to my sisters, Ruta and Skaidrite. Yes, I am special. My heart is happy. I take his hand and we walk to the house. The day is a holiday for both of us.

Then, there is a day that holds a very tragic memory. I believe that it is a Sunday morning when the telephone rings. The message it brings is that my Godfather has died. He had been found in a river near his home. I overhear a sentence that he may have taken his own life. He was a forest ranger, familiar with his surroundings, and lived in a close relationship with nature. The tragic manner of his death, I suppose, makes people wonder and question. My six-year-old mind also wonders, and my heart is filled with pain. "If he really decided to end his life", I ask in a silent voice, "how much of a difference did I make? How important had I been to him?" The day is very dark.

The funeral service is held at my grandparents' farm, his sister's home. The day is gray. I feel very sad and lost. I wander around the yard and walk to the building where my Godfather's coffin is, open the door and go in. In the middle of the semi-dark room is the coffin. There he lies, very quiet and distant. I look at his face and hardly recognize him. A sense of great loss and abandonment floods over me.

He is buried in our family's cemetery plot. I, his godchild, will have the responsibility to take care of his gravesite.

(The day we left Plikeni, I gathered a few things together, to take along some of my important treasures - my diaries and few photographs. Among those items was a snapshot of my Godfather. In our long travels and many moves, the snapshot was lost.)

Yes, my Godfather has touched me in a very profound way. Today, I wear the ring that was on his finger the day he died. It was given to me on my Confirmation Day. Thus, he is always close to me. It is my hope, that in some small measure I did bring a special happiness and lightness to his lonely life.

MY GODMOTHER, ELZA

I leaf through an old family album to find a photograph from my godmother's Confirmation day. The picture shows a group of formally dressed people, seated in a garden with my godmother Elza in a white dress. She is holding a bouquet of flowers and is seated in a place of honor in the middle of the very first row. At her feet, in a white cap and white dress, sits a cute baby girl – me.

To pinpoint the time of my first memories of Godmother Elza is very difficult. She has always been a part of my life, and also our family's life. Elza is my mother's youngest sister, who came to live with her after the death of their mother. My mother was the oldest in the family of nine children, and Elza was the youngest, therefore, it was only natural that Mother assumed responsibility over her fifteen-year-old sister.

In the early years, my Godmother, as I have been told, was also my babysitter. Later on, she became my mentor and advisor. She tells me now that she really did not like her babysitter's role because it tied her down. But she performed her task with a great sense of responsibility and, I believe, true caring. Elzina, as the family affectionately calls her, related the following story to me. When I was still a very small child, perhaps not even a year old, I became quite ill. I cried and cried, and could not be comforted. It was obvious that the child was hurting. As Elzina was watching my misery, she wholeheartedly wished that she could take on my pain. At that moment, her head started to ache and her godchild stopped crying. Was it a supernatural event? Or was it a coincidence?

I remember Godmother Elza as a protective angel, almost always being in the background, keeping watch over me, correcting me, instructing me, and guiding me. I believe that deep in her heart she felt a great responsibility for her godchild, Astrida.

After Elza finished college and started to work as a teacher in Bauska, a city not far from our farm, she returned home on holidays and vacations. She was a very pretty girl, with a serious disposition. In her personal relationship with me, at least to some degree, she continued to be a teacher. We often sang together, and she taught me many folksongs. I loved to sing. I couldn't always carry the tune, but my heart was in the songs and in the singing. I do not remember Elza being a playful person. In the early years of my life, our relationship was, and mostly remained, on the level of a child and adult. She was my substitute mother.

Elza married her college sweet-heart Martins Vasmanis The wedding was on our family farm, and I remember it as a very grandiose affair. Relatives, friends, and neighbors were invited and the celebration lasted for several days, as it was customary in Latvia. After the wedding, the young couple moved to Riga, the capital of Latvia, where uncle Martins was a Headmaster of one of Riga's secondary schools.

Our parents placed great emphasis on their children's education and wished to provide the best. The regional boarding school was not up to the standards of Uncle Martins' school and, therefore, Ruta and I were sent to Riga to live with the Vasmanis' family and to attend school there. Thus, Godmother Elza and Uncle Martins became our surrogate parents. I felt that they were overly strict parents and too protective of us. Now, being much older and wiser, I see the wisdom of their actions. They taught me responsibility, the necessity of working hard at my studies and the importance of education. I learned discipline and how to structure my time. The city living and city friends showed me a more sophisticated way of life, a life quite different from the one I had been exposed to on the farm. I was introduced to culture. My godmother took me to theatre, and we attended ballet and opera together. It was all new to me, and it was exciting! In Riga I also attended church on a much more regular basis than it was possible in Plikeni, and that left a permanent mark on me. I remember these services with great affection.

Years passed. Summers were spent on our family farm. Tante Elza and her two children were with us when, because of the Russian advancing forces, we left our farm and eventually, also, Latvia. Uncle Martins had been called into the military service and we had no news of him. He never rejoined his family after the war. "Lost in action". Elzina was now left to carry on the responsibility of raising her two children as a single parent. She never wavered from this responsibility, and raised two wonderful human beings, our cousins Astra and Aivars. Since we have always lived in a close proximity to each other, our relationship with Aivars and Astra is more on a level of a sister and a brother.

After my mother died, Godmother Elza's importance in my heart and my life became paramount. Even now, in the twilight years of her life, she is always there with her support, love and advice. I love and cherish Elzina, and am immensely grateful for the rich gifts I have received from this wonderful woman. As a golden thread, our relationship weaves through the fabric of my life.

UNCLE MARTINS

What are my first memories of Uncle Martins? When did I first meet him? I vaguely recall his visits to Plikeni, when he came to see my godmother Elza. He was very handsome, I thought. He also sang beautifully. Elza and Martins's courtship had started in Jelgava, where they both attended the Teachers' College and fell in love. Their wedding was a grand affair, and Plikeni was where it all happened on August 8, 1936. The memory of this very special occasion is very clear and alive. From this day on, Uncle Martins became a part of my life.

Usually the weddings in Latvia were not a simple affair, especially country weddings. And the preparation for this specific marriage celebration took about a week: lots of cooking, baking, arranging, and rearranging. A professional chef, who made sure that all was done properly and according to the menu requirements, was hired. I remember the happy scurrying around in the kitchen, my mother in the middle of it all, directing and supervising. I sneaked in and out, just to be able to feel the excitement and not to miss the mood of something very special in the making. What a responsibility it must have been to carry off this huge happening!

I believe that the wedding was the biggest event our farm had ever seen. All Elza and Martins's relatives and friends from all corners of Latvia, and most of our neighbors were invited to partake. Among the hundred plus adults, there were at least sixteen children. I still have a photograph that shows the children lined up by their size, standing in the courtyard. As I remember, the wedding celebration lasted about three days, maybe even longer, because some of the guests had covered long distances to attend and enjoyed the opportunity to visit with relatives and friends. In many of the photographs from that occasion, I see Elza and Martins, young, beautiful, and happy. Martins' family was very gifted, musically, and they shared their talent with the rest of us. The days were wrapped in music, songs, and lighthearted happiness. Uncle Martins' favorite song was "Kur tu skriesi, vanadzini?"(Where are you flying little hawk?), a familiar Latvian folksong.

After the wedding, Elza quit her teacher's position in Bauska, a small city approximately 20 km from Plikeni, and moved to Riga, where Martins taught grammar school. When their son, Aivars, was born the following September, my mother and I visited them in Riga. That was my first train trip to such a far away place, and the excitement of this journey still vibrates in my heart. The apartment was spotless, and to a country girl from Plikeni, exquisite! Elza, was an immaculate housekeeper. One morning, as I was blissfully munching on a piece of delicious store bought bread in her living room (in Plikeni we only ate Mother's baked bread) and she pointed to the many crumbs I had dropped on the shiny polished floor. The living room was then "off limits" to any kind of food. I quickly learned that life on a farm gave me lots of freedoms but did not teach me city manners.

My encounter with Uncle Martins on this visit was very limited. He was kind, but I was too shy to keep up a conversation. Everything was so new there, not enough time to feel relaxed and at home.

I came to know Martins on much more intimate terms a couple of years later when my parents decided to take me out of the local boarding school and transfer me to the grammar school in Riga, of which Uncle Martins was now headmaster. Scholastically, this was a much better school, and since their children's education was high on our parents' priority list, the arrangements were made for Ruta and me to live with Elza and Martins during the school year. They had a spacious apartment on the top floor of the school building. In the mornings, we just had to run down a flight of stairs to enter our classrooms. During the war, the school building was used by the German military, and our classes were held in another school building quite a distance away.

My relationship with Uncle Martins was a rather formal one. Because he was first and foremost the headmaster of the school I attended (and sometimes my teacher), it was only natural for me to feel somewhat inhibited and restrained in his presence. He loved music and relaxed by playing his violin or sitting in front of the small organ in the living room, improvising melodies on its keyboard. I enjoyed listening to him. During those moments he evolved from a formal and slightly feared schoolmaster into a person of warmth and sensitivity. Now, I wish that I could travel back to that period and meet Uncle Martins as he really was, to get to know him without the distance of age and position. In my mother's eyes, Uncle Martins belonged to the community of saints. He was a person of great moral stature: honest, just, highly principled with a great sense of duty and fairness. He was also deeply religious. I felt that. His faith was part of his personality.

My memories of Uncle Martins as a schoolteacher are several. The most distinct one is from our morning prayer sessions. Before classes started, all the students gathered in the main auditorium where Uncle Martins read from the Scriptures. We all said the "Our Father," and a hymn concluded the short gathering. He also was the choral director and conducted the school choir. For a short time, I was a part of this choir. The only class that Uncle Martins taught me was religion. And from here comes my only real negative memory of him. One day, as the class started, I was asked to recite the day's assigned lesson. I had studied, knew the subject matter, and thought that I gave a good presentation. He marked my answer "C." I was deeply hurt and felt that he had treated me unfairly. To get a "C" in religious studies was very unusual. At home, I mentioned to Godmother Elza what had happened and how hurt I was. I think her opinion was that Uncle had overdone his sense of fairness. Because I was a relative, he did not want to play favorites. Favorites! My goodness! I just wanted and deserved to be treated equally, I thought to myself.

On August 25, 1940, Astrina joined the Vasmanis family. I have a feeling that she was the "apple of her father's eye." Both children, Aivars and Astra, were the center of their parents' life and received a lot of attention and love. Since Uncle Martins' obligations at the school took most of his time, Elza was the one who was responsible for the household and the children's needs. In the evening, we all gathered in the kitchen for supper. Astra's favorite spot was her father's lap. She sat there twirling her blond hair with her index finger, and paid very little attention to food. Eating was not her favorite activity. One of the "musts" for all the children was a spoon full of cod liver oil that Elzina religiously handed out to us. I held my nose to avoid the taste. A piece of rye bread also helped to quench the unpleasant flavor. After supper, Ruta and I went to our rooms to finish our homework. I remember studying, often late into the night to complete all the homework assignments.

The war continued. We all felt the hardships that this conflict imposed. Food was rationed, and many packages from Plikeni went to the city relatives to supplement their rations. In 1943, the Germans instituted a draft, and a Latvian division was formed with a strong agreement that these troops would fight only in the Eastern front against the Russians. In the spring of 1944, Uncle Martins received his draft papers. I believe that this turn of events was a shock to everyone, especially to Elza.

It was a Sunday afternoon in late June, 1944. Uncle Martins had come to Plikeni to say "goodbye" to his family. We were all gathered in the dining room. A cloud of sadness surrounded the small group. Martins was wearing his military uniform. He was standing in a doorway leading to our parents' bedroom, somewhat separate from the rest of us when his beautiful tenor rose up in a song: "Balta roze mana darza zied" (A white rose is blooming in my garden). It is a soldier's farewell to his beloved before he leaves for war to defend his fatherland. It tells about a white rose, which he takes along from his beloved's garden. This rose follows him into the battle and eventually, when he is killed in combat, covers his lonely grave in a distant place. The sad melody and the words lingered around us, in us. The heaviness only slowly lifted. The gentle Sunday evening held a dark foreboding.

We saw Uncle Martins one more time when we visited him in Kaucminde where he was stationed. He accompanied us to the railroad station. Little Astrina, in a white dress and a white bow in her blond hair, held on to her father's hand happily skipping along his side. Those are my last memories of Martins. He never rejoined his family after the war. His fate was never openly discussed or, possibly, never known. He joined the many thousands of fallen heroes who tried to save Latvia. But the destructive forces that engulfed his country no measure of heroism could stop.

Like an avalanche, the Soviet occupying forces and the subsequent regime, swept away the dream of independent Latvia, and sent Martins family, along with thousands of others into exile, destroying what had been built up in the years of independence.

Many years have passed since the summer of 1944. In 1992, Latvia regained her independence and is now in the process of rebuilding the country. I look at Martins' children, Aivars and Astra, and see in them his enduring legacy. Aivars, who not only looks like his father, also carries his father's values in his own life and personality. And like the white rose that her father once sang about, Martins continues to live through Astra's love and admiration.

SNAPSHOTS OF NEIGHBORHOOD FRIENDSHIPS

Many happy and joyful memories are brought to mind when I think of my childhood friendships. My early friends were mostly children from the neighboring farms. Our parents also enjoyed friendly relationships, therefore our visits were most often family events.

My parents were especially friendly with two neighborhood families, the Andreika family who lived a short distance away, and the Kula family, whose farm was a stone's throw away from us, on the other side of the Svitenis River that snaked through and separated our lands. Both of these families had children that were close in age to ours. We exchanged infrequent visits with the Kula family's twins, Zigurds and Velta, and a much closer friendship tied us to the Andreika's three girls, Velta, Aina, and Modra. The reason for this was that the two families had three daughters each, and that made the children's visits more fun.

Our parents, in general, were quite restrictive about our visits, but we did not usually meet much of an objection when we asked for a permission to walk the short distance to Andreika's farm for a playtime. Our visits there were always filled with spirited joyfulness and with lots of games and laughter. Mr. Andreika was an amateur photographer, and I still have a group photo of us, the six girls, dressed in Sunday outfits. I treasure this photo as a keepsake from times past, a reminder of the carefree times we enjoyed together.

The Andreika's farm, with its gardens and buildings, was a wonderful place to run and hide, a place where our childhood exuberance and joy could be freely expressed. The farm was perfect for our favorite game, hide and seek, finding hidden corners and secret places to disappear without being easily found. Much running and carefree joy was part of our outdoor games. Tag was another fun game. It allowed us to run and chase in frivolous gaiety. Our visits usually ended indoors where we told stories, made pictures or played board games. Those were the times before television, computers, and digital games. We needed to use our imagination to invent playtime activities.

In my memory album, the visits with the Andreika's girls are times of good fun and sharing. Our friendship was warm and affectionate.

Another very special memory for me is also tied to the visits with the Andreika family. Here, I met a boy, a relative of theirs, Ilgonis. Ilgonis became an object of my dreams and captured my heart and imagination. He was a very friendly boy, a couple of years older than me, and at our meetings paid a special attention to me. Our relationship never evolved into anything serious, but in a dreamlike way Ilgonis significantly influenced my life, and the memory of him was often the light that guided me through many difficult periods. I cherished his memory. Ilgonis lived in my heart, walked beside me, and held my hand.

Ilgonis was present at all Andreika family celebrations. At our first meeting, he invited me to a dance when I really did not know how to dance yet. Was I thirteen then? I wore my first dress shoes with heels, and felt awkward, but also very grown up, when Ilgonis gently guided my unsure steps around the dance floor. It was a new experience for me to dance with a boy and to be that close to one.

Our next meeting was at the wedding reception for Velta, the oldest of the Andreika's daughters. It was Christmas time. The air was crisp and cold as my sister Skaidrite and I walked through the snowy fields from Plikeni to attend the wedding party at their farm. We entered the pleasantly warm house filled with happy people and were greeted by sounds of joyful celebration. Among the guests, I noticed Ilgonis, and my heart gave a happy leap. Later on in the evening, we were sitting side by side holding hands. Did we talk and what did we say? Words were not important. I was intensely aware of being next to Ilgonis and feeling blissfully happy. In my young and innocent heart, this evening's magic made a permanent imprint. I fell in love. How did Ilgonis feel about me? Did he dream about me as I dreamed and thought about him? I will never know for sure. I sense, though, that his heart was also touched by this tender, dreamlike magic that so completely filled mine.

The following summer, which was our last summer in Latvia, I met Ilgonis two more times. These were chance meetings, happenings planted by the kindness of fate. The first meeting happened on a beautiful, warm Sunday morning in June. Tante Elza's family and I were taking a train to pay a visit to her husband Martins, who had been drafted into the German military and was temporarily stationed in the village of Islice. The train proceeded at a slow pace, and I stepped out on the platform to more fully enjoy the warm day and the passing landscape. There, standing on the platform, was Ilgonis. To meet him so suddenly and unexpectedly was a total but a very pleasant shock. We exchanged a few words. Our meeting was too much of a surprise for both of us. Soon I had to get off and wave good-bye to Ilgonis. This chance meeting changed my day. I walked on a cloud, filled with love and dreams.

About a month later, Ilgonis and I met again by chance, and for the last time. My sisters and I were attending a neighborhood dance. Ilgonis was also there, and he invited me to a dance. I felt blessed to be so close to him, feel his arm around my waist. Shortly after this dance, we left, and I never saw Ilgonis again. It is significant that our relationship had started with a dance and also ended with one. Through the years, I often wondered about Ilgonis. What happened to him, what was his life like, what joys and pains did he experience?

I got my answer on one of my trips back to Latvia as an adult when I visited the Andreika's farm and talked with Modra. She was the only family member still living there, and managed the farm. I asked Modra about Ilgonis. She said, "Ilgonis? Yes, Astrida, he was such a gentle and kind person. He unfortunately had an unhappy marriage and eventually divorced his wife. His life ended very tragically. He was killed by a falling brick from a house which was undergoing renovations." How very tragic!, I thought. If only I could have met Ilgonis! He was still alive in 1975 when I visited Latvia for the first time after leaving the country in 1944. How I wish that I could have been able to see him, talk to him. From the object of my dreams he would have become a real person. But, it did not happen. It was not meant to be.

Today, as I turn the pages of this album and relive the joy and innocence of the times we spent together, I inevitably come to the last page, when our relationship comes to a sudden and unexpected end. It is a day in late July of 1944 when we leave our farm to escape the approaching Russian forces.

TAKING LEAVE

The morning promises a warm and sunny day. It is midsummer, July 28, 1944, and I can feel the pleasant touch of a gentle breeze as I open the kitchen door and run down the steps. Usually my dad has given me tasks for the day: weeding the garden, raking the hay, picking berries, or any other of the many jobs on the farm. Never is there a lack of work, and the children are always busily helping out. However, this day is different. There are no tasks lined up for us.

As I look around to observe and absorb the day's beauty, a distant rumbling can be heard. It sounds serious and menacing. We all know that the Russian forces have broken into Latvia and are approaching. We also know that it means saying goodbye to our farm, to the safe and happy life we have enjoyed.

"Could it really be today?" I ask myself.

I walk down the path, noticing the rich colors of my mother's flower garden, the roses my dad had just planted this spring, the dahlia plants that I water every evening. Everything looks so very perfect. I continue through the cherry orchard. The berries are red; we have just picked some yesterday. What about tomorrow? I walk by the lilac bushes. Their blooming season is over. Will I be here to enjoy their wonderful fragrance next spring? My heart gives a sudden, sharp pang. I run to the big barn, where the hay and the grain are stored. It is my favorite place on the farm: it smells of safety and fertility. It symbolizes all the riches of the earth. How can I leave this behind? How can I take it with me?

I continue through the apple orchards my father had planted. I touch the trees, their round, perfect fruit. In all of this is part of my heart, a piece of my childhood, my care free days. Wherever I look, I notice something familiar and special. "Why had not I seen this before?" I marvel. The answer is right there - because I live in it, it is me! And now, I am in danger of losing the very foundation of my life. "No!", my whole being is crying out in pain and disbelief. I have to see my friends, the animals! I run to the pasture. The children each have a pet cow, their very own. Mine is Guce. Her coat is dark brown and shiny. Her big, round eyes are looking kindly at me; the black, slightly damp nose pushes gently at my sleeve expecting the usual treat. I give her the apple I have brought along from the orchard, kiss her smooth cheek, pat her back. "Guce, I love you!" A hard lump is filling my throat. My head is hanging low as I slowly walk away.

I pass the vegetable garden: all in perfect order, no weeds, just beautifully lined up rows of cabbage, peas, carrots, tomatoes, everything ready for picking! Who will pick them?

I walk back to the house. There are many questions in my head, in my heart. "What will we do? Are we really going to leave our home?" Nothing is definite. Many unknowns. Hope against hope that life would go on as before, undisturbed. Days filled with routine tasks, predictable.

Father is very quiet. I can sense the heavy burden of the decision he is facing a decision that would change our family's future.

The distant menacing rumbling continues, disrupting, contrasting the sunny peacefulness of the perfect midsummer's day.

I see Mother going through the house, trying to select some necessary clothing and food to take along on the road if the final decision is to leave the farm. I run to my Godmother Elza. She looks concerned, worried. Only a few days ago she had said goodbye to her husband, Uncle Martins, who is being sent to the eastern front to fight the Russian forces. No doubt she is wondering about his whereabouts, his safety. She and her two small children, Astra and Aivars, are spending the summer on our farm. Our Aunt Marija and her two children are also part of our extended farm family. Her youngest, Maija, is just a tiny baby, born only this April. Uncle Edis, her husband, is in Riga, working.

Our farm is a welcome summer vacation place for all of our city relatives and friends. It is a happy place, a busy place usually. But today, the whole house is saturated by a dark cloud of concern and worry.

I go upstairs to my room and look through my personal things, letters, photographs, my diaries. I love to record my daily activities and feelings. My diary holds my heart's secret thoughts and longings. Letter writing is also something I enjoy. All this is kept in a drawer in my room. Should I hide these very personal witnesses to my inner life? Can I take them along if we leave? Slowly I separate from the rest the most important photographs and letters, and my diaries. These I will take with me. The rest I tie together securely with a string and go to look for a good hiding place.

Next to the hay barn is a structure where leftover building materials are stored. Deep under the boards I hide my treasures. They will be secure there until we come back. And we will return, I am sure of that!

The day slowly turns towards evening. Father has made his decision: we are going to leave. A call is made to his brother's house to encourage his family to come along with us. Juris, dad's brother, has already left, leaving the responsibility of his wife and two daughters to our dad. Aunt Mice and our cousins, Gunta and Aija, will join us. A meeting place is arranged.

We all rush around, getting together some of the items we would need on the road. As I look back now, I think that even our dad believed that within a very short time, probably in two weeks, the Russian army would be forced back and we would be returning home. Little did we realize that we would never return, that this is our very last goodbye to Plikeni, to the way of life we have known.

Mother sends my younger sister Ruta and me into the garden with a basket to pick some berries to take along on the road. The warm, friendly sun basks our bodies as we are bending down to gather the red and black currants and gooseberries. Many times we have picked berries; this is one of our regular jobs on the farm. However, today all seems to be different. A sadness, a sense of nostalgia, fills my heart. The bushes are covered with an abundance of berries, and soon the basket is filled to the brim. We place it next to a bush to pick it up later, before the start of our journey. In the haste of getting ready for the departure, however, nobody remembers the berry basket. Is it ever discovered? By whom and when?

In the late afternoon, in addition to the rumblings from the front in the south, a heavy, intermittent sound is heard to the northwest of us, where the city of Jelgava is. "The Russians are bombing Jelgava," father says quietly. As the day fades and evening approaches, the skyline turns crimson. The ancient, historic city of Jelgava, founded in 1265, is burning. The night sky reflects its tragic fate. Later we learn that most of the city was destroyed that night by fire and bombs.

Jelgava's burning emphasizes the urgency of our departure. Two horses are harnessed to pull two wagons so that all eleven of us, and some of our belongings, plus foodstuff, can be fitted in. We do not have the luxury of a car or a truck. Very few farms are equipped with motorized vehicles, and Plikeni is not one of them. It is deep twilight, close to ten o'clock, when we finally start our sad and long journey. I stand in the courtyard, glance over the fields and gardens, which are wrapped in darkness, the friendly buildings now diminished in the evening's gentleness. Not far away, hidden in the night, are all the animals that we are leaving behind. So much pain and heaviness hang over the small group of people gathered around the wagons. What do our father and mother feel? They are leaving behind their home, the accomplishments of years of planning and hard work.

Skaidrite's good friend, her dog Krancis, is dancing around, ready to come along. But he has to stay behind. Helene, our maid, would be in charge of the house, would take care of the animals. For a while, until we return, she would try to manage.

And then, finally, Maija and Koza, our two trusting horses are encouraged to move. With a slow trot they start to pull the heavy wagons. We wave "goodbye" to Helene, who is holding onto Krancis who restlessly barks and pulls in his attempt to follow us. There they stand, a woman and a dog, until the distance and darkness erases them from our view. Our road ahead is distant and dark, our future is hidden in a vast unknown.

ON THE ROAD

We ride through the night. The glow of the burning city of Jelgava lights up the night sky. The darkness, through which we are riding, seems to grow even darker against this unnatural glow.

Finally morning comes. We have reached the place where we would meet with Aunt Mice and her two daughters, Gunta and Aija. From this point on we will all travel together. It was only yesterday, even though it seems years ago, when the decision was made to leave our home to escape the approaching Russian army. The one year of Soviet terror, which we experienced only four short years ago, sets us all in panic when we think of another Communist occupation. Nothing, nothing could be worse than that! We cannot, we would not ever, live under the Soviets again! The terror, the inhumanity, the death, the deportations are still alive in all of us. This is exactly why our parents have made this difficult decision to leave our home and save our family.

We have stopped next to a river. I get off the wagon, stretch my stiff legs and look around. It is early morning; I can see the sun's first rays in the eastern sky. Our two horses, Maija and Koza, are resting next to the wagons. I take out my notebook and try to put in words my feelings, the night's travel, the morning's unreality. What has happened? Am I the same girl, the same Astrida as yesterday, as the years before yesterday? No. Something in me is broken. The departure from

Plikeni, the night's journey has changed my very soul, has taken away my childhood, my innocent perception of life and the world. I have lost my home. Plikeni has always been the very center of my life, my security. I had felt safe and happy there. During the winters, when I was away at school in Riga, it was Plikeni I always returned to. So eagerly did I wait for these homecomings. To where will I return now? An invisible wall stretches between me and Plikeni. All has changed.

A short time later our aunt's family arrives. It is time to move on. The weather is kind, the sun is warm. We pass farmers as they gather their crops in the fields. It is the end of July, the height of gathering season. All seems normal and natural for them. We move on. As we travel, we are joined by other families, who, like us, are on the move to escape the Soviets. Finally, after a few days of travel we reach a farm of an acquaintance in Vidzeme, in the northern region of Latvia. There we decide to stay for a while and wait. The hope still is that somehow the Russian invasion would be stopped and we would be able to return home. August passes. We wait. The front comes closer. Instead of retreating, the Russian army keeps penetrating our land. There is no other option: we have to move on. It is mid September when the two wagons are again packed with our few belongings and the horses harnessed. Our journey continues. We reach Riga, the capital of Latvia, in the late evening. The city has an air of impending doom. Soldiers wander the streets, refugees are resting their horses in the courtyards, many buildings are abandoned, empty. We ring the doorbell of our uncle's apartment. Nobody answers. I cross the bridge over Daugava to visit my school friend Irene Abols. Irene had spent her summer vacation in Plikeni and only a couple of weeks ago had left the farm to return home to her family. They also are ready to leave. With heavy heart I say goodbye to Irene and her family. Next, I stop at my school, Namejs' Grammar School (Trešā Nameja Pamatskola), which is home to me during the school year. My uncle is the headmaster of the school, and I live with his family during winters. My room feels very empty, without life. I look at some of my belongings, taking from the shelf one of my very favorite books, "God, Nature, Work" (Dievs, Daba, Darbs) by Anna Brigadere. In this book the author describes her childhood lived in a loving relationship with nature, God and work. I feel close kinship with little Annele, her feelings and experiences. As I open the door to leave, I glance back to the silent, empty place. The years seem to blend together into one painful remembrance and farewell.

We spend the night outside with our horses and wagons. Early in the morning our journey is resumed. We would go to Kurzeme where our Aunt Marija's family lives. This is the region furthest west, and also furthest away from the front line. We would wait there. We still hope for a miracle. To leave Latvia is our very last choice.

The roads are filled with refugees, just like us. All moving west. The days grow shorter and colder. We stop at roadside farms in the evenings to ask for shelter. Some welcome us in to stay for the night, but many do not. The country has changed. People are nervous, scared of war, of the unknown future. We are tired of being on the road and of homelessness. We can sense the same weariness in our horses. They have pulled the heavy wagons for days now. They need rest. Often we sleep in barns. At times, the night sky is the only roof over our heads. It is late September when we finally reach our destination, the homestead of Marija's family. Since there is not enough room for all of us to stay, father finds lodgings for the rest in the neighboring farms. The area is very beautiful. Forests, hills, and lakes adorn the countryside. Since the weather is mostly warm and sunny, our stay in Kurzeme is relatively relaxed and pleasant. We help with the farm work whenever we can, gather berries and mushrooms in the surrounding woods.

Very suddenly and unexpectedly we receive a notice that we must leave. The front line of direct combat is almost on us. Hurriedly we pack our wagons again and early the next morning set off for the very last part of our journey. Marija is staying behind. She has promised her husband, Uncle Edis, who has remained in Riga because of his work responsibilities, that she would wait for him. Marija is standing at the roadside in the dim morning light holding a green pitcher of water in her hand. Her last gesture of kindness and love is to offer us a drink. In sadness we hug and say goodbye. Many years will pass until we see each other again.

Our destination this time is the port city of Liepaja. There is no hope left; we have to leave Latvia. I remember the last part of our journey as a cold and rainy one. Before reaching Liepaja, we spend several days in a large barn close to the city. It is raining and the water drips through the leaking roof. I turn sixteen here. I am cold and miserable. The feeling of hopelessness and loss saturate our days and nights. It is a relief when finally Father brings us the news that arrangements for our departure have been made.

On October 22nd, 1944, we arrive in Liepaja. The day is sunny. In the evening, we plan to board a ship that would take us to the German city of Danzig. Everything seems like a bad dream. How could all this have happened to us? Our two horses, our companions and friends, what would become of them? The city is filled with refugees, all waiting to leave. Foreign powers are invading our country and forcing us to leave our homes, our familiar and safe way of life.

It is very late evening, close to midnight. We are in the harbor with our belongings, standing in line to board the ship. Suddenly an air raid siren sounds. Almost simultaneously with the siren, small clusters of light, called "Christmas trees", which the bombers drop to see their targets, light up the sky. The Soviet planes are overhead. I start to run. I am panicky. The streets are empty and silent. The only sound comes from the planes overhead. I run into a side street and see a person standing at a gate beckoning to me. What a relief! I enter the air raid shelter just before the bombs start to drop. The shelter is filled with people. The ground shakes after each buzzing. There is a whistling sound from the bomb, as it makes its way down, before impact. I pray. I feel suspended in time, just waiting and hoping. It seems an eternity before the "all clear" sound is finally heard and we can leave the shelter. Where is my family, my parents, my sisters? Where are Aunt Elza and her children? I am all alone in the dark night, in the burning city. Somehow I manage to retrace my steps to the ship and find my family standing there waiting for me. I am overwhelmed with relief and joy.

The process of boarding the ship continues. Our turn comes. For the last time, we pat our horses, our faithful companions. We stroke their gentle faces. My heart aches. We all feel the pain and loss, and also guilt. Now, when my thoughts turn back to that time, I have to think of our father and his feelings. How much strength was required of him, how painful and difficult were all the decisions he had to face and make? He was a man of few words, but of great wisdom and strength. He was the rock we all leaned on. But what did he really feel? How deep was his pain?

We spend the remainder of this night on the ship in the harbor. It is no luxury liner! The ship serves as a troop transfer and provides transport for the refugees after dropping off its military baggage. We try to sleep on the floor, but mostly just rest. We are too tense to sleep. I write in my diary. My final goodbye. (Now, when I re-read these entries, I feel again the pain of this much, much younger Astrida.) My promise is to never forget Latvia, to return there, to always love this very dear country of my birth.

Morning arrives. We stand on the deck and look over the harbor buildings. We see Maija and Koza. They stand there alone. We have abandoned them! The ship starts to move. My eyes are glued to the two horses. The colorless, stark buildings behind them seem to emphasize their unknown future and our fate. The ship slowly picks up speed; the distance between the land and us widens, grows ever larger. Maija and Koza, Latvia, slowly disappear from our view.

ON FOREIGN SHORES

From Danzig to Berlin

All seems to be gray: the morning, the world, the people. We have arrived at the German port city of Danzig. (After the war, the Baltic Port of Danzig was given to Poland, and its name changed to Gdansk. Almost fifty years later in this city, the Solidarity movement led by Lech Walenssa was born. This movement, and the events that followed, laid ground for the collapse of the Communist regime and rang in the birth of democracy in Poland.) The voyage from Liepaja, after leaving Latvia, has taken about twenty-four hours. We have been lucky; the Soviet planes did not attack our ship and we have avoided running into mines. Many ships have been destroyed in the Baltic Sea during these short crossings. Yes, we are fortunate to be alive. We have reached these foreign shores safely; it is something to be thankful for.

As we disembark, a bit dazed and stiff, we huddle together, waiting for our few possessions to be unloaded. Father is the one point of strength in our common weakness, and we all rely on him. He will know; he will lead us through! However even his choices are limited. We are guided to a standing train, which will take us somewhere. Where? I do not remember if anyone informed us of the train's destination, or of what would happen to us from then on. We are refugees at the mercy of a foreign government and forces. We are joining the vast river of homeless people who flood the war-torn Europe. We come from all directions, from many countries, and speak different languages. But we are united by our similar fate and understand each other's suffering.

There is one very pleasant surprise while we are waiting for our train to move. My godmother, Lonija, and her daughter, cousin Ilga, who had left Riga a couple of weeks ago, suddenly appear at the train. They had decided to remain in Danzig, at least for a bit, and made it a habit every morning to come to the port and wait for the ships to arrive from Latvia, just in case someone they know would be on board. This chance meeting lifts our spirits. The land seems friendlier, the morning brighter; we are not totally alone here.

Our train starts to move through a seemingly peaceful countryside. It is late fall, the fields have been ploughed. We pass farms that look prosperous and untouched by the events that are closing in on them. I think of our peaceful life only a very few months ago. So suddenly and abruptly all had changed for us. These people still live normally, as if the world were still a safe and normal place. We know better. Looking out through the train's window on the passing countryside, my wish and hope is that nothing will change here, that somehow, the people and their peaceful life will be protected from the war's destructive flood. Late in the afternoon our train stops at the very pretty town of Schneidemuel, southwest of Danzig. That night, we sleep in a military barracks.

The following morning, my sister Skaidrite and I take a walk through the town, and this short but pleasant excursion removes some of the dreariness of our days and makes us feel almost carefree, lighthearted. We meet laughing children, playful and happy, shoppers going in and out of stores, houses with gardens and curtained windows. This is their town. They live here, work here, laugh and cry here. They belong. Yes, it is good to belong, to be at home!

Our stopover in Schneidemuel lasts a few days. We sleep in barracks on three level bunk beds, on bare boards. At least we are inside and relatively warm, but always, always hungry! From then on the hunger never leaves us. There is never enough food to eat. Our menu consists of a dish of gray soup with a couple of vegetables floating in it. It is served to us on a regular basis, maybe once or twice a day, with a slice of dark bread and a very thin piece of margarine. (Only the end of the war ended this constant feeling of never having enough to eat.)

Our next stop is Berlin. This once beautiful city, with samples of grand architecture, prewar center of culture and art, was mostly destroyed by the Allied air attacks. Our temporary home is in Friedrichsfelde-Ost, a suburb of Berlin. Again, we live in barracks; we are cold and hungry and often scared. The sound of sirens announcing another air raid is so frequent that going to the shelters for protection is a daily and nightly routine. Our family lives in a large room, sharing it with four other families. My godmother, Elza, with her two children, Astra and Aivars, are part of our family; we are one. Nothing has been heard from Uncle Martins. He is in the eastern front helping to resist the advancing Russian army, and we hope that he is safe and unhurt. In some strange and blessed way, all of us are joined together in one community. We have become one large extended family, caring for each other, supporting each other, carrying each other's sorrows, and sharing a few small pleasures. Our mother brought along from home a sack of dried rye bread. This is a lifesaver! We share it with everybody, and I truly cannot remember anything tasting as good as these slices of dried black bread!

Rows of three-level bunk beds line the two walls, leaving a space between them for a long table and a few chairs. I spend my days reading and writing in my diary. They bring me back to the winter days in Berlin, cold, hungry, and scary days. At times, the mail comes. I receive letters from my cousin Ilga. They had left Danzig and are living in the northwestern part of Germany. There, they should be safe from the Soviets!

Christmas comes, our first Christmas away from Plikeni. Someone somewhere finds a branch of a fir tree. We set it in a bottle of water, decorate it with a few wax candles, and light them on Christmas Eve. The sound of carols fills the large barren room and our hearts open to receive the message of this Holy Night.

Not all days are totally dark and dreary. There is also a sprinkling of some joy and lightheartedness. I remember an evening around New Year's Eve, 1944. Skaidrite, our oldest sister, decides that we should entertain the people in our barrack. We find some scarves, wrap them around our waists, holding others as spreading wings, and whirl through the large semi-dark hallways in happy dance steps, visiting the surprised audiences in the adjoining rooms. We are applauded and greeted with smiles and very soon our performing group grows in numbers and gaiety.

The cold winter, the ever present hunger, and tight living quarters bring in many diseases. The children, especially, become ill. There is hardly any medicine available, medical help almost nonexistent. Two of our community members, Mrs. Ezers, a middle aged lady, and a little seven-year-old girl, Elga, die. I especially remember Elga. She was a shy, pleasant, quiet child. Elga never looked very healthy. Thin and pale, she wandered around the room or sat close to her mother. She was an only child. When she contracted pneumonia, she had no resources available to conquer the disease.

Our small cousins, Astra and Aivars, are very ill with whooping cough. Their thin bodies are wrenched by the extended coughing spells.

Long, hard days are followed by restless nights, often spent in the air raid shelters. When will this end? And how will it end? What will happen to us? These questions are in everybody's mind, haunting us. Berlin has become a dangerous place, a target of relentless air attacks. Also, the Russian forces from the east are continuously moving west. We have to get out!

Then a miracle happens. We receive a letter from a good friend, Mrs. Lula, who lives in the southern part of Germany. She invites us to join her family. Mrs. Lula has found a place for us, a shelter for refugees in a large monastery in the town of Neresheim where we can stay. What a relief! Our father begins to investigate the train schedules, to find the easiest route out of Berlin.

On February 3rd, we are ready to leave. We pack our belongings a day before our scheduled departure. Early in the morning Father, Tante Elza, Skaidrite, Ruta, and I take our few belongings to the local railroad station and board a train to the center of Berlin. Mother, Astra, and Aivars remain in the camp. Anhalter station is one of the major stations in Berlin from which trains are running to the southern part of Germany. We take our luggage to the Anhalter Station to have it checked in before our next day's departure. As we are waiting on the railroad platform to be helped, the familiar air-raid siren announces an approaching attack.

"Here come the Americans", our father remarks. American planes usually attack during the daylight hours, are more destructive than the British, and always leave behind much devastation and ruin.

We leave everything on the platform and run down the steps into the subway station, which is directly underneath the main building. Subway stations also serve as air-raid shelters. The attack comes almost simultaneously with the siren, and before we reach the lower levels of the U-Bahn, the whistling sound of approaching bombs is heard. In our rush down to the shelter's safety, we get separated from each other. Elzina and I are together, and we position ourselves next to a big pillar somewhere in the center of the large underground area. We find out later that Ruta, my little twelve-year-old sister, is all alone during this time, surrounded by strangers for company and comfort. None of us know where the others are. The bombs fall, and fall, and fall. At least one is a direct hit. The lights go out. Dust fills the air. People scream. Time seems to stretch into eternity. We stand motionless; just waiting. Finally, with a tremendous relief, we hear the "all clear" sound.

The masses of people start to move toward the exit. Elzina and I join them. As we climb the stairs and reach the street, an unforgettable sight comes into our view. It seems like the whole city is in flames and ruin. Buildings are torn apart, some revealing rooms still with furniture in place, just as their occupants had left them. We see injured and confused people, a city in shock. There we stand, looking around, trying to comprehend the reality of this unreal, unacceptable destruction.

We find the rest of our family. It is decided that Father would go back to where we had left our belongings, hoping to find them still there; and the four of us would walk back home. No trains are running; the railroad tracks have been destroyed. We walk, as in trance, among the burning buildings. The bombing and the resulting fires have created strong winds. It feels as if I am in the middle of a dream, looking into an unfamiliar world, observing, but not part of it. We keep on walking. Towards evening, it starts to rain. I am immensely tired. My feet hurt. In a deep twilight we reach our camp. We have walked about six hours, covering twenty-six kilometers. The barracks have also received some hits, but nobody is hurt. All are glad to see us, and we are tremendously happy and relieved to be back.

Berlin to Neresheim

A couple of days later, we are able to leave Berlin, traveling in trains with standing room only. As we are moving south, more and more people join the already overcrowded train, climbing in through the windows when the doors could not be opened. People, refugees, are running away from the war, from the continuous bombings, searching for a safe haven, a place of relative calm. At times we have to change trains. When there is a wait, we do some sightseeing to pass our time. The sights we see are almost impossible to describe. Most of the cities are in total ruin, destroyed by bombing attacks. (If there is a building still standing, I do not recall that. All I can remember and see from this journey is the immense destruction and devastation -- the horror, the senselessness of war.)

Our destination is the town of Neresheim in the region of Wuertemberg in southern Germany. Neresheim is untouched by war. A scattering of forests, rolling hills, and meadows surround it. It is situated in the middle of farming country where the farmers live in villages in close neighborhoods. Life is peaceful here. The undisturbed pastoral beauty of the region is such a contrast to what we had observed in the previous months that seeing it is like looking at a beautiful surrealistic painting.

A country road leads up a hill to a large complex of buildings. An iron gate opens to a spacious courtyard that is encircled by buildings from all sides. An impressive looking castle dominates the building complex. Circular stone steps lead up to a double oak door. This grand castle is going to be our temporary home. It is a tremendous improvement over the cold barracks we had left behind in Berlin. The buildings and the surrounding woods and fields belong to a monastery. I suspect that in times past it was a home of German nobility. An old, very beautiful baroque period church stands to the left of the castle. This church is the very center of the monastic life. Its doors are always open for regular services and prayers. All are welcome to enter. Every morning a service with music and singing is held and we are invited to attend. I remember that our mother is a frequent visitor to the church. She is a deeply religious woman, and during these troubling times she seeks, and also finds, comfort there. I often join the services or just visit the church. I enjoy the peace and the silent mystery of this holy place.

The monks are farmers and have beautiful gardens which we can only observe through a large fence. They are off limits to us, refugees. We are allowed to visit the barns and pat the animals. We can also take walks through the surrounding woods and enjoy their silence and tranquility. I have always loved woods and would pass many of my days wandering through their shadowy comfort. Hidden among the trees, not very far from the monastery, is a small chapel shaped like a pagoda. It is old, partially neglected. Very likely, it was built during the time when the noblemen occupied the property.

During my stay in Neresheim, two interesting things happen. One day we hear about a family in a neighboring town who is looking for someone to live in their household and be a playmate and companion to their daughter. This seems like a good opportunity for me to live outside the refugee complex and, possibly, have sufficient food to eat. I take the job and move in with the Mateus family. They live in a small house, Dr. Mateus, his wife, and Amarillis, their daughter. Amarillis is a spirited happy girl. We enjoy each other and have a very good time together. I have my own room. What luxury! The only problem is that I am terribly homesick and miss my family, but on weekends I can visit them. (I still remember the snow covered fields that I literally flew over just to rejoin my family. The happiness I felt just to be with them!) Even though the food at the Mateus household is better, the portions are very small, and my hunger never disappears. I want to be home! My father agrees that it would be wiser for the family to be together since the times are dangerous and the future unknown. So I say goodbye to my newfound friend Amarillis and move back to the castle.

The second significant event is a very painful one. We have heard that some of the people from our camp have gone to the neighboring village farmers to supplement their meager food rations. My little sister, Ruta, and I decide to do the same. "Perhaps we could get some bread, eggs, or anything! Just something extra to eat!" It is a sunny, beautiful spring morning when we start off on our journey. The village we go to is about five kilometers away, a charming place. The small houses seem friendly, inviting. We gather up our courage and knock on the first door, then the second, the third. The doors that open to us close very quickly when our request is heard. The answer is "No". Some doors never open. It is the most humiliating experience. I am a beggar! A good-for-nothing! To ask is very difficult, but to be refused is immensely denigrating. (To this day I find it very hard to ask for anything, to walk in the shoes of a beggar. The scars of this sunny, beautiful spring day have never left me.) As we make our way back home, empty-handed and empty-hearted, I sit down on the roadside to rest, feeling desolate and tired. If only I could erase this day from my life!

By April of 1945, the war begins to wind down. The collapse of Hitler's armies is expected. It is April when the Americans occupy our region. Some soldiers come up the hill, but nothing really changes in our daily lives. Only one marvelous thing happens after the Americans arrive. On my way down to the village, I find a whole loaf of white bread by the roadside. A whole loaf of bread! A miraculous find. I take it back to the camp and we have a feast!

THE WAR HAS ENDED!

It is May 8, 1945. Clear blue sky covers the green earth. The sun generously spreads its warmth and light over Neresheim. Godmother Elza and I are sitting on an embankment near the monastery, enjoying the beauty of the surrounding landscape, relaxing in the warm gentleness of the spring morning, when the news of the war's end reaches us. Germany has capitulated! Peace! Peace! The sound of this magic word seems to ring like a clear joyous bell over the fields, the hills and villages, over our world, entering our hearts. Can we really believe it? Is it true? What will it mean to us? Will we be able to return home? Will Latvia be free again? Free from the occupying forces of the Russian army, free to shape her life, her future? Many questions need answers. We will leave them for tomorrow! Today, on this perfect spring day, we will allow the sound, the joy of peace to totally envelop us. Peace is a magical word. The word that says: "You will not have to be afraid again! No more alarms, no more air-raid shelters, no more bombings! No more killings and destruction!"

Great relief, as well as sadness, comes along with the news: sadness about the senseless destruction, the tragic loss of human life, and sadness and concern about Latvia. The Russians have taken over the country. Kurzeme was the last bastion that the Latvian 19 Division and the Germans still held. Now the fighting has stopped. What would happen to all the soldiers who are now captives of the Russian forces? (I do not remember if we even tried to imagine how the German nation felt. Yes, I wonder now, how did they react to the news? Their country was ruined. They were the conquered nation; their fate would be decided by their enemies. But Hitler's reign was over! For many Germans, that was a much welcome and long awaited change.)

Much of Europe is destroyed, peoples displaced from their homelands, countries devastated by war, overrun by occupying forces. An order had to be established, decisions made concerning not only Germany, but also all the countries in Eastern Europe. A series of conferences are held. At the meeting held in Yalta (Crimea) in early 1945, Roosevelt, Churchill, and Stalin decide the fate and the borders of postwar Europe. Here, the fate of Latvia is sealed; the Baltic States would remain in the control of Soviets. As Churchill later remarked, an iron curtain is drawn across Europe, separating the free world from the enslaved one.

We feel betrayed and abandoned. How could it be that the Western leaders are ignorant of the evils of the Communist regime? Don't they know that Stalin is a soul brother of Hitler? That he runs a regime of terror and rules over an evil empire? That Russia is covered with slave labor camps? That innocent people are imprisoned, tortured and starved to death? In Ukraine alone, 6,000,000 farmers were destroyed by starvation. Don't they know that deportations of whole groups of people are a common practice? We know the truth, and we can tell, but nobody seems to be interested in listening. That Russia is a vast killing field, is nobody's concern at this point in time.

With the war's end, the administration of the refugees in Germany becomes the responsibility of the occupying forces. Since we are in the area held by the Americans, the American military takes over our management. The first act that directly touches us, and is of great concern to us, is the establishment of a Military Screening Board. This Board's responsibility is to relocate all refugees back to their homelands. Our father is repeatedly called for questioning. He has to persuade the Board that we cannot and do not want to return to the Soviet-occupied Latvia, that we left our country because of the Communist invasion. Also, we would most probably never reach Latvia and, as traitors, would be sent directly to one of the slave labor camps in Siberia. Finally, these screening sessions end and we are allowed to stay.

SUMMER IN KOENIGSBRUNN

In early summer, it is announced that we would have to leave Neresheim. All the Latvians will be transferred to Koenigsbrunn.

Koenigsburnn is a small valley town in the heart of Wuertemberg. Our new home is a settlement of barracks on a hill directly overlooking the town. The barracks may have been used to house the German military at one point or another, or could have been a site of a summer camp. All the buildings are one story high. The enclave is embraced, almost protectively, by a beautiful, silent forest, creating a fairyland effect for our camp. Green lush moss covers the earth under the tall trees, like a soft carpet.

I have mostly pleasant memories from the summer we spend in Koenigsbrunn. The nightmare of the previous year is over. The feeling I have is as one would experience after a severe, violent thunderstorm. When the rain stops, the dark clouds part, and the sun's warmth and gentleness touches the violated earth. A great sense of relief, and a freedom from fear overwhelms us. And, at last, we have more than enough to eat! We all gather in a large common dining room for our meals, with plenty of delicious food. I am sure that we all gained weight, at least I did!

One of the big events of the summer is our gymnastics spectacular, which we present to the camp residents and the American military. In the photographs taken of us in our white gymnasts' outfits, we look happy, graceful, and fit. It is a carefree summer; a charmed summer. We pick mushrooms in the forest, go for hikes, play games, do some fancy embroidery work on fancy ladies' underwear, though it is not clear to us who would be wearing these very fine, hand embroidered garments.

I have a favorite spot just outside the compound - a big rock sheltered by towering trees. Many an hour I sit there in my own safe world, reading, writing in my journal or just dreaming. From early childhood on, dreams have been my favorite companions, so this is a good place, and a good time, to allow my heart and my head to weave wonderful fantasies about a future, that for all of us, is hidden in a great unknown.

A couple of interesting events happen this summer. The American military, stationed in the Koeningsbrunn village, invite the women from our camp to their dances. A "pick-up truck" (I use this term with a bit of a chuckle) comes up the hill to our camp, gathers the waiting girls and women, and drives us down to the village hall for these socials. I attend two of them. I don't remember having much fun there. I feel quite awkward and out of place. At the second dance, as I am standing forlornly in the doorway leading to the big dance hall, a pleasant looking soldier comes up to me. Instead of inviting me to dance, he asks: "What is a nice girl like you doing here?" I just stare at him, dumbfounded. A sudden realization dawns on me: we are being used. We are here to entertain, not to be entertained! This is the last "ball" I attend.

Another amusing incident happens on Sunday morning. I have gone down to the village to get the morning paper. On my climb back to the camp, which leads uphill through the woods over a steep winding path, I suddenly hear somebody following me. A young soldier soon catches up with me and starts to say something. At first, since my English is rather limited, I cannot understand what he is asking. Then I realize; "Chocolate? Chocolate?" is what he is offering me. I run up the hill as fast as my legs would carry me! This encounter puts a stop to my solo trips to the village.

During our stay in Koenigsbrunn, my little sister Ruta,

becomes ill with what is called the "infection of lung glands". She is placed on a strict bed rest regime and thus is deprived of the beautiful summer days that the rest of us are enjoying. Just when our lives have entered a much easier and happier path, it must have felt like a real punishment to her to be confined alone to a dark room.

(Reflecting on those times, I asked Ruta recently; "How do you remember our summer in Koenigsbrunn?" "Terrible!" she said. "I missed out on everything! Remember the beautiful mushrooms we used to pick in the woods? I had so much fun before I was placed under the house arrest! And who has ever heard of "lung glands?")

Koenigsbrunn is only a temporary home for us. A more permanent location is explored and eventually found by the UNRRA (United Nations Rehabilitation and Reconstruction Adminstration) which has taken over the responsibility of the refugees, or Displaced Persons (D.P's) as we are now called. Regretfully, we have to say "goodbye" to Koenigsbrunn and the carefree days we have enjoyed there. After the difficult and painful events of the preceding year, life in Koenigsbrunn had given us a chance to recoup and rebuild our mental equilibrium. Our home for the next four years is going to be in Esslingen am Neckar. A new chapter is about to start in our lives.

YEARS IN ESSLINGEN

Esslingen is an old picturesque town in the Neckar valley, hugged by sloping grapevine and hillsides covered by apple orchards. It is approximately ten kilometers east of the city of Stuttgart, in southern Germany. The river Neckar separates the old part of the town, which dates back to the Middle Ages, from the more recently developed community. Our home for the following four years would be in this new section of Esslingen.

It is late afternoon on a day in October, 1945, when the buses carrying us, the newly created population of people, the "Dee-pee's" (Displaced Persons), arrive in Esslingen from Koenigsbrunn and stop at a large complex of long four-story buildings. These are gray concrete apartment houses, seemingly cloned from one mold. Our family is directed to a house at 24 Stuttgarterstrasse. Tante Elza and her two children are settled close by in a similar building at 2 Tannenbergstrasse. We are spared all decision-making. Everything has been planned for us ahead of time by UNRRA's officials. All we have to do is just move in and feel at home. And at home we feel! After a year of wandering and moving around, we finally have our own place; two rooms our family can call our own, plus a kitchen and a bathroom we will share with the Berzins' family, who will occupy the other two rooms in this four bedroom apartment. We feel like kings! Our very own place!

Before our arrival, these houses have been the homes of

German families. What has happened to them, I wonder, and where have they moved? How do they feel about us, the foreigners, who displaced them from their familiar surroundings? Not too kindly, I am sure. It is ironic that we, who have lost our homes, are the cause of other people's displacement!

The administration of the Latvian community in Esslingen is the responsibility of the Latvians themselves. A chief administrator is assigned to supervise the overall function of the compound. He also serves as a liaison between the "Camp" and the IRO (International Refugee Organization), which has replaced the UNRRA as the organization responsible for the post World War II refugees. Most of the residents find some form of work. Our father is in charge of the Food Distribution section. Tante Elza also works there. My sister, Ruta, helps out in the publishing office after school.

My days are mostly taken up by schoolwork, since the curriculum in the gymnasium (high school) is very intense and requires substantial effort and time spent in studies. My favorite subjects are literature, language, and history. I have always loved to read. As soon as I learned how to put letters and words together, books became my best friends, and reading my favorite entertainment. Mrs. Cebere, who teaches us language and literature, is an excellent teacher and guides me into the world of enlightened reading. I learn to analyze, distinguish bad from good literature, understand poetry and styles of writing. She teaches me to think! She is instrumental in my intellectual development. If I had to pick one person out of my gymnasium years who really made a difference to me, I would choose Mrs. Cebere. I owe a lot to this wonderful lady!

Esslingen soon develops into a large and very active Latvian community. We have lost Latvia, the country we belong to, our homeland. Forces, stronger and more powerful than we, have ripped us away from the land of our origins. But no force or power can rip from our hearts the love, the spirit, the culture, and the traditions which embody Latvia to us. The spirit will survive! From the ashes of crushed hopes arises, like a golden phoenix, a new renaissance of Latvian cultural, intellectual, and spiritual expression. Esslingen becomes "Little Latvia", the capital of the Latvian refugee population. Many of the exiled intellectuals, writers, artists, theatre people, and teachers become part of this community. A Latvian gymnasium and grammar school are established to enable the children to continue their education. Ruta, and later our two small cousins, Aivars and Astra, attend the grammar school. I study in the gymnasium. Soon, a Latvian newspaper is published and books are printed. A number of professional actors who have escaped from Latvia establish a theatre, producing high quality and well acted plays. My sister, Skaidrite, joins the theatre, first as wardrobe assistant, and slowly she works herself into playing small parts. Her life's dream has always been to become a stage actress. Here, she is getting professional training and a chance to perform under the guidance of Mr. Veics, a famous actor and stage director from Riga. A well-known men's double quartet "Tevija", originally also from Riga, finds it's home in Esslingen, as do other musicians. Cultural life is very active and rich. Concerts, art exhibits, and folk festivals are frequent events.

A beautiful church, the South Church, just a short walk from our "Camp", is made available to the Latvians. Every Sunday, services in Latvian are held. In this church, I am confirmed on May 16, 1948. It is a sunny bright Sunday morning when 60 young people, in a procession, walk up the hill to receive their First Communion and become members of the Latvian Evangelical Lutheran Church. It is a meaningful and important day in my life, forever etched in my memory and heart.

When a folk dance group is formed, I join it. Dancing has always been my very special joy, and here I have a chance to dance my heart out. My childhood dream had been to become a ballerina. Well, that was, and does remain, only a pipe dream. But for a short period of time, I take ballet lessons and also learn ballroom dancing. In dance, I can express my soul. It is a feeling of total release, total immersion in what is me.

Our folk dance group participates in school events, folk festivals, and is quite frequently invited to give performances in other parts of southern Germany to Latvian refugee communities as well as American military audiences. We usually travel together in rented buses. These trips blend us into one lighthearted, congenial family. Time is passed in singing, joking, laughing. Innocent fun is the hallmark of our travels. An added bonus is the chance to see new sights, and visit interesting and historic places, such as the "crazy" King Ludwig's castles in Bavaria, Hitler's' underground hideaway in Berchtesgaden, and the grandiose, magnificent Alps!

We are young! Because of our recent experiences, we probably have an increased need to enjoy the present moment; the importance of just "being" is intensified. Thus for me, the years in Esslingen are relatively carefree and good. In addition to the many exciting trips, I enjoy wonderful walks on the banks of the Neckar River, or joining friends on short excursions in the scenic Wuertemberg countryside. Whenever there is a reason to celebrate we do. Often, we sing and dance through the night. One early Sunday morning, on my return home from a night of fun, I meet a teacher who has assigned extensive work for Monday's exam. She comments; "Is this how you are doing your studying? See you tomorrow in class." Naturally, there has been no time to study, but I am determined to show her that pleasure does not interfere with my schoolwork. I spend most of Sunday cramming in the assigned texts and pass the next day's test with flying colors.

I form close friendships. Especially deep and lasting ties develop between my school friend, Ruta Karklins, and me. We dream together, we walk together, and we play together. We share secrets and expectations. We support each other's dreams and share the heartache of falling in and out of love. We are young together, and there is excitement and magic in our friendship. When Ruta and her family leave Esslingen to find a new home in Australia, a light seems to go out in my life. It is a gray morning at the Esslingen railroad station when we say our goodbyes. I feel immensely sad. Esslingen is never the same without Ruta.

At all times, the love and security of my family gives me a shield of protection. My greatest concern is to do well in school, to study, and to pass exams. I never believe that the road home will be closed forever. Our stay in Germany is only a temporary respite; soon, an "all clear" will sound and we will pack our bags and return to Latvia and resume our normal life. That is how I view the situation. I am sure that more rational and objective minds do see our fate and future so clearly.

Now and then a shipment of white boxes arrive, marked in large black letters, "CARE". Also, from the United States, come crates of clothing, shoes, and other household items. They are all piled up on long tables, and we go through the piles looking for something useful. I inherit a pair of pea green suede shoes and a hot pink woolen dress. Under Skaidrite's creative fingers, that dress becomes my best party dress!

Soon, a black market develops. I can sell a bar of chocolate for fifty German marks! I spend most of my money on books, which are printed in Esslingen from previously published Latvian editions, and later new works written by the exiled Latvian authors. (I still have many of these volumes. At times I leaf through their yellowing pages. A musty smell, a memory from a long-gone age surrounds me. Ghosts from times past come to visit.)

One by one, the men who have fought in the Eastern Front against the Soviets rejoin their families. Some never return, lost in action. Nothing is heard from Uncle Martins. What has happened to him? All sorts of rumors keep circulating, but no substantial confirmation of his fate. For Tante Elza and her two children, this is a time of hope and despair.

The year 1949 brings many significant changes to our family's life. In February, Skaidrite, my beautiful and vivacious sister, marries Juris Anderson. Juris is working for the American military as a translator. He often joins our social gatherings, where he meets Skaidrite and they fall in love.

In June, I graduate from the gymnasium. The last month before graduation is spent in serious study for the final exams. The exams are difficult and require long hours of study, taking over my days and even nights. Coffee beans help to keep me awake during the night hours. Finally, the day of the last exam comes and goes. We, the graduating class, are overwhelmed with the joy of achievement as well as a sense of freedom. We have left behind five years of hard work and one month of torturous brain exercises! To graduate from a gymnasium is indeed an honor. On the day of graduation, I feel proud and happy when my name is called to receive my diploma. The next step will be university, I hope.

As time ticks away and our hope of returning home with it, a decision has to be made about our future. Where to go, where to start a new life? The United States, Canada, Australia, and South America have made special quotas to allow the D.P's to immigrate to their countries. However, in order to resettle there, sponsors who will guarantee that the immigrants work for a year, as well as assume general responsibility for them, are necessary. In addition, a stringent health screening is a must before entering any of these countries. Many are rejected because of health reasons.

My mother's cousin, Elmars, has already immigrated to the United States and is working for an old Yankee family near Boston. This family, the Merrills, own a horse farm in Virginia and have offered us jobs there. We are ready to move on. Tante Elza and her children will follow later. Since Juris is still employed by the Military, Skaiddrite and he have to remain in Esslingen, at least for a while.

In late August, 1949, we say goodbye to Esslingen. The day of our departure is very painful for me. It feels like I am leaving behind not only Esslingen, but also my youth, my carefree and happy days. I cannot stop crying.

The last person I say goodbye to is Vala (Valentina) Vasilevskis, my friend since grammar school days in Riga. We hug, cry, and promise to keep in touch, and will hopefully, meet again in the United States by the same lucky chance that had brought us together in Esslingen.

We board a train for Bremenhafen, a port city in northern Germany. From there, a ship will take us to America.

CROSSING THE ATLANTIC;
A JOURNEY TO NEW BEGINNING

The final chapter of my life as a displaced person in Germany is coming to a close. The last days in Esslingen, the very sad good-byes to my friends, the tears, hugs, and promises not to forget to keep in touch, are now a part of the final "good-bye" to Germany. Over these few years since we left Latvia, Germany has become to us a home away from home, an island in the sun. Now, a ship is waiting in the Bremerhafen Harbor to take us across the Atlantic Ocean, to a new life in the United States of America. I feel excited, but also scared. Another journey into an unknown is opening before me.

It is a large troop transport ship, "S. S. General Muir", onto which I step in the late evening of September 6, 1949. Before departure, the passengers are invited to sign up for volunteer work on the ship to help the crew. Since our passage is paid by the U.S. Government, our help would defer some of the cost. I sign up. The volunteers have to board the ship a day ahead of everybody else. We are given a tour around the ship, instructed as to our duties, mostly to help families with small children and to serve in the dining room during mealtimes. Our sleeping quarters are on the upper deck, a big room with rows of bunk cots. These arrangements were meant to serve military personnel and have no frills, just basic necessities.

My first night on the ship is a very long and sleepless one, and I am happy to greet the morning and report to duty. The day is calm and sunny. In a few hours, all the passengers are settled in, and the ship is ready to depart. As the ship slowly pulls away, we wave to the departing shores of Europe with a measure of sadness. And there, before my eyes, unfolds another departing, another shore drifting away. Latvia! The tragedy and hopelessness of that day, however, cannot be compared to this sunlit morning. Ahead of us is a promise of a new beginning. America! "Land of the free and home of the brave!", as we have heard. There, we will be given a chance to mold our lives according to our wishes and our abilities. Yes, our lives will have a new tomorrow!

The seas are calm. We pass the British Isles and our ship slips into the open waters of the Atlantic Ocean. I work in the dining room and help mothers to tend to their children. The first few days are uneventful; no strong winds trouble our passage. But on the fifth day, things change. The skies become gray. Threatening clouds drift above the ship. The wind that had been quite mild at first, increases its force creating large, white-capped waves. The friendly ocean turns into a tumultuous cradle, which rocks our ship up and down and side-to-side. Most of the people are sick; they are lying on the decks, hanging over the railings, some are in their cabins trying to overcome the horrible seasickness. I feel sick, but not to the extreme as many others. Also, my duty is to help. And I try to. Calm waters, stable foundation under my feet is my greatest wish.

Finally, the storm stops. The ocean calms. The ship regains its balance and its passengers their sense of relative well-being. We are nearing the Promised Land. "America, here we come!" The port of entry would be New York. Late in the evening of September 16th we notice some flickers of light appearing and disappearing in the distance. Could it be New York? Excited viewers gather around the ship's railings. Happy voices and laughter fill the air. "It is New York!" "Yes!" "We have arrived!" One can almost touch the excitement, the spirit of jubilation. For a while, the ship continues to proceed and the distant lights grow brighter and more numerous. But, before reaching the shore, the ship stops. It would be in the morning when we enter the harbor.

Very early the next morning, I return to the deck. I feel restless and excited. New York is dimly visible through the dawn's grayness. To my right, also wrapped in the mist of the early morning, stands the grandiose Statue of Liberty. I have read about it, heard about it, but to see this monument, the proud and stately woman holding a torch in her extended arm, is an immensely moving experience. I feel that along with the many others before me whom she had welcomed to these shores, now she is beckoning to me: "Send these, the homeless, the tempest-tossed to me, I lift my lamp beside the golden door!" Yes, a door is opening to a new beginning for me, my family, for everybody on this ship. In a very short while all of the ship's passengers would step on the shore of this vast and unknown country. What will be our road ahead? Where will it lead? What will the future hold?

LIFE IN THE UNITED STATES:
THE SOBERING FIRST YEAR

Our sponsor, Mrs. Merrill, has come to New York to meet us. She is a petite, silver-haired lady. She is pleasant, as she welcomes us to America and tries to make us feel at ease. Mrs. Merrill also explains that we will be taking a train to Washington, D.C., and from there will travel by car to their farm in Virginia. She talks slowly, carefully pronouncing her words to make sure that we understand. Since my English is more fluent than the rest of the family's, I become the family's interpreter.

The train we board is very comfortable, its soft seats covered in blue material. "Plush!" I think. I have a window seat, and watch with great interest the fast moving scenery outside. Four hours later, we are in Washington, D.C. The Merrills' chauffeur, Mr. Appell, meets us at the railroad station. He is a kindly looking gentleman dressed in a black uniform. We all settle into a large station wagon, and with Mr. Appell at the wheel, we are ready to go. Our first stop is a self-service restaurant. This presents a completely new experience to me. I have never seen such a restaurant, where each customer takes a tray and walks along a marvelously rich display of food and makes one's own selections. So much food and such a variety! "Yes, this is a land of plenty!"

After a good meal, we are ready to start the final stretch of the journey to our new home. The road winds through farm country; mostly we see open fields with horses and cattle grazing. The country looks somewhat like Latvia.

At one point Mrs. Merrill interrupts our mostly silent ride: "Not far from here behind the trees on the right of us is the Potomac River. This river also flows through our farm. It is a good place to fish!"

Does Mrs. Merrill know that our father's favorite hobby is fishing? In Latvia and in Germany, whenever time and weather allowed, he departed with his fishing pole in hand to return home many hours later. He loves to sit quietly by the water, enjoying the serenity of nature and the excitement of an eventual catch.

After about an hour's drive, Mr. Appell turns into a gravel driveway, lined by tall juniper trees. At the end of the road, facing it, is a small bungalow-type clapboard building. Mr. Appell stops the station wagon in front of it. Mrs. Merrill turns to us and says: "This is your new home."

We get out of the car and follow Mrs. Merrill into the house. She walks us through the kitchen, the small dining room, and the two bedrooms. Everything looks new and attractive. The golden rays of the late afternoon sun shines through the windows, making the little house inviting and friendly.

"Welcome home!" says Mrs. Merrill. "This house is now yours."

"Thank you!" Our response comes from the heart.

The day has been very long. It seems like an eternity has passed between the time we had left the ship in the morning and our arrival to this small clapboard house in Herndon, Virginia. Much has happened. It is difficult to absorb all the events. Emotionally and physically, we feel drained. It is good to be left alone, to be able to relax and rest.

In the morning, we are summoned to the main house, a big rambling ranch with a small apartment above the garage where the live-in help, Nellie and George Appell, live. We are invited into Mr. Merrill's study where he greets us. He is a large, imposing man, a retired Admiral of the U.S. Navy. After we are seated, he explains to us our responsibilities. Father would work in the barn with the animals, and in the fields when needed. Ruta would help Nellie with the housework and also in the kitchen. Mr. Appell would drive me to Massachusetts where I would live with the Merrill's daughter's family and take care of their one-year-old son. During our short meeting, we fail to mention that Ruta needs to go back to school to complete her high school education. We feel too shy, and we clearly understand that the Merrill's expect all of us to work. Later on, however, when the question of Ruta's return to school is raised with Mr. Merrill, the answer is: "It is impossible."

A long day's drive takes me to my new job in Middleton, Massachusetts. Joey is a delightful little boy, and we enjoy our time together. I take him for short walks and longer carriage drives through the golden New England fall. The brilliant colors of the trees, and the sunny, crisp autumn days spent with little Joey create warm memories for me.

Soon, my stay in Middleton comes to an end. The Merrill's own a large estate in Pride's Crossing, Massachusetts, where they spend most of their summers. A helper is needed in the kitchen to assist the cook. I say good-bye to Joey and move to their large mansion on the Atlantic Ocean. Mrs. Merrill's father, who was a multimillionaire businessman, built the grandiose house at the beginning of the century. It is surrounded by a beautiful park and manicured gardens. In my free time, I walk through the gardens, visit the seashore, sit on the beach, and enjoy the vast expanse of the open sea. Often at night, the foghorn's lonely sound resonates in my soul. The loneliness I feel is captured by this sound.

Christmastime brings me a wonderful gift - a train ticket to Washington to visit my family. My joy is overwhelming! It makes me forget all the humiliating incidences, the small misunderstandings, and my difficulty in accepting the position of a servant. To be a maid and a kitchen help is a totally new experience for me. My separateness from the family that had invited me to this country, but not as an equal, is somewhat of a surprise to me. In my childhood home, Plikeni, the servants were considered part of our family and treated as equals. It is not so in the Merrill's household. I have a lot of learning to do, and to be a cook's helper is not the most difficult of the lessons.

Soon after Christmas I am told that in the early spring I will be returning to Virginia with the Merrills and will cook for them. To be reunited with my family is a very happy prospect, but to assume the responsibility of a full-blown cook is something else! My training has been very brief, and I feel incompetent. But return I do, and a cook I am. My sister, Ruta, serves the meals that I prepare; she is the butler. We both wear uniforms. Ruta's is a dark green dress and a small white apron; mine is a light gray dress and a much larger apron. What a team! Two young girls from distant Latvia are working for a millionaire family in America, in jobs that they hardly know and have no experience in. Nellie helps us when larger groups of people are entertained, but usually we manage alone. One ridiculously funny incident happens on an evening when the Merrills have invited a couple of friends to dinner. At the last moment we realize that the steaks we were supposed to serve are still in the freezer. But steaks are ordered, so steaks would be served! Appropriately sized T-bone steaks are removed from the large freezer and broiled to a nice dark brown color. Ruta serves them without a comment and they are consumed without a comment. To our surprise, nobody ever mentions the steaks.

We also help Nellie clean the spacious house. The house is beautiful. Each room displays antique furniture, valuable artwork, books, numerous paintings, and many other lovely things. It is a house filled with treasures. The library is my favorite room; its walls are covered by bookshelves filled with handsomely bound volumes. I am sure many of them are rare and valuable collector's items.

The spring turns into summer, and the time has come to discuss our future with the Merrill's. Mrs. Merrill invites me into her study and tells me that my salary would be raised to $60.00 a month from the $50.00 I have been receiving up to now, and that I would return with them to their Pride's Crossing residence. My dream has always been to continue my education; to go to college. I explain that to Mrs. Merrill. She is silent for a while and then tells me that she would have to discuss my plans with her husband.

A few days after my meeting with Mrs. Merrill, I am serving supper to Mr. Merrill. Mrs. Merrill is away, and Ruta is not working that evening. The bell from the dining room notifies me in the kitchen that Mr. Merrill is expecting his meal. I enter the elegant dining room. The heavy antique Spanish-style furniture gives the room a distinguished look. Mr. Merrill is sitting at the end of the long dining table. I serve his dinner and am about to leave the room when I hear his voice: "Wait!" I turn around. He looks at me coldly, and his voice is filled with anger. He says that I have been very ungrateful, that he had picked my family and me up from dirt, given us a home and jobs. Going to school? How can I, who am practically nobody, expect to go to college? On and on goes the angry flood of words, hitting me like poisoned arrows. I want to escape, to hide, but am glued to the floor, paralyzed. As his monologue continues, my heart begins to pound. My body starts to shake uncontrollably. Finally, I hear: "Go!" I turn around and flee the room. In the safety of the kitchen my calm eventually returns, my heart stops pounding, my body trembling. I know that Mr. Merrill is wrong and unfair. He has great wealth but he does not own me. He has no right to humiliate me, no right to tell me what I could or could not do with my life. The encounter with Mr. Merrill has been a very shocking and painful experience but, in a rather curious way, I feel liberated. A bond is broken. I do not owe the Merrill's anything. My respect for Mr. Merrill is destroyed by his uncontrolled anger. After the encounter, I am told that my help in Pride's Crossing would not be needed. When the Merrills leave to go to their summer residence, I remain in Virginia. During the following weeks, I spend my time picking berries, walking in the woods, or joining my father on his fishing trips. I am enjoying my freedom, my short vacation. At times, Ruta and I visit Washington to see a movie or sightsee.

Virginia's summer is very hot and humid. Our father works in the fields under the mercilessly hot sun. The work is hard and the days are long. On the evening of July 28, I am sitting on a bench in front of our little house when dad comes home from work. The day had been especially hot and humid. He looks old and tired. His back is bent and his gait slow. Only two months earlier, we had celebrated his fiftieth birthday! The work on the farm is wearing him down. I can see that. He stops before entering the house. "Daughter," he says, "we will have to write to uncle Janis to see if we can move to Iowa." Uncle Janis is dad's brother who has recently immigrated to Iowa and works there as a physician. He has written to my dad and suggested that we move to Iowa. Yes, tomorrow we would write the letter.

"Come! Come!" I hear my mother calling. It is dark; it is the middle of the night. Ruta and I run into our parents' bedroom. Father is struggling for breath. He is asleep. We try to wake him. "Dad, Dad!" A few more labored, gargling sounds and then silence. He has stopped breathing. "It could not be!" I think. I put my mouth to his and try to breath life into him. Nothing happens. He remains silent and still. Our father is gone! The tragic fact of his death finally becomes reality. It is July 29, 1950. It is the exact time, when six years earlier, he and his family had said good-bye to Plikeni.

Can we predict our passing? I wonder. Just a few days before our father died, we had been sitting around a supper table when he'd said: "We must be prepared to live a long life, but be ready to die tomorrow." Did he have a premonition?

The Merrill's help us with the funeral arrangements. Our father is laid to rest on July 31 in the local cemetery in Great Falls, Virginia. A Latvian pastor, Pravests Veinbergs, presides.

Among the people who come to say good-bye to our father, and to be with us during this time of grief, are Tante Elza, who also had left Esslingen and now lives with her children in Connecticut, and my childhood friend, Irene, and her family. Their presence and the offerings of support and love break the clouds of darkness that surround us.

Soon after the funeral Mr. Merrill visits us. He reminds us that now, since our father is gone, we need to vacate the house. He would appreciate it if we do so promptly.

In ten short months, all has changed. Only a year ago in

September we had been welcomed here and had entered the little house in hopes of a happy beginning, a secure future. The door to the Promised Land had opened to us, but it had not been a golden door.

WE BEGIN AGAIN

Father's death brings our family into a new reality. He had always been the family's stronghold. We relied on him. He was there when we needed advice, support, and guidance. Now, we feel like a ship without a rudder. Somehow we need to go on, make decisions about our future. Mother's cousin, Elmars, who also used to work for the Merrill's, has left their employment and has rented an apartment in Boston. He has a spare room there that he would make available to us if we decided to move to Boston. It seems like the simplest and safest plan. We notify Elmars that we have decided to accept his offer.

During the final weeks in Virginia, we visit our father's gravesite every Saturday to say a prayer and to place flowers. To visit our father in this place of the dead feels very unreal to me. I do not, I cannot, accept the finality of his death. My dreams very often revolve around him. One night I see him in his formal dress suit. He looks at me seriously and says, "Daughter, everything would be in order, but your soul is not ready." It is more of a vision than a dream. I feel that he has come to tell me that my time to follow him has not come yet. I do think about death often.

In September, we move to Boston. Skaidrite has remained in Germany with her husband. Mother, Ruta, and I share a large room in Elmars' spacious apartment. It is quite comfortable. Ruta decides not to begin school in the fall, but starts to work at James O. Welch Company, a chocolate manufacturer. I find a job in a dressmaking shop. From eight o'clock in the morning until five o'clock in the evening, I tie ribbons on little girls' dresses. My work area is a long table in a large room, where many women sit at sewing machines, diligently stitching together seams. Their end product comes to my table. At first, it is quite an effort to make the ties look symmetrical, but soon I gain speed and proficiency, and the ribbons I tie need no improvement. The supervisor, a darkly handsome man, compliments me on my work performance.

In November, we visit Tante Elza and our two cousins in Norwich, Connecticut. Elza works as a housekeeper for Mrs. Merrill's aunt, while Aivars and Astra attend the local grammar school. A tremendous wind and heavy rain engulf us as we step from the bus in Norwich. At that time, we had no knowledge of the hurricane season, but now, looking back, I believe that our trip fell right in the middle of one of these violent storms. Our visit, however, is most enjoyable! It is so good and relaxing to be together with Elza's family to reflect, share our experiences, and cry on each other's shoulder. The weekend speeds by, and Sunday afternoon we board the bus back to Boston.

During the late fall, my health begins to deteriorate. The smallest effort makes me short of breath. My heart races, my hands tremble. In the evening my legs look like two round logs. Physically and emotionally, I am a total wreck! What is happening to me? I recall that during the summer, while still in Virginia, my thyroid had started to become overactive. Apparently, father's sudden death, and all the changes that followed, had contributed to the flare-up of this condition. At Massachusetts General Hospital I am diagnosed as having Grave's disease, a hyperactive thyroid, and surgery is suggested. Since I have no medical insurance and no funds to pay for my treatment and hospitalization, I am given an offer to enter a research program in lieu of payment. That I do. I undergo all sorts of tests, and am placed on various drug regimes. In the course of my treatment, I meet some very nice and interesting people who help me along, encourage and support me. It takes quite awhile for my thyroid to calm down to the point where it is safe for me to undergo surgery.

The great negative of this period of my illness is my inability to work. I do not know how we manage financially.

Ruta continues to work, and her income has to cover our basic needs. The great positive is that I have all this time available to read. Elmars' wife, Dudina, is a passionate reader. With her help, I acquire a library card at the Boston Public Library. Dudina and I visit the library regularly to borrow books. I read and read. I become familiar with Charles Dickens works and read "David Copperfield" from cover to cover, plus a few of his other publications. My favorite author is Somerset Maugham. I read most of his novels, and am especially impressed by the thoughts on the human condition expressed in "Human Bondage" and "The Raiser's Edge". I read Emily Bronte and J.B. Priestley. This improves my knowledge of the English language. I list and learn all the unfamiliar words. (Just recently I glanced through my "self-made" dictionary. It is interesting to see what and how much I had to learn.)

My surgery is in early February, 1951, and in the beginning of April I am ready to return to work. The dream of furthering my education has to be put on the "back-burner", at least for a while. Ruta's education is of primary importance at this time, and she enters high school to complete her studies. I need to find work and look for an office job. Soon, I am employed as a file clerk/typist in the Crowel-Collier magazine sales office. I make $35.00 a week, and for a while am the only breadwinner in our family. It is during this time that I meet my future husband, Arvids, and he is very impressed by my position of responsibility. Every penny counts, and I walk a considerable distance to catch a bus just to save a nickel. I do very well in my job and am soon promoted to a higher position and given a raise.

In general, this is a relaxed and happy summer. I join a Latvian folk dance group, make new friendships, begin to date, and have fun. Arvids is my most frequent date. Even the question, "Where are you from?" that is generally asked when I say something in English, does not bother me that much anymore. My response: "From Latvia," most often is followed by another question: "Where is that?" It is tiresome to explain, and astounding to realize that so many people have little knowledge of geography. My accent always gives me away, sets me apart.

The Latvian community in Boston grows, as many of the refugees leave Germany establish a new home in the United States. We join a Latvian church and take part in the Latvian community life. Our goal and hope is to return home to Latvia, and organizations are formed to actively work to reach this goal. Much the same as in Esslingen, Germany, we find security and companionship among our own kind. We feel safe and at home among other Latvians.

Early in the year, our family moves out of Elmars's place and rents our own apartment on the top floor of a three-decker house on Minden Street in Jamaica Plain. We have four rooms, a kitchen with a black-bellied stove, and a deck. Our mother immediately finds some flowerpots and window boxes for the deck, and as soon as the weather permits, plants vegetable and flower seeds in them. In summer, the deck looks like a colorful garden patch, growing marigolds, nasturtiums, and zinnias. We also have our own homegrown tomatoes and cucumbers! Our mother is a natural nurturer; she makes sure that Ruta and I are well taken care of. As she had in Plikeni, she welcomes friends and relatives into our new home. (Her warm hospitality is still remembered by the people who enjoyed it. My friend, Alise Staris, who at that time came to visit me quite frequently, recalls how mother always offered her tea and cookies and invited her to rest up after the meal.)

To save money on groceries, we walk a considerable distance to a discount grocery store, Blairs, which is located near Dudley Station in Roxbury. Many of our Latvian friends shop there, since all of us are just starting out and establishing our lives in the United States. Life is not easy for any of us. Lawyers, educators, actors and many other professionals are working in factories, cleaning houses, starting out in low-level jobs in hospitals and offices. Some work as live-in household help. Many go back to school to be retrained.

In my own personal life, bad luck does not step aside, but keeps following me. My dad's death seems to place my life in a "free-fall". In the late fall, I become ill with a very bad flu and cannot shake it. I feel tired and listless and have many migraine headaches. An x-ray of my lungs shows a suspicious shadow, and it is just before Thanksgiving, when during a visit to MGH, a doctor calls me into his office and announces: "You have tuberculosis." Tuberculosis! If he had said: "You have been sentenced to die," I would not have been more shocked. I am in a daze as I take the subway home. As I look at the people around me, at their smiling faces, listening to their happy chatter, I think: "You don't know how lucky you are! You are healthy! You are free!" I feel isolated and very alone as I am trying to comprehend and accept what I have just learned.

What follows, then, are long weeks of tests and discussions of what would be the best course of treatment for me. The minimum of a year in a sanatorium is generally an accepted treatment for TB. I have only a minimal disease, but because of my youth, and to be sure that I would be completely cured, a decision is made to place me in a sanatorium for a year.

In the early spring of 1952, my sister, Skaidrite, arrives from Germany to join us in Boston. At the time of our departure from Germany in 1949, Skaidrite's husband Juris was employed by the American military as an interpreter, and both of them stayed behind. Now, Skaidrite, has come alone, and Juris will follow later. Ruta and I are very glad to welcome our sister. She has always been a stabilizing force in our family, and it is especially true now, when we acutely feel the loss of our father. It is deeply comforting to me to have her support while I am waiting to be admitted to the Sanatorium in Rutland, Massachusetts. Early in June, Ruta is confirmed, and our family has a small celebration in honor of this special occasion. Among the guests are Elza and her two children, our cousin Ilga and her family, and Elmars and Dudina with their little son, Ilmars.

Late in June, I enter the Rutland State Sanatorium in Central Massachusetts. Thus, my third year in the United States is spent in bed with daily injections of streptomycin. I count days, weeks, and months, waiting for the eventual day of freedom. I feel like a prisoner, and envy all the lucky people who are free to come and go as they please. There are two very different worlds: one within the Sanatorium walls, and the other enjoyed by the rest of the population on the outside, the world of freedom and opportunity. I begin to understand how the people in jails feel, and have compassion for them. The sunny side to this year of "imprisonment" is the availability of books to read. Also, I learn interesting crafts and make close friendships. (Some of these have lasted to this day.) I meet very kind and caring people, not only among the hospital staff and patients, but also among total strangers who come to visit us and bring gifts, especially their love and compassion.

Tuberculosis is a serious and contagious disease. All the caring people who visit us take a risk. But they still come. One can never forget that! I will always remember Mr. and Mrs. Hahns, a Latvian couple, who live in a neighboring town and frequently visit me, never coming empty-handed or empty-hearted. Their kindness means a lot to me. Naturally, my family comes to visit whenever they can get a ride. Also Arvids' visits are quite frequent, especially towards the end of my stay. On Sundays, my eyes are turned to the door in expectation!

I learn, after the fact, (the family does not want to upset me) that while I was in the hospital, Ruta had to undergo an emergency surgery for an ovarian infection. I suspect that the ruptured appendix that almost took her life in childhood is responsible for this latest incident.

The lesson this difficult year teaches me, again, is that in every darkness there hides a ray of light, that pain and misfortune can be a way to deeper joy and understanding. I have learned to appreciate the value of physical freedom. I take pleasure in the small opportunities that every-day life presents. It is a treat to go shopping, to wander through city streets, to take walks in the woods, to be together with friends and family without restrictions, and most importantly, to be able to greet each morning in my own place and in my own way. All these are joyful experiences, never appreciated in full measure before. My year in confinement highlighted their importance, and for that I am grateful. Also, I value the gifts of the human heart more deeply; that a common destiny, in this case illness, can bond strangers into one caring family is a very important lesson.

A SUMMER OF ADJUSTMENT

Spring, my most favorite season, is greening and coloring the countryside around Rutland. My stay at the sanatorium is ending, and the door is now open for me to leave. I am cured! I can start to live again. Physically, I look and feel healthy, and I am ready to go out into the world with a new spirit of hope. My heart is filled with happiness, as I step into Arvids' car in the late morning of June 16. He has come to pick me up and drive me home to Boston.

I am embraced with the warm, welcoming, and loving arms of my family, as I walk up the three flights of stairs and enter our apartment. Twelve long months have gone by in anticipation of this day, and now, I allow the luxury of homecoming to flow into my soul. It is so very good to be home!

I soon realize, however, that the year of seclusion and absence from a normal way of life has changed me. I feel timid and unsure. My former friends and acquaintances are friendly and accepting, inviting me back into their circle. It is I who feel strange among them; it is I who has difficulty fitting in. I feel scarred, blemished. Invisible to all others is the sign of Cain I wear on my forehead, though actually, in my soul. What has happened to my psyche? My self-confidence, which had always been fragile, has reached an all-time low.

(Today, as I reflect and try to understand the Astrida of that time, I am deeply puzzled. I see a girl who seems to have lost her center, her identity, her will. Is it possible that too much had been thrown at her in too short a time, or was there not enough space between the setbacks for her to recoup, for her soul to be healed? Like a bird injured in flight that, in time, feels strong enough to rise up to the sky, then a sudden burst of wind catches its wing, pushing it back to the ground. The bird rests for a while, then extends its wings for a new attempt to fly. But, again, is pushed back; falls to the ground. The bird gives up. Did I give up? I see a girl who is painfully uncertain, afraid to make a decision. She walks in a shadowy world, allowing circumstances to lead and guide her; permits the opinions of others to overrule her own judgments, to influence her decisions.

In my effort to understand myself, I think back to my childhood; to the time when my secure and safe world fell apart; the warm midsummer evening when we left Plikeni; the morning in October when Latvia's shores drifted out of our sight; our journey through war-torn Germany; our stay in the refugee camps; the lost hope of returning back home; and, finally, the new beginning in the United States; a beginning with many setbacks and painful experiences.

Yes, I begin to understand.)

I see Arvids a lot this summer, we have regular dates, and my family has accepted him as my steady boyfriend. Our relationship, however, lacks true openness and trust; it has many ups and downs. Our walks around Jamaica Pond, our trips in the country are pleasant and enjoyable. But our discussions are often marred by misunderstandings that are followed by days of silence. The silences are Arvids' way of telling me that he is disappointed and angry. I am often sad and puzzled, very unsure of myself, my feelings, and his feelings. But we continue to date and eventually decide to get married. But the joy that an engagement should bring to one's soul is missing in mine. Even the ring Arvids gives me has a crack in it and needs to be returned for exchange. I have many misgivings about our future together; probably Arvids does too. My action is to not take action. I allow events to take their course.

I give myself a bit of a time to readjust to the real world, to being home, and then I start looking for a job. I am timid at first. My previous employer, the Crowel-Collier Company has invited me back, but many of the people I used to work with are gone; the administration is new. I would like to explore something different also; to take some courses, acquire new skills. I look in the Help Wanted pages of the newspaper and start my search. A rude awakening! One of the questions asked on the job application form is: what have you done in the previous year? What have I done? I have spent it in a sanatorium; I was treated for tuberculosis. I soon realize that an honest answer about my illness, even though I am cured now, closes all doors. It is painful and humbling. I have committed no crime, but feel like a criminal, someone to be avoided. I learn not to tell the truth, and soon find a job at the Harvard Law School Library, working in the cataloging department with varied responsibilities.

It feels good to work again, to get up in the morning, to get ready, to take the train to Cambridge, and to meet my co-workers. Such simple, everyday activities give me a lift. I feel useful and normal, just like all the others around me. I like my fellow workers and what I am doing. The best of all the benefits that this job offers me is that I will be able to take courses at the University, tuition free! A new season has begun in my life.

PHOTOGRAPHS FROM THE EARLY DAYS

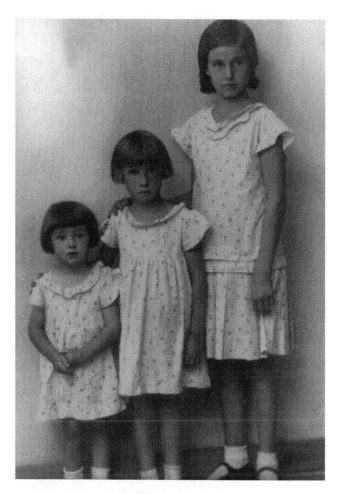

**Me with my little sister, Ruta, and
older sister, Skaidrite**

My father, Karlis, and me

Neighborhood children and good friends

Our Family's Offical Immigration Photo
(top left is me, Ruta in center, Skaidrite on the right)

Our Home in Plikeni

My High School Classmates in Esslingen

Me, Ruta and Skaidrite

Uncle Martins and my godmother, Aunt Elza, and their children, Aivars and Astra

Our last summer in Esslington, Germany (I'm on the left, Skaidrite in center, Ruta on the right)

Part Two:
Marriage and Motherhood

"Life wonderfully provides solutions, fills voids, and eases pain. Blessings often come from unexpected sources.....God takes away and God gives back...

Astrida

THE START OF A NEW LIFE

On Christmas Eve, 1953, a new chapter starts in my life. Arvids and I are married that day, and we begin our life together in a three-room apartment on the top floor of a two-family house in Jamaica Plain. We both have a difficult period of adjustment. Our expectations of each other, the projections of what a married life should be, fall short of the reality. The first year is especially hard, at least for me.

Gradually, our life begins to fall into a regular pattern. On weekdays, we are both busy at work. On Saturdays, I am very busy cleaning our small apartment. I scrub, dust, and vacuum. I wonder if all newlywed wives are such meticulous housekeepers. Our house is spotless! On the small kitchen stove that has only two burners, I manage to create a variety of new dishes. I learn to enjoy cooking and become quite good at it. To my family's surprise, I buy a sewing machine. The comment is: "Who would imagine that Astrida, the bookworm, the reader, the dreamer, could be interested in such a practical task as sewing?" In time, it becomes one of my favorite hobbies. My family remains very important to me; my relationship with them continues to be close, but our circle-of-friends are mostly Arvids' former friends.

Eventually, I terminate my employment at the Harvard Law School Library where I have worked for three years, and find a job at Massachusetts General Hospital. During my time at Harvard, I have taken evening courses at the Bryant Stratton

Secretarial School, have acquired new skills, and feel ready, with Arvids' urging, to start a new career. The change of work is only the beginning of other important changes in my life. By a lucky coincidence, I find a job in the Hospital's Medical Records Department. (It is "lucky", because there I form close and important relationships, meaningful friendships; and it is a "coincidence" because Mary Converse, the director of that department, had not yet filed a requisition for the position I was to fill.) As I am sitting in the personnel department's waiting room expecting to be interviewed, Mary, on her way to meet someone in the office, passes by me, notices me, likes my smile, as she later would note, and hires me as her secretary and office assistant the same day. She becomes my boss and most importantly my mentor and friend. She promotes my development, professional, as well as personal. Under Mary's guidance, I assume responsibilities far beyond my job description, and develop skills and gain experience that greatly help me in the future. Mary invariably believes in me and trusts me. Eventually, she guides me into the field of medical records administration, which opens the door to my future professional life of a cancer registrar and research assistant in the Department of Gynecology at Massachusetts General Hospital.

Mary Converse is a tall, stately woman with a permanent smile in her blue eyes and friendly dimples in her cheeks. She is the mother-hen type, taking under her wings those who, in her opinion, need help and encouragement. She runs her large department as a family unit, and her employees feel like members of a close-knit and caring group. Mary was born in Nebraska. The openness of those spacious farmlands, the caring for one's fellow travelers that must have been necessary for each individual's survival there, seem to be a part of her personality and soul. Mary often talks about her origins. I believe that she never really separated herself from her life in Nebraska and always felt rooted there. She is a very special human being, a broad-minded, capable professional, a leader in her field.

At that time, another very special friendship develops

between Hilda Sequeira and me. Both of us are new to the department. We share coffee breaks and lunch times, and eventually our relationship grows into a close and intimate friendship. She becomes my true soul sister. (I have written more about her and our friendship in the chapter called Those Who Have Taught Me Important Life Lessons in Part V . Cancer ends Hilda's life in 1992, but in my heart she will always be alive. There, she is immortal.)

WE ARE HOMEOWNERS

In 1957, Arvids and I buy a house in South Natick and leave our small apartment in Jamaica Plain. It is a sunny, gloriously colorful day in October when the movers deliver all our belongings to our new home on Glen Street. After the truck has unloaded everything and has left, I sit on the floor in the middle of the living room and enjoy the delightful feeling of ownership. I look around. Everything is new, clean, and bright. The house is only a year old, and it is ours! It feels like a dream, but it is not a dream. And the reality is beautiful and exciting.

Best of all is that our new house is surrounded by almost an acre of land that needs care and development. Here, we can exercise our imagination and create a garden; we can dig the soil, plant trees, bushes, and flowers. We start on this project almost immediately. That Fall, we plant our first tree, an apple tree. Whenever the weather is kind, our free time is spent outdoors. In time, our small house is surrounded by apple trees, pear trees, cherry trees, and peach trees, bushes of all sizes and shapes, an arrangement of flowerbeds, and a large vegetable garden. The vegetable garden is Arvids' domain, his "golf course", as he often says. My joy is to plant and care for the flowers. I often consult my sister Skaidrite, whose profession is garden design, and I value her advice. She gives me good hints of what to plant, and where. The rock garden is my most creative effort. I spend many hours planning, moving, and arranging large and small rocks. In between them, I place a variety of flowering and foliage plants. Ours could be called a country garden. Its informal setting reminds me of my childhood in Latvia, the garden in Plikeni. Something is always in bloom there. Spring brings a burst of color, as if a rainbow had come down from heaven to rest around our house. In the mornings, with my coffee cup in hand, I walk around the garden, checking on the new buds, the opening blossoms, breathing in the magic of spring air and allowing my soul to rest in its peace. The garden is Arvids' and my common interest and love. In that, we come together in our otherwise distant marriage.

We have a nice house, and a beautiful garden, but our life has a hollow sound. I never really feel complete; there is an emptiness, a longing in my heart that I cannot explain. Life seems to lack purpose and meaning. We miss children.

PAUL – PAULITIS

On May 18th, 1956, a son was born to my sister Skaidrite and her husband Juris. Little Paul, or Paulitis, as we affectionately call him, brings much happiness, not only to his parents, but also to everybody in the extended family. He has a sunny and affectionate personality, and I love to spend time with him. Paulitis is often at our house and becomes very precious to me, and also to Arvids. To a great degree, he fills our need to care for and love a child. Paul is my godchild, and that adds a special importance to our relationship. During the time when Skaidrite and Juris plan and build their house in the neighboring town of Sherborn, the family spends quite a bit of time with us and brings much liveliness and warmth to our home. To have Paulitis around is a blessing. He receives an abundance of love from everybody, and rewards us all with just being himself and bringing sunshine into our adult world. He is the center of our mother's life. She lives with Skaidrite's family and is called "Omite". Omite lovingly cares for Paul, and later for his sister, Annele.

(I am sure that Omite left deep positive imprints in their personalities, and much of their grandmother's Latvian heritage enriches their lives even today. Paul eventually marries Ann, and they become parents of two beautiful girls, Meg and Kate. He is a professional botanist/ecologist, and has a successful career. Paul has never lost his loving, informal, and caring personality. The

little "Paulitis" with his quick and, at times, mischievous ways is still very much alive in him. He enjoys woodworking and building, has helped to build a comfortable house for his family; a magnificent barn for himself, with an extensive woodworking shop; and an elegant tree house for his daughters. From his mother, Paul has inherited the love for gardening; and the spacious grounds around his house are artistically designed and beautifully planted. Paul is also a gracious host and a good cook, and together with his wife, Ann, entertain their extended families on holidays and other special occasions. Paul has an important place in my heart and the happiness he gave me during his growing-up years I have never forgotten.)

PETER'S HOMECOMING

It has been ten long months since we made our first contact with the adoption agency and expressed our wish to adopt a child, a baby, if at all possible. We were handed a long and detailed application to fill out, and also at the same time, warned that there were very few children available and that we should not place too much hope in our prospective parenthood. Regardless of the pessimistic outlook, we completed all the paperwork and waited for the agency's response. We wanted a child, a family, and were ready to do whatever was necessary. And there was a lot we had to do. Much was expected of us: we had to prove that we were worthy to assume responsibility over another human being, to nurture, to teach, to cherish, and guide, and to be able to provide for his or her physical and material well being.

Many months of regular interviews followed; lots of questions were asked, references requested. Were we measuring up to the expectations, were we good enough individuals to be parents? Before our monthly interviews, Arvids and I would look at each other and wonder this, as we opened and closed the agency's doors. The agency had become "The Great Inquisitor" and, in a way, held our future in its palm.

Summer passed, a tense summer. In between the regular trips to Worcester, where the agency was, we tended our garden. We both loved to work the soil, to plant, and to experience the joy of seeing our plantings grow. Our frustrations and anxieties went right through our fingers into the earth and helped to keep us grounded.

We have a comfortable house with two extra bedrooms, just right for a small inhabitant to move into! We cannot resist the temptation to walk through the stores that sell children's furniture and other items for little people, just in case.

At the end of the summer, the home evaluation is completed. October arrives. While at work, I receive a telephone call. It is Mrs. Bice from the agency. "We have a wonderful baby boy for you", she says, "You can come and pick him up the day after tomorrow".

"Day after tomorrow?" my voice trails off. Suddenly, my heart skips a beat, several beats. I am panicky! "How will I know how to take care of a baby? How will I know what to do?" One of the requirements of the new mother is to quit her work, if she is employed. I work full-time and love what I do. The reality of giving up my present lifestyle, the comfortable routine of my days is an unexpected shock. I want to run, to say: "No! No! No!" Then a calm sets in. A great joy replaces my panic. "I am going to be a mother!"

It is on the sunny, warm, beautiful Wednesday afternoon of October 17, 1962, when we open the door to the building that we had stepped into with great concern and anxiety for so many months. Mrs. Bice greets us and places in my arms the most beautiful, blond, blue-eyed boy I have ever seen. "Your son," she says. "My son! Our son!" My heart overflows with such tenderness, such love. I have never experienced such an overwhelming emotion. I love this little person with my whole being. At that moment, I know that if anyone would approach me to say that I cannot keep this child, I would run and hide. I would never give him up. Never!

We arrive home with Peter; a sunlit house welcomes us. A freshly painted, newly furnished room greets its new master. Peter has come home.

MOTHERHOOD

Who would have known or even guessed, that one little boy could have the power to change two people's lives most profoundly? Peter does. The sunshine that so brightly illuminated our way back home from the agency in Worcester, with Peter in our arms, came into our house with him and remains. My heart is singing. The unrequited longing, the feeling of a wasted, unfulfilled life that had been constantly with me had disappeared the instant I took Peter in my arms. It is a miracle. Something totally unexpected. Peter is a cuddly baby. He loves to be held close, and it is a real joy for me to hug and hold Peter. Arvids also loves to be with Peter, and the pride and affection toward his son are plainly visible.

Peter adjusts to his new home and parents without any apparent difficulty. Since Arvids and I speak Latvian with each other, that also becomes Peter's language. Very precious time for me, and I think for Peter also, are the moments we spend together before his evening bedtime. I hold him in my lap, give him his bottle, and sing one of the beautiful Latvian lullabies ("Aijā žūžū, lāča bērni", sleep, bear baby, sleep, is my favorite) while his trusting blue eyes hold me close. It is a peaceful and blessed time. Much love and tenderness passes between the two of us. During the daytime, before he learns to walk on his own, Peter enjoys whirling around the house in the small walker we have bought for him. Many things that happen to be in his way are pushed aside or just are broken. All of our most valuable treasures find places on higher ground. At age nine and a half months Peter, does not need his walker any more, he travels the world on his own two feet. And he is moving with great speed and determination.

When spring comes, we move outdoors. There, Peter has the freedom of open spaces, can run and play, and help me to dig and plant the garden, mostly to dig, though.

Peter can move with the speed of lightning, as I find out one afternoon. For a brief moment, as I tend to the soil in one of my flowerbeds, my attention is turned away from Peter. When I look up, he is nowhere to be seen. "Peter! Peter!" I call. No answer. I run around frantically, looking and calling for him. I am sure that somebody has kidnapped him. Such a beautiful, friendly boy! Naturally, somebody would want to take him! I become panicky. And then I notice something red moving in the neighbor's tall grass. Peter's red hat! I am overwhelmed with relief and joy!

Another spring day, my garden is in its glory: daffodils, tulips, and crocuses are blooming in the flowerbeds, covering them with a blanket of color. Especially beautiful is the crimson row of tulips that line one side of my backyard garden. For a brief moment, I go into the house. Peter remains outside. "I will be right back!" I tell him. When I return a short while later, I see my little boy standing next to a neatly stacked heap of red tulip blossoms. The flowerbed is barren; the rows of tulip stalks are the only reminders of their vanished beauty. In my shock, I cannot find appropriate words, and Peter seems to be so proud of his accomplishment that whatever I had wanted to say remains unsaid.

Motherhood brings me unexpected blessings, and I am determined to be the best mother I can be. Peter is very easy to love, but a much harder task is to discipline and teach him. Dr. Benjamin Spock's books are continuously consulted. He is my guide and teacher. Whenever I run into a problem or am not sure of what to do, I leaf through his "Baby and Child Care" and most often find answers to my questions.

KRISTINE JOINS OUR FAMILY

My secret dream had always been to have a daughter. Since I grew up in a family of girls, I feel more relaxed and at ease with girls, though Peter certainly has changed this feeling. His arrival has been a real blessing to me and Arvids. But an only child is also a lonely child. Arvids and I feel that we all would benefit from having another child in the family. We discuss our plans with the agency, and then proceed to file the papers for another adoption. This time, it is a much simpler affair, since we have already gone through the screening and have been approved for parenthood. After a few months of waiting, the agency calls us with the happy news that they have found a perfect little girl for us.

On the morning of June 1st, 1964, Arvids, two-year-old Peter and I, head off to Worcester to pick up our new family member. I have chosen her name. Kristine. It seems to be such a good and wholesome name for a girl. As we open the agency's door and walk into the waiting room, my heart gives several restless beats. The social worker is standing next to a window, holding in her arms - a little girl, all dressed in pink. She walks over to meet us, and hands Kristine to me, as Arvids comments: "Now Astrida finally has her daughter!" Yes, my wish has been fulfilled. I glance at my daughter. Slightly wavy, chestnut brown hair frames her pretty face. Her dark eyes look at me questionably, searchingly. "What does she feel? What does she think?" I wonder.

The foster parents with whom Kristine has lived during the first seven months of her life had called her Beth. Now, she will have to adjust to a new name, new home, accept new parents, and a new brother. For all of us, life will be different. I look forward to this difference with joy and prayerful expectation, and also, with some concern.

The first couple of weeks are a bit rocky. Kristine refuses to eat, just looks at me with a quizzical expression in her brown eyes when I try to feed her. I am concerned. Kristine is a thin child and needs good nourishment to thrive and grow. Within a couple of weeks, however, she starts to adjust to us, starts to eat and gain weight. A happy smile lights up her pretty face. She has accepted us! Finally, she has arrived home. Kristine develops into an outgoing, joyful little person. She is slightly timid around strangers, but with her family, is relaxed and good-natured. She is sensitive and bright, and I believe that the initial difficulty of accepting her new home and family is directly related to these traits.

Before she learns to walk, Kristine uses a most interesting way to propel herself around. She tucks one of her legs under her and uses the other one to push herself forward. This unusual way of "walking" earns her a nickname of Chester. I believe that my cousin Aivars is the first to call her Chester. Shortly before her first birthday, Kristine masters the art of walking, at first wobbly and unsure, but soon she is a real "walking champion". Kristine's sunny and friendly personality gains her many friends. She loves to socialize with both adults and children alike. Mother Goose rhymes gain a colorful dimension when Kris adds her own interpretation with gestures, mimics, and acrobatics. She is a natural entertainer!

As Kristine grows and develops, she brings much joy into our house. She is warm, funny, and friendly. She also exhibits wisdom, which is well beyond her years. Often she amazes me with her statements and judgments. In the small body of a young girl seems to dwell a woman of great insight.

At that time, I discussed issues with her that, in retrospect, were too serious and heavy for a child. But it was easy, because she listened with intentness and understanding. Besides being my daughter, she was also my friend.

FOUR MAKES A FAMILY

With Kristine's arrival, our family is complete. A sense of peace settles over our household. At first, Peter has some difficulty accepting his new sister. He is used to being the very center of our universe. A rival has entered this universe, threatening his security. I do not know how well I am doing in assuring him that nobody and nothing would ever change our love for him, that no one can or would take his place in our hearts. A child's heart is very sensitive, so impressionable, so easily hurt, so easily bruised! At times, I wonder how this adjustment period will affect Peter's personality. Will it leave permanent imprints on his soul?

Our days are filled with activity. When I do not cook, sew, or work in the garden, we play games, read, and go for walks. On good days we take walks on Glen Street. It is a long straight road, and to cover even a part of it offers good exercise to all of us. On our walks we try to spot birds on tree branches, pick roadside flowers, and find pretty pebbles to bring back home with us. Peter is especially good at pointing out birds. His favorite find is the tree-climbing woodpecker that we fondly call "putniņš dzenītis", a Latvian name for this bird. "Skaties, putniņš dzenītis (look, a woodpecker)!", I hear Peter's little voice announcing. Soon, Peter names all the birds we meet on our walks "putniņš dzenītis".

Behind our house, separated by a stone wall, spread the fields and orchards of Lookout Farm. During the spring and summer months, we like to observe the activity in the fields where the farm hands work the soil, plant crops, and in the fall gather their harvest. A special fun time for us is the apple picking time. We walk over to the orchards to gather the so-called "drops". A full bushel of apples costs only one dollar!

My kitchen is a very busy place during the summer and fall seasons. Our garden produces much more than the family can consume or can be given away to relatives, friends, and neighbors. Therefore, our kitchen is temporarily transformed into a "farm produce processing plant". I can and freeze vegetables, make jellies from our backyard grape and red currant harvest in addition to all the good things prepared from apples. Delicious fragrances saturate the air. Jars filled with applesauce, apple butter, apple, grape and red currant jellies line the pantry shelves. We invest in a huge freezer to store the vegetables and fruit that I have prepared and packaged for freezing. This is a happy time with lots of productive activity for all the members of our family. It is a pleasure in the winter months to walk down to the basement, open the freezer door, and help myself to whatever I needed for that day's meal.

NEW FRIENDSHIPS

I do not really miss work, but I miss the people I have learned to love there - my friends. To get together with them is rather difficult because of Arvids 's objections. He likes to be in control. Also, transportation is an issue, because we have only one car, and Arvids uses it to commute to work.

Eventually, I meet neighbors with small children and develop new friendships. One day while I am busily working at my sewing machine, there is a knock at the kitchen door. As I open it, outside stands a young woman holding a little boy's hand. "I am your neighbor, Edith Jones, and am looking for a playmate for my son Christopher," she says. I invite them in, offer a cup of coffee to Edith, and the two of us discuss the importance of playmates for our children. We agree to meet several times a week at each other's homes so that our sons can play together. Since they live only a couple of houses down the road from us, this poses no difficulty. Thus starts our regular meetings, and, in time, the four of us become close friends. Christopher and Peter are the same age and enjoy playing together. His mother fills my need for adult companionship and good conversation. We cover many topics, from culinary arts to world affairs. Edi was a political major in college, is well versed in current affairs, and is an astute analyst of American political life. From Edi, I learn to like politics, to be a critical reader of newspapers and magazines. Before Edi enlightened me, I tended to believe in the written word as if it were the Gospel truth. Over cups of coffee, we have lengthy discussions while our boys try to share toys and, mostly, have a good time together.

Edi's kitchen is a happy place where friends are welcome. She tells me that her mother, a German immigrant, had never had time for her neighbors, always being preoccupied with cooking meals for her family, keeping a spotless house and doing all the necessary sewing, mending, and knitting for the household. She had followed the rule of the "three Ks" that a good German housewife was guided by: "Kinder, Kueche, Kirche" (children, kitchen, church). Edi is determined not to live her mother's lonely life, and makes sure that her family has many friends, and often hosts dinner parties.

On Saturdays, the Jones's house is filled with a delicious aroma. Starting in the morning, step by step, Edi meticulously combines all the necessary ingredients in a traditional earthenware bean pot to make New England baked beans. It takes the better part of her day to prepare and bake the beans.

(Now, when I see or taste New England baked beans, I think of Edi. Do her children, Randy, Gweneth and Christopher, remember these traditional Saturday night dinners? To me they seemed to be warm, loving, and very special family gathering times. To this day, Edi and I exchange Christmas cards. We keep in touch. Our lives have undergone many changes. Unchanged and permanent, however, is the time we enjoyed together in South Natick. That chapter is safe in my memory.)

THE ARNOLDS ARRIVE

A pleasant change for the children and me begins when the Arnold family move next door. Madeleine and George have five children: three boys and two girls. Our children are a bit younger than the Arnolds', but that does not prevent them from developing close friendships. The Arnolds' youngest girl, Barbara, is a couple of years older than Kris, and the two become very good friends. Our backyard sees lots of activity: badminton and ping-pong are very popular, as are playing catch, hide-and-seek, or having lunch under the spreading branches of the crab apple tree. Steve and Teresa become Peter's special buddies. Their relationship, however, is not always harmonious, and it is usually my responsibility to be the judge, to make the decision of guilt or innocence. That is my least favorite responsibility.

Madeleine has a car, and frequently invites us to come along to shop, to sightsee, or just to go for rides. It is a welcome break from our daily routine.

HOLIDAY FROM APRON STRINGS

In the fall, the local YWCA offers a program called "Holiday from Apron Strings", for mothers with small children. "Let's sign up," Madeleine invites Edi and me. The three of us join the program, and Madeleine, the only car owner, provides our transportation. A new world opens to us. The children spend the day in a supervised kindergarten/playroom while their mothers in the adjoining rooms learn how to sew, embroider, make hats, exercise, discuss books, listen to lectures, etc. I meet interesting people, learn new crafts, and join a book discussion group. The most meaningful of all, however, is my participation in a small, intimate group that, under the "Y's" sponsorship, is formed and led by a local psychologist, Dr. Cohen. The group's theme is "Understanding yourself". Dr. Cohen encourages open discussion and sharing of feelings and experiences. It is my very first exposure to such self-analysis. At times it is truly dramatic, even disturbing. Hidden passages are revealed to me, unknown shadows of past experiences that still seem to control my reactions; my responses of today come to light. It is a very intense and intimate journey into my inner psyche. The members of this group become very close, and our friendships continue long after our formal meetings end. I develop especially close ties with Lee Shull. Our childhood experiences, our emotional makeup, our reactions to situations, for me, are like reflections in a pool of clear water. I hear her stories resonating in my soul as if they were my own. Lee and I become (and remain) close friends.

"Holiday from Apron Strings" leads me into a wonderful hobby - crewel embroidery. The beginnings of crewel embroidery, also called "painting with needle and thread", can be traced back to sixteenth century England. Trade with India and the founding of The East India Company allowed imports of fabrics and exotic designs from the East to England. One notable import was the very popular "tree of life" motif that even today takes an important place in crewel patterns. In time, the designs were adapted to express the local culture and customs. The English gentlewomen spent many of their leisure hours embroidering intricate patterns on linen or cotton fabrics with wool and later silk thread, experimenting with a variety of elaborate stitches. Valances, chair covers, bedspreads, petticoats, and bell-pulls were beautifully decorated. As the English came to America, they brought this heritage of crewel embroidery with them and in time it changed to portray the life in their adopted country.

Our teacher, Lois Derderian Holman, is an artist whose expertise and love for this old form of needlework inspires her students. Lois has an ability to reach her students on a very personal and individual level. That greatly impresses me. She recognizes our differences, and encourages us to develop our own unique character and style in color and design. It is an exciting development, and I become her devout disciple. I learn the effective use of color, and how to make my own designs. I feel very creative. It is a revelation to me that one can be so completely consumed by the process of creation. I spend many hours embroidering, choosing and combining colors, experimenting with stitches. Under Lois's guidance, my fingers create numerous colorful and beautiful embroidery pieces. My most ambitious achievement are two pairs of curtains for our bedroom windows. It is a labor of love and patience, and I am very proud with the result. To work with needle and thread is exciting and fun. In time, I develop enough proficiency to be able to conduct my own crewel embroidery classes. When I need help, Lois is always available to assist. I enjoy teaching. Also, the extra spending money helps my limited budget.

During the time Lois is working at the "Y", her personal life is in turmoil. She does not talk about it openly, but one can sense the deep unrest underneath her calm exterior. Eventually we learn that Lois had separated from her husband and lives alone with her four children in their large house in Sudbury, Massachusetts. A short time later, her son, Bruce, and a friend are killed in an automobile accident on their way home from New York City. How can one understand the loss of a child so suddenly and tragically? Lois, standing next to her son's coffin in the funeral home, a vulnerable, slight figure, will always stay with me.

(A blessing that reaches into my present life from that time is my friendship with Lois. Her gentle soul, her spirituality, and strength have been an inspiration to me. We have supported each other during tragic periods of our lives and shared laughs during the happy times.)

SCHOOL TIME IS HERE

Where did the years go? My little son has reached school age! In February of 1967, Peter turns five, and in August of that year, I sign him up for kindergarten. Since the town of Natick does not provide transportation for the kindergartners, we buy a ten–year-old Rambler. It is a real "cream puff", has very low mileage, and looks almost like new. I love my car! It gives me heretofore unknown independence and freedom, and Peter transportation to school.

On the day after Labor Day, Kristine and I take Peter to school. I am nervous. Will he be all right? Will he be able to adjust without difficulty to the school environment? As we walk into the classroom, the kindergarten teacher, Mrs. Freeman, a pleasant silver-haired lady, greets us. "Hello, Peter," she says, taking his hand and waving me goodbye. Just like that! As if it were nothing special that I am leaving my little son all alone among strangers! My heart gives a painful jolt as I turn to the door. Another glance back. Peter has already vanished in a crowd of other little boys and girls. He is OK! It is I who has some adjusting to do!

Naturally, I adjust. In another year, Kristine starts school. My children are on their way to independence, and I am left with a lot of time on my hands. There is a void that needs to be filled, and the neighborhood "coffee-klatch" gatherings leave me feeling empty. Time is too precious to waste, so I sign up for classes at Northeastern University to finish my education. I choose morning classes in order to be home when the children arrive back from school. My studies challenge and inspire me. I feel alive and excited. Life is good, and for a while, our family's ship sails in calm waters.

SOME RIPPLES

The only recognizable changes in our family's life during this time are the changes in our children. They continue to get older, to grow in size and independence. At times, Peter's independence creates a real headache for us, especially for me, because I am usually the one who bears the responsibility for the children's misdeeds.

Peter loves firecrackers! Where he gets hold of the loud and also dangerous explosives is a mystery to me. At one time, he is caught by the police in the act of exploding these "crackers". We receive a notice to come to the police station for a meeting. Arvids refuses to go. Peter's actions are my responsibility, he says. I go, with my heart stuck in my throat. I have always viewed police officers with respect, and also with some fear. To enter a police station and to face one of these officers as a guilty person (in the eyes of the law, I am responsible for what my son does) is one of the hardest things I have to do as a mother. Peter and I are led into a room where a policeman greets us and asks us to take a seat facing him. Much of what is discussed during this meeting I have blocked out of my memory. We leave the room with a promise that, in the future, Peter will abstain from using firecrackers. Peter's obsession with firecrackers, however, does not end that day. Lucky for him, he never gets caught again.

But from very early on, Peter had always been a very active child, and prone to accidents. When still a toddler, one evening he'd been happily jumping in his crib. He falls and injures his eyelid on the bedpost. A big gash and severe bleeding scares all of us, and we quickly rush Peter to the local hospital. While the surgeon sutures Peter's wound, I held my son's hand and tried to calm the horrified boy. I feel his pain as my pain, wishing to take away his suffering, his fright!

A similar incident happened several years later. I am sitting at a kitchen counter listening to the evening news as the reporter announces that Robert Kennedy has just been shot by an assailant, when behind me I hear a sound of breaking glass and Peter's cry. Quickly turning around, I see Peter outside the kitchen door with his arm stuck through the door's broken glass. In his haste to come in from playing outdoors, he has pushed on the door's glass and has broken it. I jump from my seat, run to help Peter extricate himself from the glass, grab a towel, wrap his bleeding arm in it, rush him into the car, and drive to the hospital's emergency room. "Deja-vous!" Again, as before, I am there to support my son, to feel for him, to try to calm his anxiety as well as mine. Subsequently, the glass in the door is replaced by a much safer Plexiglas.

As time goes on, Leonard Morse Hospital becomes quite a well-known place to our family. We turn there for help in every emergency. When Kris breaks her wrist falling from a bike, we both spend a whole day there while she undergoes evaluation of her injury and receives treatment. In the early summer of 1979, Peter is taken there after his motorcycle accident, when a car runs into him, almost severing his leg. After many surgeries and several hospitalizations, he still has a slight limp. And it is in the cardiac unit of the hospital where Arvids spends the month of November of the same year recuperating from his first heart attack.

As years go on, our life undergoes many changes. We, as a family, and as individuals, experience much darkness and pain, as well as lightness and joy. Nothing and nobody can erase the very special blessings that our children have brought into our lives.

OUR EXTENDED FAMILY

Close family ties are always important to us. Small arguments or minor misunderstandings never reach our family's heart; never seriously trouble its relationship. We are joined in mutual loyalty, ready to defend each other and help each other.

My sister Skaidrite's family (the Andersons) live in the neighboring town of Sherborn, just ten minutes away from us, and we spend a lot of our free time with them. Since I have a car now, and my sister does not, I provide the transportation when there is a need. Kris develops a very close friendship with her cousin, Anne. They both love horseback riding and also take ballet lessons together. Friday, in general, is our day out with the children. We go shopping, have a meal at a restaurant, and while Skaidrite and I leisurely finish our food, discussing whatever seems important and interesting at the time, the children explore the shopping mall and happily spend their weekly allowance.

A very special time for our family is Christmas. It is a tradition to spend Christmas Eve at the Anderson's house in Sherborn. A huge tree, brightly lit, reaches to the ceiling of their spacious living room, and spreads its warmth and light among the gathered. Ski starts the evening with a reading of Christmas poetry followed by the singing of carols that enfolds us all in the spirit of the holy event of Christ's birth. Our caroling is accompanied by Anne and Peter on the piano, and

Kris on her flute. This is a blessed and peace-filled family time.

My godmother, Tante Elza, and her two children have always remained an integral part of our family. Since we left Latvia, our lives have run a parallel course; we are always closely connected, keeping in touch. Eventually, they move to Boston from Connecticut. Before they buy a house, they share an apartment in Jamaica Plain with my sister, Ruta. Cousin Aivars graduates from the University of Connecticut with a degree in engineering. His sister, Astra, becomes an airline stewardess. She works for American Airlines, where she meets Captain Thomas Holmes, falls in love, and marries. Their wedding is celebrated on August 21, 1965 at the Anderson's house in Sherborn. The day is warm and sunny, as is the mood of all present; a perfect day and a handsome and happy couple! Skaidrite's picturesque garden, which exhibits her training and skill in landscape design, makes a perfect setting for the guests to gather and enjoy Astra and Tom's special day.

After a short stay in California, Astra and Tom settle in New Hampshire. California felt too crowded; they both love nature and the freedom of open spaces. In New Hampshire, they create their own Shangri-la, a charming house that displays their fine taste and love for country antiques. As one steps into the house, one seems to step back in time, surrounded by old-fashioned warmth. With Tom's assistance, Astra has planted a beautiful garden. Tom's love for building and woodworking has created what can best be described as a watchtower house and a barn workshop. For many years, we enjoy their hospitality during Thanksgiving holidays and are their guests on many other special occasions.

Aivars buys a house in Auburndale, Massachusetts, where he lives with his mother, Elza. For many years, our family gathers for Easter breakfast at their home. These special traditions hold our family together and add richness to our lives.

THE LATVIAN COMMUNITY

The Latvian community is very much the center of our lives. We are members of the Latvian Lutheran Church, and when our children reach school age, we enroll them in the Latvian Saturday School. The school's main goal is to teach the children Latvian language, culture, history, and religion. This takes away the children's free Saturdays, and also requires giving up some evening time to prepare the Latvian school homework. That is no fun for any of us. I still remember our struggle with the "Abece", the reading exercise book, and the penmanship practice sessions, where the lines drawn by the children's small hands just would not follow the lines in the exercise. book. Or the effort to learn and remember the history of the Latvian people, their traditions, art and folklore, and the geography of Latvia. Both children graduate from the Latvian Saturday School in Boston, and Kristine continues her studies in a Latvian summer high school in Quakertown, Pennsylvania. The school is named "Beverina", after an ancient Latvian kingdom. *(Today, in retrospect, I ask myself: How important was this considerable effort on our children's and our part? Did it leave any lasting and meaningful imprints and understanding of their parents' heritage in Kristine and Peter's perception? Do they feel some connection to this legacy? I do not know.)*

To Arvids and me, it was important to pass our heritage on to our children. Latvia was very much a part of us, and we wanted our children to inherit and understand our roots. Peter and Kristine can converse in Latvian; they can also, to some degree, read and write in Latvian. It is a plus, certainly. At our family gatherings when the predominant language is Latvian, they can feel at home and included.

During the time when Peter and Kris attend Latvian School, and even after their graduation, I am actively involved as a teacher of the Latvian language and literature. An interesting discovery for me is that I love teaching children and have a very good rapport with my students. My work there is a labor of love. The hours spent in preparing for the class presentations and correcting students' papers is a gift of my time that is given with pleasure. I consider this time as one of the most meaningful periods in my life, where I had the opportunity to pass on what is very precious to me, my Latvian heritage.

(A number of the children who graduated from the Latvian Schools, have now, after the Soviet empire collapsed and Latvia regained its freedom and independence, returned to their parents' homeland. They work there in various capacities and contribute significantly to the rebuilding of the country. I am glad that, in a small measure, I have been able to influence their understanding of Latvia, and thus their love and commitment to the country and her people.)

OUR LATVIAN FRIENDS

Our family develops special friendships with the Bunde and Veidis families. Rudi Bunde and Mikelis Veidis are Arvids' fraternity brothers. Arvids has known Rudi since his university years in Pinneberg, Germany. With Miķelis, his friendship develops much later when he and his family arrive in Boston from Australia via Canada. Arvids does not form friendships easily, but he likes Miķelis. A common bond among them is the Latvian fraternity, Gersicania. It gives their relationship a special significance. Miķelis' wife, Brigita, and I become good friends. An interesting coincidence is that Brigita and I look very much alike, even though we have no blood relationship. We also have somewhat similar personalities. When we first meet them, the Veidis have two children: a daughter, Valda, who becomes Kristine's good friend, and a son, Andris. A second son, Martins, was born in Boston, and my cousin Aivars and I are chosen to be his godparents. It is an honor and is also a responsibility. *(My ties with Martins have continued to be special. When I was diagnosed with cancer in the summer of 2003, Martins was a great support to me, giving his time and love. His unexpected kindness and concern have deeply touched me.)*

With the Veidis family, we take short sightseeing trips, Sunday walks through the woods during the warm seasons, and skate on the nearby ponds on the cold winter days. Miķelis is an ardent fisherman, and on many a Sunday, we join the

Veidis family on their fishing expeditions. On late fall days, we visit Cape Cod's cranberry bogs to gather the leftover berries after the fields have been harvested. On our return home from these Sunday trips, we often enjoy supper together at one another's houses.

Our family enjoys vacations on Cape Cod and in New Hampshire, especially the camping days on our church farm "Piesaule". "Piesaule" in English means "place in the sun", and it aptly describes the tranquil beauty of this old farm in the town of Bradford, near Lake Sunapee. There, our family owns a piece of land where we set up our tent, and usually spend a relaxed week of fishing, swimming, and enjoying the company of other vacationers. The Latvians love to sing, and many of our evenings extend late into the night in sing-along get-togethers. Piesaule is a center of summer activities for the Latvian community. Many people have built summer cottages there, thus having developed a surrogate Latvia, a homeland away from home. An especially beautiful and exciting event is the Midsummer Night's festivities, the celebration of summer solstice - an ancient Latvian holiday that is celebrated on the eve of the twenty-third of June, when the night is the shortest. A huge bonfire is lit in the middle of the farm's spacious meadow. Young and old gather around it and sing "ligo" songs, special songs devoted to this evening - the "Līgo vakars", as it is called in Latvian. In the northern country of Latvia, the sun has hardly set in the west when it greets a new morning in the east.

FIRST TRIP BACK TO LATVIA IN 1975

One very significant and special vacation for Kristine and me is our trip to Latvia in 1975. I had not been back since my family fled the country in 1944 to escape the Communist occupation. The fear of the Soviets has never diminished in my heart. It takes tremendous courage to go back for this short visit. For Kris it is an exciting adventure; for me a tense pilgrimage. On our way, we visit St. Petersburg (Leningrad, then) and Moscow. It is impressive, and also sad, to see these old cities where the czars had lived, where so much of the past tragic history can still be felt. In Leningrad, we board a small Aeroflot airplane that will take us to Riga. As the plane crosses the Soviet boarder into Latvia, the passengers crowd at the tiny windows to get a view of Latvia. It is an emotionally overwhelming moment for me to see my native country after more than thirty years of separation. It is a sacred moment, forever etched in my heart. Finally, Riga! A crowd of people welcome us at the gate with flowers, embraces, and smiles. It feels unreal to me, like a dream. How does Kristine feel?

Our visit lasts two weeks and flies by with incredible speed. Kristine conquers Riga and the hearts of our family and friends. She comes from the West, from freedom. She does not recognize the fear of "Big Brother" always watching her, unlike her newfound relatives who have lived under its shadow for years, and continue to do so. For them to see this young girl so free, so uninhibited, is like observing and meeting a storybook character. She brings them sunshine and the fresh air of freedom, even if just for a moment.

It is early morning when we gather again at the airport to say our final goodbyes. We are sad. There are tears as we hug each other for the last time. Kris and I are going back to our world. Our Latvian family is staying in theirs.

SUMMER VACATION

Our family's home for a week is an A-frame house in North Conway, NH. It is a friend's summer cottage that she graciously offered us for our vacation. To find it has been quite a trick! Trees, trees, streets without names, houses without numbers. We travel through this maze for some time. With a map in hand to guide us, eventually we find the right house.

The place seems a bit neglected. Tall, lush grass covers the ground and hides the walk to the deck and the main entrance. We carefully tread through it, and I unlock the door. Peter and Kris are first to explore our new home. They are excited and happy. A new adventure is about to start! We all take part in unloading the car and carrying in our luggage. The house is spacious. A large living, dining, and kitchen area takes up most of the downstairs. Two small bedrooms hide behind the kitchen area. Arvids and I will sleep there. The second floor mezzanine will be Peter and Kris's space. The place needs fresh air and good cleaning.

We open the doors and windows. I inspect the cabinets and find all the necessary cooking utensils and a good supply of dishes. My next job is to sweep the floors, wipe away the cobwebs, clean the counters, and wash the dishes. The children and Arvids, after settling into their own spaces, go off to explore our new neighborhood. I enjoy working alone. It takes up most of the afternoon, however, and much of my energy, to change a long unused house into a clean and livable home.

Finally the place looks inviting and bright and I sit down on the deck to relax and enjoy the tranquility of the late afternoon. Soon, voices through the trees announce my family's return. "Mom, we found the Saco River! Dad said that we can go fishing tomorrow." Peter is all excited. "Sounds good to me! We might have fish for supper tomorrow", I reply, leaving my comfortable position in the recliner. It is time to fix something for this evening's meal.

The next day is Sunday. After breakfast, the children and I take a walk through the woods to the river. It is a cloudy day and the grass still holds the night's mist. Peter and Kris lead me to a clearing on the riverbank. "Here is where we will be fishing later on," Peter explains. The fishing rod is ready and waiting, and he has his father's promise to join him. That is a special treat! On our way back, we pick some field flowers to decorate our house.

Our main project for the day is to explore the surrounding area and to find the nearby Echo Lake. The lake is all-important, because swimming for the children is the chief focus of our vacation.

On our way to the lake, we visit Cathedral Ledge. It is quite a dramatic sight. A shear stone ledge leads to the summit. A group of climbers, holding onto ropes and the outcroppings of rocks, slowly edge their way up! It is amazing to see this daring and seemingly dangerous pursuit. We spend some time watching their efforts, then get into our car and take the road up to the summit, the easy and safe way. "Be careful!" I call out to Peter and Kris, especially to Peter, as they get out of the car and run from the parking lot to explore the summit. Peter always seems to forget caution and likes to challenge his fate. He is only nine years old, and there is so much to be discovered! I hold on to Kris's hand as we look down the ledge to watch the climbers' progress. We wait until the first one is safely up. His reward is applause and happy calls, and, also, most certainly, his own pride and joy over this achievement.

We find blueberry bushes filled with berries just waiting to be picked and eaten. We do just that, and gather some to take along for our later enjoyment. I may even bake a pie. Today is my Name's Day. We can celebrate it with a pie. The time is getting late and our Echo Lake visit will have to be left for tomorrow. On our way home, we stop for ice cream and coffee. Arvids calls the coffee "muddy water" and I agree.

After arriving home, we take a short rest and then enjoy another walk through the surrounding woods. The silence and peace are comforting. We look for birds and try to identify them. Arvids is good at that. He also knows the species of most of the trees. This knowledge comes from his childhood days of growing up in a small country town in Latvia. Kris and Peter enjoy the seemingly limitless boundaries and freedom to run. We hear a sound of water through the trees and soon come upon a waterfall, an unexpected and delightful sight. Peter, in his eagerness to explore, touch, and feel, goes too close to the edge and slips into the water. It results in a couple of wet feet and one muddy bottom. On our arrival home, I do make the pie. Our second vacation day has been a fun day for all of us.

The next day greets us with sunshine and a cloudless sky. I pack a picnic basket, we gather our swimming suits, towels, some reading material and games, and off we go for our day on Echo Lake beach. Naturally, Peter's fishing rod is the most important item, safely stored away in the trunk.

The lake is about a 15 minute drive from our cottage. It is a picture of tranquil beauty, surrounded by mountains and woods. The beach is of golden sand, the water clear and pleasantly warm. We jump in, swim to the float, and try out our diving and jumping skills. After a while, I lie down on the warm boards to rest and let the sun's warmth cover my body. Kris and Peter swim back to the shore. It is the fishing that lures Peter away from the swimming. Arvids has remained on the shore. He will supervise, and I can relax in the sun's kindness, away from everybody. Soon, I hear Kristine's voice excitedly calling me to come back to the shore.

"Mom, mom, come quickly!" Peter has had an accident. Instead of catching a fish, he has caught himself on the fishhook. The hook is deeply nestled into his lower arm, and all our attempts to remove it are unsuccessful. Arvids cuts the line and the two of them get into the car to drive to the local hospital for help. Kris and I remain at the lake. We wait. An hour passes, two hours go by, when finally we see our car pulling into the parking lot. The hook has been removed. Only two small holes are visible, the entrance and the exit place. Peter is pale and quiet: an unfortunate ending to his so eagerly awaited fishing experience. I feel sorry for him! I hug him and say: "All will be well, Peterit!"

We are hungry and ready for our long delayed hamburger cookout. We gather twigs and pinecones for Arvids to start the fire. The first result is a lot of smoke. Eventually, a success! The hamburgers are barbecued and consumed with great appetite. A touch of smoky flavor does not seem to bother anyone.

Peter has regained his sense of well-being and is on the lookout for frogs. Arvids stretches out on the beach to relax. Kris and I decide to take a walk around the lake. A moss covered path winds through the woods, leading us into a beautiful and a bit mysterious world. I love forests! To me they seem to shelter the secrets of our very distant past, the undiscovered passages of primordial time and life, still somehow present in the hidden shadows, ready to be revealed, to be discovered. We look for mushrooms and blueberries and find some of both. It does not take long to circle the lake, and soon we are back for our final swim.

"This has been such a fun day!" says Kristine. The only black spot is Peter's mishap, but even that, now, seems to have drifted away. I make pancakes for our supper, then we sit on the deck to enjoy the warm evening while the children create and present a play for their interested parents.

The next day, day four of our vacation, is spent sightseeing. We visit Glen Ellis Falls and Wildcat Mountain. The gondola takes us up to the summit where we explore its secret hideouts and find a ledge with a splendid lookout. There, before our eyes, the world opens in its grandeur and spaciousness. I stand in awe. The earth's beauty is spiritual. God stands close by.

The Appalachian Trail, which cuts across the Eastern United States from Georgia to Maine, crosses over the Wildcat Mountain. Half jokingly, we start to follow it and come upon a hikers' shelter. One is reminded of all the individuals who have stopped here for a rest on their long journey. Our hike ends here. We take the easy road down in the gondola.

"I have a headache," Peter complains. It has been a long and hot day. We stop at the Howard Johnson's restaurant for supper and arrive home in time for a late evening swim in the Saco River.

All is quiet. The children are asleep. Arvids fixes me a drink, and I settle down with a book for an evening's rest. Tomorrow is a new day.

Day five is spent doing more sightseeing. We take the Kancamagus highway and follow it to the rapids. We park our car along the roadside and join the loud and happy crowd on the riverbank and in the fast flow of the river. To allow the water to carry one through the rapids is fun and exciting. "Hey, watch your children!" I hear Arvids call. "My children?" I mumble under my breath. And soon enough, there is a reason to "watch my children". I see Peter going over a large ledge into a deep crevice. I run to see if he is safe. Yes, he is climbing out from the bottom of the river and getting onto the shore. "My foot slipped," he says quite shaken and pale. Peterit! Peterit! He always manages to get himself into some unexpected and slippery circumstances. Arvids is angry. We decide to move on to a quieter spot along the river. Here we get out our picnic basket, sit down and enjoy our own company. After the meal, Arvids and Peter climb into the shallow waters of the river to look for trout. The fish hide under the rocks. It is quite a trick to find one. The searcher has to move very cautiously and noiselessly. Arvids spots a trout. "Oops!" It gets away. Kris and I relax on the shore and watch their efforts. The air vibrates in the August sun. Now and then a bee buzzes by, or a bird makes its happy call above our heads. It is a lazy and quiet afternoon.

The riverbanks are covered with trees, all sizes and shapes. Birches, pine trees, and maples I recognize. The sky is very clear and blue, and the green trees etch an exquisite design in its blueness. In a relaxed state of well-being, I totally immerse myself in the afternoon's gift of peace and beauty. Peter and Arvids climb out of the river. I reluctantly return to the real world.

On our way home, we shop for food and buy Kentucky fried chicken for our supper. The evening ends with a "Booby-

Trap" game in which we all participate.

"When are we going home?" Kristine is becoming restless. She misses her friends.

The weekend comes, and we welcome the arrival of the Anderson family. Thus, our last two vacation days have an added joy of pleasant companionship and fun. Kris and Peter finally have someone other than themselves to spend time with. Paul and Anne, their cousins, bring new life and excitement to their days, which had started to lose their original luster. Almost immediately after their arrival, we see the children, clad in their bathing suits, disappear in the direction of the river. The rest of us relax on the deck, sip cool drinks, and discuss the current political events and the galloping inflation, among other things. The next two days never lack for things to do. We take some short sightseeing trips to show our guests the surrounding areas of interest. We all agree, however, that the best choice is just to hang around the place, enjoy the lazy days of summer and each other's company.

The days flow by quickly. Time comes to pack up, to say good-bye to our A-frame home and to our summer vacation. We have had a fun time and many happy memories to take along.

But there is one more stop! On our way home, we drive by Nottingham, New Hampshire to visit Tom and Astra. As usual, their welcoming smiles and hugs bring us into a world of New England charm and hospitality. Even though we have just dropped by to say "hi", we are treated like long expected and treasured guests. It is Astra and Tom's unique gift of making everyone who visits them feel special. Their house is very special too. It sits on a hill overlooking the town of Nottingham, the white church in its foreground and the distant White Mountains dimly visible at the horizon line. It is a sight one wants to take along on leaving. Above and beyond everything, there is Astra's garden! It is a thing of beauty, the result of Astra's hard work and love of gardening.

We soon bid "good-bye" to our gracious hosts and head home. Our vacation has ended.

THANKSGIVINGS REMEMBERED

It usually takes years for family traditions to develop. Some live only for a while and in the passage of time are replaced by something different and new. Holidays are very important tradition builders, and for our family, each of them holds special memories. Most of these memories are happy; some have a sprinkling of sadness.

In the following pages, I would like to walk through the years and relive our family get-togethers as we celebrated Thanksgiving.

For me, Thanksgiving is the holiday that has a very special glow surrounding it. Like a string of golden beads, it winds through the passage of years, leaving especially happy and warm memories. This holiday was a total stranger to us when we first came to United States. It was not celebrated in Latvia. The closest thing to Thanksgiving was the harvest festival, however, it did not hold the significance or the traditionalism of the Thanksgiving as we celebrate here. When we started our family get-togethers, it was my home where we had the holiday meal. I enjoyed preparing the turkey dinner with all the fixings. It was fun and had a lot of happy moments. But this tradition changed when our cousin Astra and her husband Tom moved from California to Nottingham, New Hampshire. Their move to the East Coast came very close to Thanksgiving Day and they invited the whole family to a very traditional Thanksgiving feast at the Sturbridge Village. It was a very special day for all of us: the young, as well as the not so young. We toured the village before the meal, and it was an enlightening experience, since the whole place was set up to relive the very first Thanksgiving of the pilgrims. Pretty girls dressed in traditional garb served our Thanksgiving meal, and the food was also very traditional. This certainly was a day that will always live in my memory as a unique and a special experience. And it also changed our family's traditional Thanksgiving feast from my house to Astra and Tom's house. And it was all for the better!

Astra and Tom had bought a lovely house in Nottingham. The architecture of the house is hard to describe. It had its own style and charm. It seems to have climbed out of the past, when the world was a simpler place, when life styles were less crammed with busy work and anxious days, when people knew the value of peace and relaxation. Who knows, probably there never was a world like that, but Astra and Tom's house made one think of such an ideal place. It was the most perfect setting for the most perfect, traditional Thanksgiving celebration.

The family would usually arrive between twelve noon and one o'clock. One by one, the cars would pull into the big courtyard, and before we could park and get out of our vehicles, Tom's smiling face would appear in front of us with a joyful greeting: "So great to see you!", followed by a warm hug. "Please, come in!" The door to the house opened again, and cousin Astra with her usual friendly smile waved us inside. There, we were greeted by the third member of the family, their dog. First, it was Rocket, the long eared, short-legged basset hound, who was afraid of everyone but his immediate family. He loved his masters and Mozart. When Mozart's music was played, he stayed close to the source and sang along in his doggie voice. Rocket was followed by Wendy, an overly friendly golden retriever. Over the years, the four-legged family member changed in shape and temperament, but there was always one present as we stepped through the door into the house which held the spirit of the very first Thanksgiving.

Astra and Tom loved antiques, especially country antiques, and beautiful objects from the past filled their house. There was the black-bellied stove in the library that radiated a friendly glow from the burning fire. A crowd was always gathered around it. An old post office box with many little compartments and combination locks was my son Peter's object of technical exercise, in his effort to decipher the combinations. He was quite successful! The house was rich in things of the past and the beauty of the present. Tom's love of woodworking was seen in every room; the grandfather's clock in the dining room was a true work of art. One could wander from room to room and find something to admire and appreciate. But what we all admired and appreciated the most, was the warm and wonderful hospitality of our hosts. They radiated love and made us feel so much at home, so very welcomed.

The kitchen was a busy and happy place. We all tried to help out and contribute under Astra's expert guidance. And the final result was a feast in its truest sense. The table decorations displayed Astra's imaginative taste, and the meal received at least a five star rating from all present.

Over the years, the turkey was the only constant part of the meal. The fixings would change, as well as the attendance. Tom's mother, Audie, who'd been a very important part of our Thanksgiving family, parted from us to be with her Lord. She had lived in His presence in this world, and there was never a doubt in her mind that she would be with Him in the next.

Another very sad Thanksgiving came when my husband Arvids had a heart attack just before the Holiday. We visited him in the hospital before leaving for Nottingham. This would be Arvids' last Thanksgiving. As the years passed, our children grew and changed, eventually marrying and having their own families. Astra and Tom continued to welcome them. Their house was always open to the ever-expanding extended family. To go to Nottingham for Thanksgiving was very important to all of us. It was a tradition we all cherished, enjoyed, and were thankful for, a rich and beautiful gift which Astra and Tom gave us in such a spirit of generosity.

Generations change; family traditions change. Eventually, Anne, my sister Skaidrite's daughter, and her husband Jerome, bought an old and charming house in Northampton,

Massachusetts, and we were welcomed to celebrate Thanksgiving there.

But as tradition changes, the warm glow of past Thanksgivings with Astra and Tom in Nottingham never fade away. These golden moments remain with us forever.

ARVIDS' DEPARTURE

It is January 31, 1980. The day is cold and gray, and my personal world is also immersed in the midwinter cold and stillness. I sit at my desk at work and try to concentrate on the tasks before me. In the next building of the Massachusetts General Hospital, just a short walk away, my husband Arvids is fighting for his life. A pacemaker was placed in his chest yesterday to help his damaged heart to beat, however it had not made much of a difference in his condition.

Just a short while ago, I went to have lunch in Arvids' room and to help him with his food, as I have done every day since his hospitalization. To see this proud man so weak and disabled, so dependent on outside help for his every need, is very humbling and painful. And, it is surely humiliating to him.

Arvids is attached to tubes and machines; they keep him alive. During my visits, I usually just sit. Conversations are difficult. Throughout our life, through our many years of marriage, we were poor communicators. It is different now, though. We do not talk, because every word is an effort on Arvids' part. It saps his meager strength. And I don't know what to say. We sit in silence and listen to the clock ticking away his life. Three months ago, he had been a healthy person. At least he appeared to be. How did this nightmare begin?

It was a late evening on November 2, 1979. Arvids had gone to a meeting and was late coming home. I was sitting at the dining room table reading when he finally arrived. He went directly to the bedroom but soon came back. "I don't feel well. I have a tremendous pressure in my chest!" he said. His face was ashen. He looked ill. "I will take you to the hospital!" Our daughter, Kris, came along.

The Leonard Morse Hospital in Natick was only a short distance away; we were in their emergency room within 15 minutes, and within half-an-hour we knew that Arvids had suffered a serious heart attack. Naturally, this was shocking news, but there was hope for his complete recovery.

After a month of treatment, he was discharged home. It was a happy day for all of us. The late fall sun kindly warmed Arvids' homecoming. His first wish was to see the garden, and in a slow pace, he walked up the small incline to the house and to the garden, stopping here and there, looking around at the many growing things that, over the years, he had planted and tended to. I could feel his joy of being home again. This joy was short-lived, though. Within a month, Arvids had another heart attack and was taken by ambulance to Massachusetts General Hospital. There, it became clear that his heart was severely damaged, that he could not live without a heart-lung machine. He looked healthy and well while on the mechanical support but went into severe distress when it was withdrawn. It was a struggle. Day after day, he was fighting to survive. The last hope had been the pacemaker.

I sit in my office fighting away the gloom that strangles my heart. I know, and don't want to know, the inevitable. On my way home, I go back to Arvids' room. The nurse is with him. "I am thirsty," he whispers. She gives him ginger ale, which results in a severe coughing spell. The nurse asks me to leave the room. "I will wait outside," I say. "You cannot do anything here" she says. "Not tonight. Please go home." I look back at Arvids as he struggles for breath and softly close the door behind me.

I am at home with Kris. The house is lonely and dark and feels very empty. Peter is in the hospital, awaiting surgery to repair his fractured leg. He had had a motorcycle accident earlier in the year. At ten o'clock, the telephone rings. I know, even before Dr. Yurchak's voice announces: "Your husband just died." Kris stands beside me. We hug and cry.

A life has ended, Arvids' life. What was his journey like? He was a complex man, and I think also a very lonely man. He had few friends, and his relationships with friends and relatives were volatile. A word or an action could easily be misunderstood and a bond broken, sometimes never to be mended. Arvids expected perfection from himself and others. Darkness and light lived in him side-by-side; he could be very kind and loving, but also very cruel and ruthless. He felt deeply and thought deeply. Music relaxed him. He enjoyed art and literature. He avoided large crowds and public parties. Family was the center of his life, and he deeply cared for his children and their welfare. Sadly, his caring often resulted in a need to control, to dictate. This was a cause of many conflicts.

Arvids was a disciplined person, and his achievements were the result of hard work and persistence. From early childhood on, he had learned discipline and self-sufficiency. The grammar school he attended was about six kilometers from his home. He had to measure the long distance every day, rain or snow. It had not been easy for the small boy. He remembered these years with affection, though. His father had died when Arvids was still very young. He carried the pain of this loss well into his adulthood. To continue his education, Arvids went to Riga. Again, hard work, persistence, and discipline helped him to graduate from the "technikums" (technical high-school) and enter the University of Riga's architectural program. To be an architect had been his lifelong goal. But war interrupted Arvids' studies. When the Soviet armies occupied Latvia, he left his native country for Germany. There, he eventually completed his studies in architecture and received a diploma from the Baltic University in Pinneberg.

Arvids had a strong affinity for nature. This love of nature was rooted in the distant past, his early boyhood. He grew up in a small town in Latvia, Skriveri, which was surrounded by woods, hills, and water. He liked to reflect on his childhood years, years when he would freely roam the countryside, learning to recognize birds and their habits, trees by their foliage, and insect and plant life. His favorite place had been the river bank. He could sit there for hours observing the changing flow of the water or watch a tiny ant carrying a load many times its size through the tall grass. He never lost this special relationship with nature, and felt, that in nature, the creative force of God was working in the most miraculous ways. I truly believe that the garden that Arvids so lovingly planted and cared for, and where he found peace and relaxation, was a symbol of his childhood happiness.

How does one measure one's life and the value of it? Ralph Waldo Emerson wrote: "To know even one life has breathed easier because you lived. This is to have succeeded."

After Arvids' death, I found a paper in his desk titled: "If I were twenty-one years old." Here, he lists ten rules and objectives he would live by. The last two read: "I would live a balanced life, giving my time in equal measure to work, play, love, and religion." "I would find harmony with the Eternal, opening my life to higher intellectual and spiritual forces."

Only Arvids knows how many of his goals he achieved. I do hope that, in some measure, he had found peace with God and himself.

LIFE AFTER ARVIDS

It feels like an earthquake has hit our family's structure. The foundation has been shaken; life disrupted. Arvids is gone. He has always been in charge. Even through his illness, he was the manager. My responsibility for the running of our house or the family was secondary to his. Now his place is empty. I have to take over the management of the children and the running of the household. The conditions are adverse. Peter is on crutches. His broken leg has not been healing well and he has to undergo another surgery. Peter had been admitted to the hospital, awaiting surgery, when Arvids died. So, plans changed, and my brother-in-law, Juris, and I went to the hospital to bring Peter home that night. To tell Peter about his father's death is my very first responsibility as the new head of our household. A very painful beginning.

During the immediate weeks following Arvids' death, my family and friends are a great support. They stand by me and help me. Nobody, however, can take my place, make my decisions, and face my problems. The loneliness I feel is my own, mine is the pain, mine are the decisions to make, the actions to take.

Peter eventually has his delayed surgery and returns to high school to finish his senior year. Kris is sixteen. This is a difficult age in any circumstance, but extremely hard at a time of a family shake-up. She is totally out of my control. Even before her father's illness and death, our relationship had changed; she was following her own pilot and did not listen much to either Arvids or me. Arvids' death has brought a total breakdown in our relationship. We do not communicate at all. She is failing in school and spends most of her time with her boyfriend, Larry. Through the help of the school and her teachers, I try to reach her, without any success. Soon, Kris announces that she is leaving school and that I can do nothing to stop her. My pleading has no results. I ask Larry to help me to convince Kris to stay in school, but she does not listen to him either. Apparently, some time ago, he had dropped out of Natick high school and recently had tried to re-enter, but had not been accepted. This has made both of them, especially Kris, bitter and angry with the school.

I feel very alone and helpless. "What can I do? What will I do?" Soon after Kris's announcement, something strange happens. I have fallen asleep on the living room sofa and have an unusual dream, a vision. Arvids is standing in the midst of several men, all clad in black. I run to him, calling: "Help me, please!" He looks at me with indifference and walks away. I awake with an empty feeling in my chest and a profound realization that I stand alone.

In the spring, Peter graduates from high school and receives his diploma while still on crutches. He has to start thinking about his future; to make plans. He is interested in auto mechanics and applies to the Franklin Institute in Boston, is accepted there, and in the fall will start his studies. The year has been difficult for Peter: his accident, followed by a long hospitalization and several surgeries, his father's illness and death, and another hospitalization with surgery. He is understandably depressed, and I am concerned about him.

It is a late evening. Peter is asleep in his room. Kris has not come home and I am worried. "Where is she?" I wonder. The kitchen door opens and Kris walks in. Without saying a word, she goes directly to her room. A chill moves through my body. Soon Kris reappears, comes over to the dining room table where I sit frozen in place, puts a letter in front of me, and says, "I am leaving." "Leaving? What do you mean? Where are you going?" My anxious questions seem to remain hanging in the air. "I am leaving this house!" she says, opens the kitchen door, through which she, only minutes ago had entered, and walks out. I run after her in the chilly January night. "Kris, come back, please!" I plead. Without another word, she walks away, gets into Larry's waiting car, and disappears in the darkness. The chilly night air penetrates me and numbs me. If there is a place of total desperation and void, that is where I am. I walk back into the house. I look at the white envelope that Kris has left on the table and open it. It is a four-page letter. I sit down and start to read. "Ma," it says, "I'm writing you a letter ...because I can say much more in a letter than I can in words. This is going to be hard for me. I wish I could talk to you, but all you do is cry and yell at me (Is that what I do? Is that how she feels?) so I end up keeping everything inside, which after a while tears me apart and hurts, badly. We used to be able to laugh together and have a good time, but lately you haven't been able to let me grow up. I think it all started a long time ago, but really came out November 2, when Dad had his first heart attack. Because all my life it's been you and Peter, me and Dad. And when he died I felt all alone... I really needed a friend and all you would be to me was a mother." The letter continues on and on. I keep reading, trying to comprehend what she says. "Ma, I need to be away from that house, for a while at least. Now, you can make this hard and try to stop me, but you can't, even legally." I get to the last page. "I know you love me and care for me and my future. You know you will always be the first one I'll turn to because you are my MOTHER and I care for you and everything you mean and represent to me. I'm sorry I have to do this, but I think it is the best for our family." I put the letter down. What is Kristine really saying, what is hidden in all these words? One thing is clear to me that a gulf is separating me from my daughter and I don't know how to cross it.

Not only does it feel like our family's structure has been hit by an earthquake, but it seems to me that this violent force has now extended to include our physical surroundings, our house. Arvids had often said that there is never-ending work to keep the house in repair and in good shape. I soon find out what he meant. If I were to believe in a poltergeist (and I'm almost beginning to) I would say that it has entered our house. First, the outside cement steps collapse; one morning I discover a big hole in the middle of the first landing. What to do? With Peter's help, we pour cement and gravel into the hole to fill it and make a smooth cement covering over it. The result looks quite acceptable. Next to go is the freezer; it just stops working. This time, I call a professional for advice. A repairman comes, and after investigating, announces that the freezer cannot be fixed. The third item on the list is our heating system that develops a leak. Luckily, this can be repaired.

I feel persecuted. Could it really be that somebody is trying to teach me a lesson? Could it be that Arvids, from the other side, is looking in saying: "Now you see what I meant by never-ending work." Yes, but he never had so many mishaps happening in such a short span of time! Then, things start to disappear from the house: tools, my tennis racket, a silver coin collection. Where have they gone? It is puzzling and disturbing. I never find the lost items, and the mystery of their disappearance is never solved.

In midsummer, my friend Madeleine, her daughter Karen, and I, spend a week on the Cape. For the first time since Arvids' death I feel totally relaxed and at peace. We spend time on the beach; we visit art shows, stores, and restaurants. We go for long walks on the National Seashore, have picnics in the dunes, and enjoy long discussions. Madeleine is a true friend, with deep compassion and an understanding heart. She listens to my words. She understands my feelings. I talk to her about Kris. Madeleine knows Kristine well, since the time when she was our next-door neighbor and Kris was her daughter Barbara's best friend. I am very grateful for the time we spend together, for the sharing of feelings and thoughts, for her support and friendship.

A huge surprise awaits us on our return home. Kris and Larry have moved into the house, have turned my orderly clean rooms into a chaotic mess. I am in a state of shock. Madeleine's presence, her calm, and strength, are invaluable to me. She takes matters into her own hands, and in a strong and calm voice tells Larry and Kris: "You have to leave now! You are trespassing! This is not your house!" They obey, pack up, and leave. For me, it is a nightmarish situation. Madeleine helps me. I am torn by guilt and anger at Kris; by her coming back home in this way, and by my having to turn her out. The reality of my life has returned. The week on the Cape has been a short and welcome respite. Now I am back and have to face my responsibilities. "Am I really in charge?" I ask, feeling very vulnerable.

In the following months, Kris keeps returning home for short visits, accompanied by Larry. She storms in like a tornado, her long jean coat flying around her, bursts out in a long monologue of words that I would rather not hear, and storms out. I dread these visits. I also wonder about her life, where does she spend her days, her nights? What does she do? These unanswered questions trouble me. Kris needs help, I know. She is very angry; on the surface, mostly at me. I suspect, though, that her emotions have a much deeper source, hidden away somewhere in the depth of her troubled soul.

Work is where I find solace. My co-workers are very supportive, and I temporarily escape the pressing problems while concentrating on my job. Also, I live by the maxim: "Life is hard by a yard, by an inch it is a cinch." The only way I am able to manage my life during this period is to take one day at a time and to avoid thinking, either about yesterday or about tomorrow. I try to keep close to God, to rely on His strength and to ask daily for His help. And there is also my garden! My garden is my refuge. In the soil, I bury my despair, and through it, my soul absorbs energy and light.

(Years later, my friend Brigita tells me that she had wanted to help me but I had been close-lipped and aloof. Yes, that probably was true. I am afraid to start my miserable tale because to face the reality of my life as a whole would be too threatening, the burden too heavy. I cannot break! No! That I cannot, will not risk! But Brigita helps me anyway, by her calls, by her invitations to visit, by letting me know that she is close. So does my family, with their continuous support and caring. What would I do without these wonderful people?)

I finally seek professional help. One visit with Dr. Zoya

Slive, a silver-haired, tremendously kind and wise lady, gives me insight and opens my strangled heart for hope to enter in. In time, life seems less troublesome, and I feel more empowered to take charge. Life's twisted threads start to unravel and the road ahead becomes clearer as the darkness gradually disappears.

Part Three:
A New Life with Frank

"My life has gone through many phases, many periods of growth and regression. It is like climbing a mountain: one has to go through some very difficult terrain, slide back and rest for a while, but then one resumes the journey, and finally reaches the summit. One has to keep on learning and growing, keep on climbing. This is our responsibility. Life has taught me many good lessons. I have grown in wisdom in my own way. At least, I have tried to follow the road that, in my view, was the right one for me."

Astrida

FRANK AND I

Courtship

Do we meet because at some point in time, at some chance place, our roads cross? Do we meet because a Great Planner has mapped out the road we travel, and chance happenings are very few? I don't know. I would like to think that meeting Frank was organized by some Divine Wisdom; that we were destined to meet.

It happens on the evening of August 25, 1983, at a gathering of a support group for single people. In the 1980s, there are a considerable number of such groups that are attended by individuals who look for companionship, social contact, or some form of relationship, mostly short term, I think. In time, I learn that a great majority of these people are scarred by some painful experience: either by an unhappy marriage, death of a spouse, or some other hurtful past event. I am introduced to "The Next Step", as this group is called, by a friend of mine. The object of our gatherings is to meet people socially, give mutual support, discuss topics of interest, and form friendships. Frank comes to that particular evening's meeting after reading about it in the local Needham paper.

When Frank arrives, I am standing at the door and am the first to greet this tall, good-looking gentleman wearing a dark brown suit. He seems to be a bit shy. I introduce myself and welcome him in. That evening we talk about personal experiences and interests. Frank has recently lost his wife and has attended a support group for widowed spouses. He mentions that he had been impressed by the difficulties women have to endure when their husbands die, significantly more than that of widowed men. His sensitivity and caring impresses me. When the group's discussion turns to personal interests, likes, and dislikes, Frank mentions that he is interested in philosophy and has recently read works of Thoreau and Emerson. He is sitting at a table across from me (actually I am propped up on a kitchen stool). I observe Frank, and as I listen to him, I am convinced that the man who has joined our group that evening is a very special person. I like him and am hoping that he does return. Frank continues to attend most of our meetings, and thus, in an informal and indirect way we become acquainted. He confesses much later that the reason for his attendance was mainly to see me, not to discuss issues and problems. Such "round table" discussions are not his "cup of tea."

Our first date, a dinner at Hillary's, is filled with curious incidences. Our plan for the evening is that after the meal we would go to Frank's house to listen to Beethoven's Ninth Symphony. He has a good recording, and this would be a preview to our next Saturday's date at Symphony Hall. He comes to pick me up, and as I am holding my freshly baked apple pie to take along to his house, the door closes behind me before I realize that the house keys are sitting on the kitchen counter behind the now locked door. My children are gone for the evening. "My keys!", I exclaim. I hardly know Frank; he hardly knows me. "Will he think that this is a set-up?" How embarrassing!

It is Saturday, so Hillary's is overcrowded, and we have to wait for a table. I know, now, that Frank intensely dislikes waiting at restaurants, however, that evening I do not notice any sign of impatience in him. We are directed to the pub to wait. Half an hour passes, and then an hour goes by. We are not called. "I will go and check," Frank suggests and is soon back with the news that the hostess had forgotten us! We are promptly seated. Our long wait gives me an opportunity to learn quite a bit about Frank's wife, Arden, her continuous struggle with ill health, and her sudden, unexpected death - a loss that takes many years to heal.

After dinner, Frank is looking for his credit card to pay. It is nowhere to be found! Lost and gone. "Somehow I must have dropped it somewhere," Frank concludes and makes the payment in cash. As soon as we arrive home, he reports the loss and we are ready to settle down with a cup of tea and the apple pie I have baked for our "concert." At that point, listening to Beethoven does not seem too enticing, though. Frank takes off his jacket and once more checks its pockets. And there it is, the lost credit card! "Arden and Arvids are playing jokes on us!" I laugh. It has been a most unusual evening, to say the least! I keep calling home. It is after midnight when finally my daughter Kris answers. I am glad to be able to go home.

Our courtship is rather long; it lasts almost four years, and has its ups and downs. The first part is quite painful for me, and possibly, also, for Frank. Arden's presence is always felt: she sits with us at meals, accompanies us on outings, shares in our discussions. Frank cannot separate himself from his deceased wife, or rather his attachment to her, and she is threatening our relationship. When I mention my feelings, he feels that I am unsympathetic to his loss, not understanding, not being compassionate. And I feel that he does not understand me! We are in the middle of a serious dilemma. Frank had met Arden when she was nineteen, and he was twenty-two. Arden was a strikingly beautiful girl and it had been love at first sight, he says. They were engaged within three weeks but waited a year and a half to get married. The old family albums show a handsome couple surrounded by three blond, beautiful children. An ideal family: Karen was the first-born, two years later came Joseph - Joey, as he was called, and last to arrive was Robert - Robby.

Meeting Frank's Family

Almost at the very beginning, Frank introduces me to his family - his parents and children. His son, Rob, is a senior at

Northeastern University and is still living at home at the time Frank and I meet. At times, Rob, his fiancée Linda, and the two of us share dates together. Quite often, the two bachelors, as they like to call themselves, invite me to dinner. These are light and friendly occasions, most often observed by Annie Rooney, the tailless family cat. Very early in our relationship, Frank takes me to meet his parents, Mathilde and Joseph Ramrath. I like them instantly. Omi and Opa, as the family affectionately call them, hold close to their German heritage. Their home is filled with books, paintings, and a collection of beautiful things. Omi is a very intelligent, well-read lady. Books are her constant companions and she loves discussions and intellectual dialogues. I grow very fond of her, and in time, she becomes my second mother. Opa's personality is quite different from his wife's. He is an extrovert and a storyteller. He loves to remember and share past experiences, like the one about the sinking of the Titanic. He had been the first in his family to hear about the news and had run home to tell them all. He was only seven then. A memorable day for a little boy. Opa likes to be the center of attention.

Mathilde and Joseph first met on a ship during their return trip from the United States to their native Germany. In the late 1920s, times were hard in Germany, and unemployment was high. Many young people looked for jobs outside the country, especially in the United States. After completing his studies, Joseph had traveled to the United States and had found an engineering position in Philadelphia. He was on his way back to Germany to spend a vacation with his family when a mutual friend introduced him to Mathilde, who was returning home from a year's adventure in the United States. For Joseph, it was love at first sight. A shipboard romance blossomed. During his brief stay in Germany, Joseph pursued the beautiful girl. He invited her to visit his parents in Eslohe, his hometown, and during that visit, presented Mathilde with an engagement ring. Before his return to the United States, Mathilde's parents gave them an official engagement party. That same fall, the two were married in Philadelphia.

Next, I meet Frank's daughter, Karen, and her husband,

Dave. They invite us to dinner, or, rather, Frank invites us both to their house for a meal. To bring along as a house gift, I have baked a large torte, beautifully decorated with fruits and nuts. Well, life is a learning experience, and this evening I learn that Karen is very allergic to nuts. However, she graciously removes the dangerous nuts and enjoys the cake.

Frank's son Joe is away in California, attending a law school there. He and his wife, Debbie, are introduced to me much later, when, after Joseph's graduation, they return to Massachusetts and settle here.

Initially I feel rather awkward at these family introductions. Frank and I have just met. I hardly know him! I would have rather liked to get to know him better, to feel comfortable with him before making all these family acquaintances. I understand now why we had to climb these steps in our developing relationship, before it could proceed into a more serious and possibly permanent alliance. Frank likes directness and clarity. He lives his life as an engineer, not as a poet or a dreamer. He is seriously interested in me. His family is very important to him, and their approval of me is equally important. Luckily, we all like each other. "If it were not so, what would have happened?" I wonder.

Till Death Do Us Part

It is on a Wednesday evening in August of 1986. I am standing in the doorway of Frank's home, about to leave after our customary spaghetti dinner. He pulls me back, holds my hand and asks: "What would you think about getting married?" It is totally unexpected. My heart does several somersaults and I say: "I'll think about it." I am happy and also concerned. I have promised never to get married again. My marriage to Arvids had been unhappy. For many years, I had been locked into a relationship that had brought much heartache to me, and also, I am sure, to Arvids. I do not want to make another mistake. Marriage is a risk, a leap into the dark. What do I want? What is the right decision? I love Frank. We enjoy each other's company and have developed a good friendship. But there are also moments when he seems to be worlds away. Arden is still a part of his life; not as strongly as in the beginning of our relationship, but I always know that his feelings for Arden overshadows the love that he has for me. My acceptance of where Frank is in his emotions, at that point, is very important, more important than my place in his heart. I pray. The answer comes. A light, a knowing, fills my heart. I am sure of the answer I will give him! "Yes."

May 9, 1987, is the "day that the Lord has made"; it is our wedding day, and it is filled with sunshine and color. Spring has opened its doors to nature's awakening, spread its rich blessings over the earth, and over us. Frank and I are married at my church, the Latvian Lutheran Church in Brookline, by a Catholic priest, Father John Arens from Frank's parish, and a Lutheran minister, Imants Kalnins, the pastor of my church. Our families and only our closest friends are with us this day and share the moment of our mutual promise of love and respect. It is a solemn but also lighthearted and festive celebration. It is God's day, and "we rejoice and are glad in it." We start our life together.

After the wedding, we take a short honeymoon trip to Philbrook Farm Inn in Shelburne, NH, a charming old farm in the White Mountain region. Since then, every May, we return there to rest our souls and our bodies in this lovely ancient house, where each corner tells a story about times past when the world had more silence, and people greeted days with less turbulence in their hearts. We go there to celebrate our marriage and our life. We walk through the surrounding woods and meadows, hike the mountain trails, listen to the toads' evening concerts, and enjoy conversations with the Philbrook family members.

Hand in Hand

Beginnings are not always easy. There are adjustments to be made, goodbyes to be said to the familiar and routine of the past; a period of learning and acceptance must be faced. Frank and I have to do just that: get used to each other, learn much more intimately and directly about each other, understand each other's needs, face the shortcomings, and appreciate the positive points.

I pack my belongings at my home on Glen Street in South Natick and move into Frank's house on Sargent Street in Needham. A year before our wedding, Frank had bought a two-family dwelling to make room for his parents. They have become too old to live by themselves and take care of their house in Hyde Park. At first it had been hard for Omi and Opa to part from their home of many years, and to lose a measure of their independence. However, to have their son watch over them and take care of their needs gives them a great relief and comfort. As a small boy, Frank had told his mother: "I will always take care of you." This promise he keeps. Frank has always lived within a short distance of his parents. When their house needed a repair or some sudden emergency arose, it was Frank who was called to help. It is only natural that Frank would continue to be his parents' stronghold and guardian in the last part of their life. When I arrive in May of 1987, Omi and Opa have already settled into their very comfortable first floor apartment. This is a perfect arrangement for all of us. I have never felt really at ease in the house where Frank and Arden had raised their family. The spirit of the past still lived there. Arden's presence was very immediate, and I felt that I was intruding into a world where I had no place. Frank knew, and considered my feelings, and this gave him an added reason to put his one-family house on the market and buy the one on Sargent Street.

It takes awhile for me to separate myself from my Natick house, especially the garden. Arvids and I had planned, had landscaped, and planted our garden. It is part of me, and in leaving it, I am leaving part of me behind. During the first year, I go back often. Mostly these are sad, nostalgic visits. The garden is mine, and at the same time it is not mine anymore. I feel like a traitor; I am abandoning what I so lovingly had created and nurtured. My son, Peter, continues to live in the house. He and the garden are the two reasons why I do not sell the house. Peter still lives there, but the garden has lost its beauty and shine. Like a child, it needed continued care and nurturing to grow and develop.

When I move to Needham, my black dog, Suzie, moves in with me. Early on, Frank had realized, not with great enthusiasm, though; "Have Astrida, have her dog." That is a prerequisite. Frank is not keen on having an animal in his house. He had plenty of them in "his previous life." Birds, cats, dogs, rats, and even a monkey had shared their household. "Another dog?" Frank understands, however, that Suzie is very important to me. She is my closest friend. She has been with me since her birth and has shared my joys and my pain. We are bonded. When my heart was heavy and burdened, I would wrap my arms around her black body and feel comforted. Suzie knew. Suzie understood.

The first few months at our new home has some unexpected hurdles. Suzie does not adjust readily; she is very insecure without me. She follows me everywhere like a black shadow. One evening, especially, comes to mind. I am returning home rather late from a meeting, and as I turn the car into our driveway, Suzie's frantic barks are heard from the house. My heart gives a jolt! "Suzie, be quiet!" I silently pray. She is waiting for me at the kitchen door, still barking. When Suzie sees me, she quiets down, but Suzie's barks have wakened Frank up. He sits in his bed, stiff as an arrow, pretending to read. His face is frozen. I know that he is angry. "I'm sorry," I mumble. From then on, if I need to return home late, I switch off the car's motor before coming into the driveway and glide the car silently into the garage.

Within a couple of months, however, Suzie adjusts to her new home, and Frank adjusts to Suzie. Soon, they become the best of friends and daily walking companions. A tall man accompanied by a black dog is a familiar sight in our neighborhood.

Our past shapes us, molds us, and conditions us. We carry our experiences within our souls and our psyche and often react to present situations from a wrong and outdated perspective. At the beginning of our married life, and even some time later, I sense that my feelings and reactions come from the past. I also see this in some of Frank's responses to my actions and words. He often seems to be threatened or accused by my words when nothing is intended. His responses come from the shadows of his past experiences. A long time has to elapse before he realizes that today is not yesterday, and we can start building our relationship on our today's reality. I also need to adjust to my new reality. I do not have to be afraid of Frank or hesitate to ask or tell him things that in my previous life were taboo. Even now, after so many years, at times I feel the old insecurities in me and am surprised to see how slowly time erases the footprints left by old hurts and conditionings.

Honeymoon Trip to Germany

Meeting Frank's German Relatives

Later on that year we travel to Germany on an extended second honeymoon. Frank wants to show me the country of his birth and introduce me to his family. We fly by Lufthansa Airline from Boston to Frankfurt, and from there, we board a Lufthansa sponsored luxury train to go to Dueseldorf. On board, we are treated to a champagne breakfast while enjoying a ride along the scenic Rhine River. In Dueseldorf, we rent a car and proceed to Eslohe, a small village in Sauerland where Frank's father was born and had spent his childhood and youth. It is the most charming and picturesque village, embraced by evergreen tree-covered hills and mountain meadows. Sheep farming and forestry are the main industries there. The sheep in their white woolly coats roam the green pastures, adding a feeling of peace and comfort to the pastoral scene. Rows of colorful lupines line the winding roads that connect one village to the next. I am totally captured by the extraordinary beauty of this area. "Paradise would certainly look like Eslohe," I thought.

Tante Adele, the sister of Frank's father, lives in Eslohe and we pay her a visit. Adele's husband had died some years back, and she lives alone in a charming house on the outskirts of town. Her architect husband had designed the house. Tante Adele has suffered a stroke recently, and her speech is slow with intermittent pauses. Her gentle face is lit up by a welcoming smile as she beckons us inside. She shows us her house, pointing out some of the special treasures that were collected over her long life. We stand at a window; practically the whole wall is a window, overlooking her small garden and the beautiful countryside beyond. In her measured speech, she is telling me some bits and pieces of the family history. She has three children, two daughters and a son, who have all done well. Especially the son. He has followed in his father's footsteps, and is a well-recognized architect and dean of the department of architecture at the University of Munich. The visit gives me a chance to exercise my rusty German.

The next day, which is a Sunday, we attend a church service together. It is the same church where Opa had served as an altar boy. In front of the church stands an old oak tree. I look at the tree and think, "This tree was here when Opa was just a boy. He was standing before it just as I am today." A most unreal feeling touches my heart. The relativity of time! The past and the present merge together in that one moment.

The following morning we say goodbye to Tante Adele and Eslohe. "We will have to return again!" I say to Frank. *(Years later we do, together with Frank's mother. But Tante Adele is not there to greet us. She had gone to meet her Maker.)*

We Visit Muenster

Our next destination is the city of Muenster in northern Germany. There are two main reasons for our visit to Muenster. Frank had lived there with his maternal grandparents, Omi and Opa Rump, in the early 1930s. Frank's parents had lost their jobs then, during the heart of the Depression, and had sent their children, Frank and Eleanor, to live with their parents: Frank to Muenster, and Eleanor to

Eslohe. The second reason is to attend the Latvian Song and Dance Festival that is held in Muenster in August of 1987.

Muenster had been a beautiful medieval university city that was almost totally (96%) destroyed by Allied bombs during the Second World War. Now, it had undergone a nearly total metamorphosis. Walking through the winding streets, one can hardly see the signs of war and destruction. One structure, however, still bears the wounds of the war: St. Paul's Cathedral in the heart of Muenster. The foundation of the original church had been laid in the ninth century. The church had been built in the Romanesque style, and even though it has undergone major changes and additions in subsequent centuries, the original architectural style never changed. The last major work on the cathedral was done in the 1500's, and for four hundred years until its destruction in 1943, the cathedral had remained the unchanging landmark in the center of Muenster.

As Frank is guiding me through the city, showing me the main points of interest, personal as well as historical, we visit the cathedral. In its foyer is a markedly impressive display of photographs. Back to back, it shows the cathedral, before the war, in its magnificent beauty, and the ruins of it at the end of the war. One cannot but reflect on man's folly and ignorance. The historical heritage and beauty that the human spirit had created over many centuries can be so easily and thoughtlessly destroyed within minutes by the dark side of the same human spirit. Very hard to comprehend, accept, and justify.

As we walk through the grandiose building that has undergone almost complete restoration, Frank remembers that his grandfather had taken him there many years ago to show him a very unique clock inside the church. The clock had contained the figures of the twelve disciples of Jesus, who marched out in a procession at 12 o'clock noon and at 12 o'clock midnight, one at a time, as the gong marked the hours. The clock has been reconstructed, however, without the twelve disciples. Cardinal Von Galen, who was the pastor of the church during the Nazi era, is buried in the cathedral behind the main altar. He had been an outstanding and courageous man. Because of his stand against the Nazi policies and outrageous acts, he was called the "Lion of Muenster."

Frank remembers an interesting story about the Cardinal, as his grandmother had related it to him. She had attended a service when the Cardinal, during his sermon, strongly denounced the Nazi policies and had said: "One has to be ashamed to be a German today." The next day, the Gestapo officials arrived at his residence to arrest him. "Gentlemen, excuse me while I get dressed," the Cardinal had said. A short time later he appeared in his full Cardinal's regalia, in the red robe and cardinal's hat. Meanwhile, a crowd had gathered outside the residence. It was a moment of decision. The arrest was not made. The Gestapo officials left, and the Cardinal survived the Nazi regime and the war.

The Latvian Song and Dance Festival

In the early 1950s, Muenster had become an important center for the Latvian refugee community. Most of the post Second World War refugees who had escaped to Germany in order to avoid the Russian occupation, had eventually immigrated to other countries. For the Latvians who had remained in Germany and settled there, Muenster had become their cultural and political center. A Latvian secondary school was established here. Children from all over the world could come to Muenster to continue their education in Latvian. The school continued to exist until its closure in the late 1990s, when, after the Soviet Union's collapse, the children could return to the newly-free Latvia for their education. Muenster had served its purpose. In 1987, Muenster was chosen as an ideal site in Europe for the Latvian Song and Dance Festival.

In between our visits to the places that are significant to Frank from his stay with his grandparents, we also attend the program of the Latvian Festival. This Festival is organized by the Free World Latvians. Latvians have gathered here from all around the world to sing, dance, display their art, make friends, meet old acquaintances, and be happy together. I meet several old school friends from my years in Esslingen. Ausma Steinbergs is one of them. Just before our graduation in 1949, she had developed pneumonia and had had to stay in Germany because of resulting complications. (To enter the United States, one had to be in perfect health!) We share and compare our experiences. It is like shaking hands over time and space and developing a new closeness. There are other chance meetings, "hellos", and "goodbyes". "Hope to see you again. Let us keep in touch!" are often repeated phrases. The program lasts a week and its motto is "Remember Latvia." It is a colorful exhibit of Latvian culture: music, art, folklore, dance, but above all, the strong spirit of their ethnic heritage and identity. For me, this time is an emotional journey. I touch my beginnings, my roots, and am again reminded of how deeply connected I am to being a Latvian. During that week, the German city of Muenster is turned into a "Little Latvia." It is Frank's first real immersion into the Latvian soul and culture. What are his feelings? Hard to say. I believe that he is overwhelmed by all the pageantry and a bit bewildered. Even now, at times, Frank finds it hard to understand my deep attachment to my national heritage. It is also one of the "hurdles" in our life together that needs some overcoming and accepting.

Visit With Tante Elsbeth in Wellingsholzhausen

On August 9, we leave Muenster and our charming temporary home at "Hof zur Linde," an old Manor House which had been converted into an inn. "Aufwiedersehen!" Our next destination is Wellingholzhausen to visit Omi's sister, Tante Elsbeth, and her family. On our way, we travel through the fertile farm country of Westfalen. The road takes us by large, wealthy farms. One can judge their wealth by the cluster of well-maintained red brick buildings and the miles of fields that stretch away from this center. "This is the bread basket of northern Germany," Frank explains.

Within a couple of hours we are in Wellingholzhausen, where Frank quite readily finds Tante Elsbeth's house. He has been here before, together with his sister, Eleanor, when both of them had gone on a pilgrimage to Germany in 1984. Tante Elsbeth shares her house with her son, Karl-Benno, his wife

Irmhild, and their boy Stephan. A perfectly groomed house in a perfectly groomed garden! Everything here expresses order and neatness. Tante Elsbeth lives downstairs, where on our arrival we are served coffee and cake from exquisite china, placed on a beautifully hand-embroidered linen-tablecloth-covered coffee table. Everything in Tante Elsbeth's house is beautiful and of value. She is proud of her antiques, and one cannot but be impressed by her elegant taste. Karl-Benno's family live upstairs. It is also a very nice place but much simpler and more "lived in." Irmhild is a superb cook, and during our visit with the family we have meals upstairs. I enjoy playing with little Stephan. He is a friendly fellow, and we are about equal in our knowledge of German, therefore have no problem communicating. Karl-Benno's dental practice is on the first floor of the house, and he shows us his office with pride. During our tour, I mention to him that I have some complications with my recent dental work. "I'll look at it!" he immediately offers. "No, no. It will be fine, I am sure!"

Elsbeth's husband, who had also been a dentist, has recently died following an accident - a fall down a flight of stairs. The family cemetery is almost across the street from the house, and we walk over there to visit the resting places of Frank's grandparents, his Muenster Omi and Opa, and other members of the Rump family. The cemeteries in Germany have the appearance of well-maintained parks, and this is no exception. One is greeted by a sense of silence and peace. Tall trees shade the well-groomed gravesites marked by tombstones, most of them individually carved and personalized. We lay flowers on the family gravesites and keep a moment of silence. For me, cemeteries have always held a special significance, a glimpse into the past, a narrow opening into lives that had been and now were silent. "What was your life like? Who were you? What did you feel? What were your successes? Failures?", I ask while reading the names, the dates, and the inscriptions on the tombstones. Each grave holds an untold story, a mystery never to be revealed.

Tante Elsbeth is a good hostess. She introduces us to some of her friends, and takes us on a tour to interesting and historical places. The most memorable is a church in Melle-Oldendorf, Ev.-Luth, Marienkirche, which has survived the war untouched. It is a small Gothic church with beautifully designed interior arches and an altar piece of magnificently carved biblical figures in oak.

We Journey to Stuttgart to Meet Uncle Werner's Family

After several days of visiting, we said goodbye to our Wellingholzhausen family and resume our trip. On our way to Stuttgart to visit Omi's brother, Uncle Werner, and his family we make several stops. The first of these is the Vincent van Gogh Museum in Amsterdam. The Museum holds the largest collection of Van Gogh's works, and it is very exciting and interesting to view so many of this talented and tragically complex painter's works together in one place. We are negatively impressed by the city of Amsterdam, especially by the area where the museum is. Pornographic pictures and magazines are generously displayed in the newsstands; graffiti covers the building walls, and streets are littered with rubbish. We walk across the Amstel River, which flows through Amsterdam, to briefly visit the other side of the city. We like this part much better and regret that time does not allow us to explore more.

On our way south, we make a short lunch stop in DieKirch, a border town between Germany and Luxembourg. By pure chance, we come upon a church that has been built on Roman burial grounds and is undergoing archeological excavations. We are allowed to go into the dig site and find several stone sarcophagi holding petrified skeletons there. Frank reaches into one of them and "shakes a leg" of an ancient Roman. A memorable experience, indeed! We take quite a few pictures of the place, but by an unlucky course of events, the film falls out in the trunk of our rented car and is never recovered.

Next, we visit the city of Trier, which was founded around the time of Christ's birth. Here, one can trace history from the Roman era, to early Christian times, through the Middle Ages, to the present. A very impressive historical monument is the gate to the city, "Porta Negra," which was built by the Romans, and to this day is among the city's most significant landmarks. We visit the Roman bath, a round open-air structure that is encircled by beautiful gardens. Lots of color and brightness! Since the day of our visit is sunny and warm, it adds a special glow to this ancient city that is famous for its wine breweries and seemingly lighthearted and happy people.

We continue our journey through the Mosel Valley and spend the night at a hospitable bed and breakfast. We toast our hosts, Paula and Alois Kaes, with their delicious homemade wine, and enjoy a leisurely evening walk around the picturesque town, marked by vineyards and flower gardens. The next day, we travel to Freiburg, a city remarkable for its history and some very impressive architecture. One could spend days here exploring and enjoying. Again, restraints of time! We do visit a uniquely beautiful church with exquisite stained glass windows that have survived the war. In the afternoon, we drive to Berzaine a retreat for Latvian war veterans, Daugavas Vanagi. We have some difficulty finding the place because of the many one-way streets and lots of ongoing roadwork. Eventually we see a sign for Berzaine, and pull into its driveway. We are greeted by a group of "happy warriors" who are enjoying the afternoon with the help of some alcoholic spirits. The compound functions also as a bed and breakfast, and we spend the night there. Our short stay with these old soldiers makes me reflect again on the tragic events of the Second World War. Here, I see a sampling of human tragedy: broken lives, broken hearts, lost battles. The goal of these men, freedom for Latvia, has not been attained. Past war experiences and memories bind them together in kind of a patch-work family. "Old soldiers never die, they just fade away," said General MacArthur. How true !

Uncle Werner and Tante Helen

The next day, we arrive in the Bad Canstadt region of the city of Stuttgart, and are warmly greeted by Uncle Werner and Tante Helen. We are embraced by their warm hospitality. They cannot do enough for us! I am impressed by the deep love that Werner and Helen share. The glow of their relationship makes our visit with them especially meaningful and memorable. In his young days, Uncle Werner had been very handsome, sort of a ladies' man, as Frank remembers. He is still that; a charming gentleman and a perfect host. And he admires Helen. Their love has endured severe trials and a long separation. Shortly after their marriage, Werner had been drafted into the German army and was captured by the Russian military just before the war ended. Eventually, the Soviets released him, and he made his way home through Niederschlaesien, where Helen's family had lived, in hope to find his wife there. After the war, however, this part of Germany had been signed over to Poland, and all of the German population had been relocated to the West. In today's terms, it was an act of ethnic cleansing. Unfortunately, Werner was recaptured by the Poles, who had no love for the Germans, to put it mildly. Werner spent ten years at hard labor in Poland's coal mines. Helen waited. Eventually, her husband returned. I can only imagine the happiness that these two long-separated lovers experienced. Soon their only child, daughter Angelica, was born. On our visit there, we also meet Angelica's family, her husband and their daughter.

The visit with Uncle Werner's family ends my introduction to Frank's German relatives. It is a unique experience to have personal and close contact with these great people, to be in their midst as a family member, as one of them. To revisit Germany with Frank gives me a different perspective of the country, a more intimate look at German life. Even though Frank maintains that he is a "man of the world" with no specific national identification, his ancestral roots are in Germany. He was born there; it is his native country. I am grateful for the gift of memories I carry home with me.

PHILBROOK FARM INN:
OUR SHANGRI-LA

"...Where the welcome mat really says "Welcome," and the latch-string is always out for those seeking peace, quiet and contentment in a world turned upside down", is the invitation from the Philbrook family to all who enter the rambling white house that opened its doors to its first guests in 1861. The inn is located in Shelburne, New Hampshire in the picturesque White Mountain region. The most striking feature of the area is the beauty of the white birches that grow in abundance along the road leading to the town of Shelburne and on the Philbrook Farm property along the banks of Androscoggin River.

The original farmhouse was built in 1834, but over the years, it has undergone several additions, and has grown into an 18-bedroom guesthouse. The building holds the treasures of the Philbrook family's long history, five generations of it. As one opens the door, one steps into the warm embrace of the Philbrook family, past and present. The rooms are filled with antique treasures, family pictures, artwork, paintings, beautiful hand- braided rugs, and a collection of embroidered pieces that have all been, and still are, being created by members of the family. So much to see, feel, admire, and enjoy!

For us, it is a place where we find an escape from the pressures of daily life, where we can enjoy peace, and come into touch with something permanent. It was on May 11, 1987, when we first came to the Philbrook Farm Inn for a short honeymoon retreat, two days after our wedding. Every year since, we measure the four hour ride up north to celebrate the anniversary of our special day. In the fifteen years of return visits, the Philbrook family has become our family. For us, it is a homecoming; a warm and tender place to be. It is a real joy to say hello again to Connie and Nancy, the Philbrook family's senior sisters, and to Connie's children, Ann and Larry, who gradually have taken over the management of the inn.

Our room is prepared. Usually it is either "Gracie's Room" or "Grandpa Gus's Room" on the second floor above the main dining room. All the guest rooms are uniquely furnished and decorated with antiques and family memorabilia. These two rooms, to me, feel especially cozy and comfortable. They both face a spacious green meadow that ends at the Androscoggin River, and in the distance beyond, one can see the Presidential Range. As I look out over the pastoral scene, I feel its calm replacing all the feelings of stress and anxiety that I had carried along with me. Here, all is well with the world.

Over the years, Frank and I have developed a certain routine that we follow during our stay at the inn. It is usually a late afternoon when we arrive. First, we unpack our bags, take a brief rest, than go down for a short visit with the family, or just walk around the spacious living and family rooms to enjoy and admire the family treasures. At 6:30 p.m., the bell invites us to dinner. Our usual table in the dining room has been set for us. For the family to remember our special place adds to the warmth of being cared about. It is a special treat for Frank and me to sit across from each other at the same table year after year and to enjoy the home cooked meals together.

After dinner, we enjoy a walk along the North Road that runs by the inn. Going east on it, we come to the family's cemetery plot; going west, we reach the town of Shelburne after crossing Androscoggin River Bridge. We can also choose to walk directly across the meadow to the river to admire the magnificent white birch growth along its banks. Usually the family's dog, Valkyrie, a German shorthair pointer, is more than happy to accompany us. The evening's silence is filled with the loud chorus of frog voices. They seem to be coming from all directions. "Where are the invisible creatures?" we wonder. Gradually the daylight recedes, the sky darkens, and the stars mark their usual pattern in its deep blue distance. The brilliance of these distant objects is awe-inspiring.

Directly behind the inn's buildings rises the Mahoosuc Range. Several hiking trails lead to mountain ledges with magnificent views over the Androscoggin River valley, the White Mountains, and other surrounding areas. Each day's plan for us includes hiking one of these trails, reaching the mountain top, and enjoying a well-deserved lunch, while resting and feasting our eyes with the immense beauty of God's world before us and among us. My task before we set off is to pack our lunch, while Frank reads the literature describing the trails. Our backpack includes water (very necessary!), sandwiches, fruit, and hard candies for a treat. These hikes are exciting, at times quite difficult, but always most enjoyable. Valkyrie just loves to join us and usually is impatiently waiting for our departure. She has an admirable familiarity with the trails, and we can depend on her guidance. She is swift as an arrow when chasing some invisible target in the woods, but always faithfully returns to us.

The hardest part of each hike, for me, is the very beginning. My heart races, and my legs hurt. As I proceed, however, these symptoms recede, and I happily climb over rocks, tree roots, jump across narrow brooks while admiring and enjoying the awakening of the spring around us. The soft greens in the opening buds, the tiny blossoms among last autumn's leaves, the birds chirping in the woods, and at times (what luck) a surprised deer, disappearing among the trees, are the memory treasures that I carry back home. I always learn something, something of value for my own soul. The awareness of being part of nature, one with all creation, is forever a valuable discovery.

Our stay at the inn lasts two to four days. Each day is different and each day is the same; all very predictable and, most importantly, relaxed and peaceful. On rainy days we take short rides in the country or just sit around, visit, read, or join the family in putting together wooden jigsaw puzzles that have been created by generations of Philbrook family members.

The last day of our Shangri-La vacation never fails to arrive. We pack, have breakfast, pay our bill, bid "we will see you again next year" to the family and our faithful friend and trail companion, Valkyrie. Our car pulls out onto North Road. The friendly buildings of the inn disappear behind the trees.

FRIENDSHIP WITH THE BOOKERS

How does one define a friend? A commonly used colloquialism comes to mind: "A friend in need is a friend indeed." There is much truth to it. Recently, I heard another definition: "A friend is someone who knows the song in your heart and sings it back to you when you have forgotten the words". I like that. To me it says that a true friend knows your innermost self, your song, and in your darkest hour, is there to call you back to light. How do friendships start? Life brings us together with many people. They come and go. We touch and part. Most of the time, with most of the individuals we meet, it is only a casual touching. Some meetings are different, though. There is something special, one can call it chemistry, a spark, that connects people on a deeper level. It is a subliminal recognition of a kindred spirit.

We first met Inara and Bill Booker about fifteen years ago at a dinner party at a home of mutual friends. I knew Inara's father, Dr. Mednis, long before I met his daughter.

Dr. Mednis and my family shared mutual friends from Latvia, the Lulas family, and quite often I had met Dr. Mednis at their house. He was a charming, distinguished gentlemen; tall, with a twinkle in his ice-blue eyes and a good sense of humor. Dr. Mednis was a prominent, well-recognized surgeon in Jelgava, Latvia. I remember very well the reverence and respect with which Dr. Mednis' name was mentioned in our family! Inara reminded me of her father. She is also tall, and her blue eyes, blond hair and fine facial features are so much like her father's. While Ina is blond and fair, her husband Bill is darkly handsome. His profession as a teacher had given him ample practice in the art of conversation, and it was never boring to be in his company. We continued to meet the Bookers socially and got to know them quite well. They were gracious hosts and gave elegant dinner parties. Most of all, we admired their sincerity, intelligence, and obviously caring and sensitive hearts. They had many friends and were devoted to their family, especially to their three children, Ingrid, Billy, and Krista.

The Bookers have invited us to visit them at their summer place in Maine. So, in the summer of 1990, on our way back from a camping vacation to Nova Scotia, we stop in Rangeley, Maine for a visit with them. On a sunny, mid-august day in the late afternoon, we arrive at the "camp", as Bookers called their summer home, and are warmly welcomed by our hosts. Immediately one senses their genuine hospitality. Heart: that is how one would define the essence of the house and their masters. Instantly, we feel expected and welcome. The "camp" sits on the banks of the picturesque Dodge Pond, one of the many beautiful lakes of the scenic Rangeley Region. Ina and Bill have been residents there for many years. Their family had enjoyed Rangeley's lakes and mountains every summer and for parts of each winter. All of the Bookers love nature. Outdoor sports are close to their hearts, and they are very good at all of them. They are expert skiers, swimmers, boaters, plus any other activity connected to outdoors.

We spend a relaxed afternoon in sun and water. Supper is served on the veranda with the view to the pond, the surrounding forests, and distant mountains. The setting sun paints the evening sky in all shades of crimson, giving us a magnificent view of the departing day. After the meal, we are invited to have coffee by the lake. "How romantic!" I think. Ina lights a fire near the water's edge, and serves us mugs of coffee. A perfect evening. Peace and tranquility. We talk some, but to be silent is better. The stars brilliantly outline the almost black sky, the moonlight dances in silver patterns over the peaceful water, and at times, we hear the lonely voice of a distant loon.

The evening has a soft magic. I recall Samuel Johnson's words: "We cannot tell the precise moment when a friendship is formed. As in filling a vessel drop by drop, there is the last drop that makes it run over". The same with the heart. A moment comes when we know that something has changed. A friend has entered our life.

Inara and Bill have a very special gift: love for their fellow man, readiness to help, to open their hearts and their home to their friends and anyone in need of special attention. In the years following, we are often recipients of this gift, as are so many others. It is hard to count all the people whom we have met at their home during the years of our friendship. There is always someone knocking at their door, being invited for a meal, spending hours or even days in their home. Their doors are always open. And Ina and Bill are standing in front of these doors, ready to give the arrival a hug and a smile: "Welcome! So nice to see you!" So many a time we hear this greeting at the end of our five hour ride from Needham to Rangeley. So many a time we feel thus welcomed and expected. If all the people who have enjoyed the Bookers' hospitality, in thanksgiving, would plant just one flower in Ina's lovely garden, it would be ever blooming!

An immensely tragic event happens in the Bookers' family on September 27, 1990. Billy, their only son, was killed on a Vermont country road while driving home at night. The darkness that comes into their lives still lingers there, and the pain can be seen and felt when Billy's name is mentioned or some memory comes into the present from the past. At times, we talk about it, about the pain, the deep loss. Talking eases one's burden. Hopefully.

Life wonderfully provides solutions, fills voids, and eases pain. Blessings often come from unexpected sources. The Booker's daughter, Ingrid, and her husband Bill, are very close to their parents. Two delightful people. I have a feeling that the young Bill has become a substitute son to Bill Sr. Certainly, nobody can ever replace Billy, the son they lost, but Bill, the son-in-law, is a perfect companion and shares many interests with his father-in-law. God takes away and God gives back...

A time when we most distinctly feel our friends' hearts and help is when Frank is diagnosed with prostate cancer. The Bookers are there immediately with their support. After Frank undergoes surgery, we have an open invitation to come and stay with them, to recoup and relax. "You know", Inara says, "your room is always ready and waiting". After the surgery, Frank experiences some difficulties and a slight complication. Rangeley is where he becomes well again. It is like a miracle cure. He arrives there filled with pain and discomfort. The peace, the love, the caring, and the relaxed comfort of our friends' home does what no medicine could completely accomplish.

Then, when Frank's mother, our Omi, is in failing health, Bill's aunt Peggy is also in a similar situation. It is a difficult period for both of our families. This is a time when we can help each other with support, and share our similar experiences. Peggy is the sister of Bill's mother and had brought Bill up after his mother died when he was just a little boy. Peggy had never married, had no children of her own, but had assumed responsibility for her extended family. She was the stalwart of the family, a proud and stately woman. Peggy was born, grew up, and lived all her life in Maine. I first meet Peggy when her health has already started to fail, but even so, I am deeply impressed by her genteel manner and grace. During the last years of her life, Bill and Ina are responsible for Peggy's care, and together with Ina's sister Margaret, at whose house Peggy lives, they provide her with comfort and love. Margaret, fondly called Marite, is another person with a deep attachment to this remarkable woman. Bill's love and gratitude to Peggy, the only mother he had ever really known, was obvious.

Our roads cross and come together many a time. We spend wonderful, meaningful times in Rangeley and on Cape Cod, where the Bookers have a winter home. Eventually they sell this property and move permanently to Rangeley. The "camp" is then converted into their primary residence. It is cozy and comfortable; they love their house and their life in Rangeley. Upstairs is a room where we always find a bed made and a bouquet of fresh flowers welcoming us.

Through the years, we canoe, hike, and cross-country ski with our friends, Bill and Ina. Especially remarkable is our Windjammer cruise through the Penobscot Bay. Another most enjoyable vacation is our trip to the Azore Archipelago, the island of Sao Miguel, a place of perfect beauty. We enjoy a "back to nature" camping experience on the totally isolated Warren Island in Maine's Penobscot Bay. Without the Bookers' boat, this could not be possible, since the only access to the island is by boat. It is quite a chore to transport all the necessary equipment and food to the island, but once we are there, we pitch our tents close to the water's edge and settle down to enjoy a communion with nature and each other. There, we can view the sea and listen, as the ocean comes in and goes out; especially during the night when all is quiet and the only sound is the water. Each day we start with a hearty breakfast, pack our daily provisions, and take off to cruise around the waters, visiting the nearby towns. Bill is a capable captain and Ina his ever ready and willing mate. In the evenings, we watch the gloriously colorful sunsets while enjoying a glass of wine before our home cooked dinner. Thanks to Ina's sense of beauty, our table is always covered with a tablecloth, and a vase of field flowers completes the décor. Here, we live very close to nature and very close to each other. We share a lot, and grow to know each other more deeply and intimately. The water, the trees, the isolation from the world outside is a healing and restoring experience. Ina and I talk. She is the one person I can totally confide in. I know that she cares and understands. She keeps my words with her. I treasure her advice. About Inara I can say: "She knows the song of my heart and plays it back to me when I have forgotten the words."

Before and after our Warren Island vacation, we visit and spend a night with Ina's sister Margaret – Marite. Marite is very much like Inara, a giving and caring person. She owns a wonderful small farm on the banks of St. George's River, not far from Lincolnville (from where we start our Warren Island vacation), and we stay there in one of her charming little cottages overlooking the river. The river rises and falls with the tide. It is like being in a fairyland! The roadside to our cottage is lined with blackberry bushes. In August, they are covered with berries; a multitude of sweet, juicy, most delicious berries! A land of plenty.

Our friendship with the Bookers can be compared to a "land of plenty". We have received much love and caring from them, and are in God's "state of grace" through His giving us a chance to enjoy our special friends.

LOST AT SEA

It is August 26, 1999. We have arrived and settled into our tents to enjoy our annual camping vacation on the charming Warren Island with our friends, Bill and Inara Booker.

Warren Island is an uninhabited picturesque piece of land in the Penobscot Bay, a short distance from the town of Lincolnville and close to the Island of Islesboro. In the late 1890's, the island was purchased by a Philadelphia woolen manufacturer William Folwell. His plan to build a 22-bedroom "log cabin" there was carried out by his son, as he died before its completion. The end result was a grandiose place to enjoy parties and good times. Eventually, however, the building was left empty, was neglected, and finally burned down in the summer of 1919. Today, one can still find a few reminders of the past, a few stones and bricks where the house had stood. The island belongs to the State of Maine and is open for camping and picnicking.

To reach Warren Island, one has to rely on one's own means of transportation. As a result, the island enjoys lots of privacy. The four of us treasure the peaceful, relaxing days together. It is a special time for us; time to deepen our friendship and to share conversations under the magnificent sunsets during our pre-dinner "happy hour". Nothing can be more beautiful! The island invites us back year after year to enjoy its charm, its peace, and our friendship.

This year we have a small problem, though. Bill's 19-foot

motorboat, equipped with all the current state-of-the-art safety instruments, has been in an accident and is still in the repair shop at the time of our departure. His smaller boat, which has a compass, but none of the more sophisticated safety tools, has to be used for our transport and short sightseeing trips.

During our five-day Warren Island camping vacation, we enjoy day trips to points of interest along the shores of the Penobscot Bay. Today we plan to go to Belfast, an old scenic fishing town north of Lincolnville. The morning is perfect. After a hearty breakfast, prepared under the cover of the lean-to, we board our small boat. The sky is cloudless, the sun shines brightly, and our moods are, likewise, sunny and carefree.

Bill is a master boatsman. After settling ourselves comfortably into his boat, we can relax and enjoy the views of the passing shoreline. Many of the houses we pass are summer estates of the "rich and mighty" and it is quite impressive to see, from a distance, how some of our contemporaries are enjoying their days in the sun. Through our binoculars, we can be "peeping toms", and use our imagination to enter for a brief moment their lives. Interesting!

The waters are calm, and we reach Belfast in record time. After Bill ties his boat at the dock, we step out to explore the town and do some shopping. The day continues to be warm, the sun shines friendly and bright, and we feel relaxed and carefree.

"Let's have lunch at The Weathervane, Ina suggests. We have good memories from our last summer's visit there. "A perfect choice!" all agree.

We are seated at a table overlooking the bay and are enjoying the calming sight of small and large boats idling in the harbor. There is plenty of time for our journey back. Our seafood specials are excellent and we savor them in a relaxed leisure.

It is early afternoon when we start our voyage back. There are a few clouds in the mostly blue sky but nothing to indicate what awaits us ahead. We clear the harbor and come into the open waters. The waves are a bit rough and, considering everything, Bill predicts that it will take us about two hours to reach Warren Island. Soon, seemingly from nowhere, a fog settles over us. We are wrapped in its increasingly thick blanket, the shoreline hardly visible. The waves grow more restless and higher. The boat rocks in their rough grasp. The sky, which was blue and friendly only a short while ago, is gray and menacing. Bill steers the boat closer to the shore, trying to ride the waves and avoid the ever-present rocks. The sea gets increasingly rougher; at times, the shoreline disappears completely from our view.

"Get down from your seats and sit on the bottom of the boat," Bill yells over the sound of the wind and waves: to make the boat more stable, he later tells us. We do, as he says. "Will we get back to the safety of the land?" is a question in my heart and very likely in everybody's. I know that Bill is an experienced boatsman. He knows how to handle his boat and the waters. Ina is his first mate, she is by his side helping and guiding. "The ocean is in charge", Bill says. A man can do only what is in his power to do. The rest is in God's hand and the elements. As I sit quietly on the bottom of the boat, I am very cold, but surprisingly not very scared. In a way, I have come to terms with my finality. We read stories about "people lost at sea". It does happen. It can happen to us. We are in a very small boat in a large, restless, menacing ocean. There are no landmarks to follow, only the drifting shoreline. The compass in this situation is useless.

It is starting to get dark. "How long have we been going? Where is Lincolnville?" We should have been there a long time ago.

Then, a miracle. The curtain of fog parts and reveals a lonely fisherman in a rowboat. He seems to have climbed out of a Winslow Homer's painting to come to our rescue. "Where is Lincolnville?" asks Bill. The man points with his hand away from where we had been heading: "That way. Approximately a mile from here." Bill turns his boat to the pointed direction, and lo and behold, soon, from the gray mist, emerges the silhouette of the harbor of Lincolnville. The most welcome sight! Our relief cannot be measured. We are chilled to the bone. I cannot stop shivering even after consuming a warming mug of tea at the local eatery. One more problem remains, though: "How will we get back to Warren Island, our camping home?" The wind is fierce, and the waves high, and too dangerous for our boat to cross. Then we are handed a second miracle; a wonderful man comes to our rescue. His name is Mel, a retired FBI Agent, a former police officer from Florida, who now lives in Maine and has a business transferring passengers between the islands. He offers to guide our boat to Warren Island.

It is dark when we finally arrive home, dead tired but immensely thankful and happy for the comfort and safety of our tents.

MORE FAMILY PHOTO'S

Peter and me, outside our Natick home

Arvids, Kristine, Peter and me - Christmas in Natick

Kristine, Peter and me

**Skaidrite, Juris, Anne and Paul -
Paul's Confirmation**

**My nephew Paul and his wife, Anne with their
girls, Megan and Kate**

**My neice Anne and her husband Jerome with
their children, Piper and Ethan**

Frank and me on our wedding day – May 9, 1987

My New Family!

Frank's parents, Joseph and Mathilde

My granddaughters (from left to right) – Tara, me, Erin, and
Larissa, at Erin's wedding

Part Four: Always a Part of Me...Latvia and its People

"... I have been grounded in the soul of Plikeni. It is my living water, the rock on which I am standing. Plikeni is and will always be part of me...

...my promise is to never forget Latvia, to return there, to always love this very dear country of my birth."

Astrida

GAVA

The telephone rings. It is my cousin Ruta from Chicago. "Gava died today", she says. "Gava died", I repeat silently. He had been fighting cancer for over a year, until now, always being the winner. His will to live had been remarkable. Gava had faced many challenges, had fought, and survived many tragedies. At times, I had wondered if he would outwit his cancer. Ruta's message tells otherwise.

Gava was a very special person. To me, he is a symbol of survival, and an exceptional human being. I allow memories of him to take hold of me, allow my thoughts to honor his life.

When and how did I meet Gava for the first time? It was in June of 1975, when my daughter Kris and I visit Latvia. Cousin Ruta had married Gava's son, Yuri, and we were invited to the family's seaside home in Bulduri. On our arrival, we were greeted by a distinguished and handsome gentleman. "Welcome," he had said. "'How good to meet you. Please come in." Beside him stood his smiling wife, Lala. We were introduced to their younger son, Andrey. Their son, Yuri a world-renowned silent film specialist, was away on a lecture tour. The welcome was warm, and we felt embraced by a special, kind hospitality. In later years, we learn that Gava's and Lala's hearts and house were always opened to people they loved. And there were many that they loved! A glow of friendliness and humor surrounded them. I looked at Gava. "He could be an aristocrat," I had thought. There was a special dignity and a detached authority in his personality. He was warm and friendly, but at the same time a bit distant. It is some time later that I learn about Gava's life, about the many tragic events of his past and the many miraculous survivals. Gava never discussed his past with me. It is only through other people that I came to know his family's history.

Gabriels Civjans, Gava's real name, was born in Riga of Jewish parents. His father was a recognized physician. When the Nazis invaded Latvia, his family was arrested; his parents and a sister were executed. Miraculously, Gava managed to escape, and was hiding for a while with the help of a Latvian relative. He acquired a passport, changed his name to a Latvian sounding one: Gunars Cirulis. Through a series of lucky events, he was able to leave Latvia and, through Germany, managed to escape to Switzerland. There, he graduated from a university, majoring in journalism. He fluently spoke several languages. In addition to Latvian, he knew German, French, and Russian. During this time he started to write, first as a journalist and later writing detective stories. During his stay in Switzerland, he was able to help out a Russian diplomat as a translator. After the war, Gava had to leave Switzerland. With the help of the Russian diplomat, he returned to his native Latvia, now a Soviet occupied Latvia. He was deeply shocked to find his family gone.

Gava was apolitical, and the regime allowed him a certain literary freedom. He seriously turned to writing, and under his adopted name of Gunars Cirulis became well known as an author of detective novels and short stories. He published about 30 literary works.

In 1975, when I met Gava for the first time, he was a well-known writer and publicist. But, above all, he is a warm, caring, and compassionate person with an ever-present twinkle in his eyes and a smile on his lips. The love for his family is all-inclusive. Family is the center of his life. His wife, children and grandchildren are the people who give him the most joy. His many friends are a close second. Gava has a very special relationship with cousin Ruta's mother, Marija. Both of them are gifted with a great sense of humor and their engaging dialogues are lively and entertaining. Whenever I have visited Latvia, I have also been a guest at Gava's home. Many a time I have enjoyed the interesting conversations and shared the exquisite meals in their hospitable house. As a well-known and recognized author, he enjoyed certain privileges, even during the Soviet Regime. One such luxury was the use of a yacht. My visits to Latvia were very intense and often tiring. During one of these visits, I am especially exhausted. Gava offers me a day of relaxation on the yacht, cruising the river Lielupe. The calm waters, the sun, and the blue sky is a wonderful therapy for one's tired body and soul. I am renewed and ready to face another tomorrow. The day is a gift that I will always remember.

Another special memory involves a visit to a fisherman's village, Bērzciems, in Kurzeme. The area is a military enclave and is off limits to outsiders, certainly foreigners. (There were many areas in the Soviet Latvia where foreign visitors were not welcome. Pliķēni was one of those places then too) I believe one needed a permit to enter. However, Gava feels that we should visit a special friend of his, an old sea captain. Every summer the family rents a room in the sea captain's house to spend a week or two close to nature. It is a special house, a special family and a special day. We listen to the captain's stories of the far gone days, how he and his family were shipbuilders, how he took his boats on the open seas, the visits to foreign shores and adventures in foreign lands. Behind the captain's house is a garden that reminds me of the garden we used to have in Plikeni. Lots of bushes filled with delicious berries, ready for picking and eating. It is sort of a homecoming, a glimpse back into my happy childhood days..

Before lunch we go mushroom picking in the nearby forest. Cousin Ruta is a great mushroom picker. It is relaxing and peaceful to walk through the woods and search among the leaves and grass for the round mushroom heads.

The day's most exciting, though scary, incident happens on our way home. We are enjoying our ride, laughing and joking. From seemingly nowhere a policeman steps on the road in front of us and waives our car to stop. A thought flashes through my head. This is it. He will arrest both of us, my sister Ruta and me, and our next trip will be to Siberia. I try to become invisible. Gava steps out of the car, and he and the young police officer have an animated conversation. At the end, they shake hands. We can proceed. "Oh, it was nothing", Gava says, "He just wanted to see my license, wanted to know where we are going, where we have been". Now, in retrospect, being familiar with the history of Gava's life, the dangers he had to face and somehow manage to survive and outsmart his opponents, I do realize that Gava had a special wisdom, a canny sense of what to do when the chips are down and danger looms.

My last visit with Gava is during our visit to Latvia this summer. Sister Ruta and I visit him in the hospital. He is very ill. But soon, his health improves. He is discharged home and we visit him in Lielupe. He has improved considerably and is very hopeful about his recovery. Yuri and cousin Ruta have come from Chicago to be with the family. That is a great support and joy to Gava and also his wife Lala. Yuri and Ruta now live in Chicago where Yuri is a professor at the University of Chicago. The arrival of his children has given Gava a new energy. He starts to write again with the help of his daughter-in-law, Ruta. He dictates, Ruta writes. Sadly, the disease is more powerful than he is. In the end, it is the one enemy that he has not been able to beat.

It has been a privilege to know Gunars Cirulis. There is a great void and sadness that his passing has left behind. However, memories survive; his books continue to live! Through the written word, his voice, his humor comes through, clear and loud. Through the memories, he continues to live in the hearts of the people whom he loved and who loved him.

A CHANCE MEETING IN 1993

My visits to Latvia are quite frequent, I return there at least every other year. I am pulled by a longing to go back to the place of my origins. To look for what? For a place in the sun, for a lost paradise? Again and again I have confirmed to myself that this special place exists only in my memories, in my dreams. And still...I return. Every time, it is a homecoming. I realize, however, that Latvia and I have changed; we have become estranged.

Latvia regained her freedom from the Soviet rule in 1991 when the Soviet Union collapsed. Now, people can travel around freely; no restrictions, no "off limits" signs stop visitors from moving on. The country is starting to breathe again, to rebuild her shattered life. However, life for many people is very hard. It is a real problem for a great number of families to make ends meet. Especially hard off are the senior population and multiple children families. To make life easier, the Latvian community in Boston has developed ties with these folks and tries to help them with clothing, food, medicine, and other necessities. Through this aid effort, many personal relationships have developed, and during our visits to Latvia, we try to meet our new friends and to learn about their life and their immediate needs.

It is the summer of 1993. I am in Riga, staying with my aunt's family and enjoying their warm hospitality. Also, my plan is to meet some of the families that our church supports.

Today I have made arrangements for a visit with Baiba Beitins, a mother of six children, most of them in poor health. I have brought along medicine and some gifts. The doorbell rings. I open the door to a young woman and a pretty blond girl. "Hallo", I greet them, "please come in". I make a special effort to make them feel welcome and at ease. We sit down in my aunt's living room, and cousin Maija brings in tea and cookies. It is always a bit difficult to open conversation with people one has never met before, but soon we feel comfortable enough, and our conversation flows naturally and openly. The little girl, Velga, is four years old. She is very thin and suffers from asthma. I invite her to sit next to me, put my arm around her, and offer a cookie. Her mother, Baiba, tells me about the difficulties the family faces of just getting along day to day, of the children's illnesses, and husband's struggle with drinking. It sounds overwhelming to me!

As our visit continues, I share some of my past experiences, especially my childhood before I left Latvia. I mention that I lived on a farm in Zemgale and how difficult it was for my family to leave our homestead Plikeni.

"Plikeni"? Baiba repeats. "Was it in the township of Svitene?" "Yes", I nod in response. "I lived in Plikeni after the war ended", Baiba continues. "After the Russians nationalized all the private lands and created collective farms, my dad, who had a degree in agriculture, was put in charge of the garden center of Svitene's collective farm. Plikeni was the natural choice for this center because of its already existing orchards and fruit and vegetable gardens. I loved my life there. It was such a beautiful place! I remember the flower gardens, so much color!"

I look at Baiba, and listen to her words in total disbelief. "How can this be? Such an almost impossible coincidence!" Through this woman's story, my childhood Plikeni, the only place that symbolizes home to me, has come out of the shadows of the past and has started to live again. I met Baiba, a complete stranger, only a short hour ago, but now a deep connecting tie binds us together, shared memories of a life in Plikeni. She lived there, she walked the same paths, looked at the same gardens, lived in the same house, slept there, had meals there.

My heart is filled with a myriad of emotions. I am happy to hear that Plikeni kept living and prospering after we left, but in some strange way, I also feel that this woman sitting across from me in my aunt's living room has invaded my sacred space. By what right can she call "my Plikeni" "her Plikeni"?

Strange, how at times, life seems to come around to complete a full circle, how a chance meeting can bring past into present and start to live in a new dimension. Baiba and I are bound by a common thread. For a brief moment in time, we have shared the magic of a small piece of our world, a place in the sun called "Plikeni".

VISITING PLIKENI WITH FRANK AND RUTA

It is just past noon when we arrive in Plikeni. Frank is at the wheel of our rented VW Gulf. This is the third and final week of our visit to my homeland, Latvia. For Frank, these three weeks have been an introduction, and also a revelation. Before our trip, Latvia to him had been a distant land, somewhat backward, where Mafia ruled the scene and nobody could feel really safe. He says that he gained these impressions from us, the Latvians, who had lived there and had revisited. But the visit has revealed a totally different Latvia to him, a charming country with rich and often tragic history and beautiful women. If someone asks him now, "What did you like best in Latvia?" His answer is: "The beautiful women."

Today, Tante Marija from Riga, my sister Ruta, Frank and I have come to visit Plikeni. Frank wants to see the place where I grew up, and spent, as I have often told him, the most carefree years of my life. I had painted for him a memory picture of the farm: the buildings, my dad's apple orchards, the fields, the animals, the river Svitenis that bordered our land and where we used to swim; where, in its waters, our dad fished, and I got my very first catch.

Today's Plikeni has acquired a new landmark. A stork family has found a home on top of a tall chimney that has remained from the Soviet era green house. Latvia has become one of the storks' favorite nesting areas. Approximately 10,000 birds have been counted this year. The increase of marshlands due to neglected and abandoned farms has increased the frog population, the very favorite food for storks. On our rides through Latvia, we saw many delightful sites of stork-nests on rooftops, trees, telephone poles, or other high places convenient for nest building. Numerous times, we passed these graceful, long beaked, long legged birds walking in the fields or on the roadsides.

The road that used to lead to the farm is gone. We approach the house by a new route. To me, everything looks different and new. We pass the place where the animal barn, my very favorite building, used to stand. An empty spot looks at us; only markings from the old foundation are visible. Cousin Ilmars, who now manages the farm, has told us that during the Soviet era the barn had deteriorated to the point that it could not be successfully reconstructed. He had no choice but to tear it down. The main house is still there, however. It has undergone a face-lift, and has been repainted and repaired. Colorful flowers adorn the front entrance. We drive into the yard. Frank stops the car and we step out. Ilmars and his family come to greet us: his daughter Anna, her husband Rihards, and their five-year-old daughter Eline. We exchange hugs and smiles. "Please, come in," we are invited, and follow our hosts into the house.

As I step over the high threshold, I step into a place that is, and yet is not, my childhood home. It feels foreign and different. Many years have passed since that July evening when, for the last time, I stepped over that same threshold to leave behind my life of security and innocence. Today, I have to strain my memory to bring the past together with the present. As we are lead through the house, it takes a great effort to make it feel familiar and alive. Was it Thomas Wolfe who said: "You can never go back"?

After a short visit around the coffee table, we are ready for a tour outside. Rihards and Eline are our guides. Little Eline, Elinite as we affectionately call her, holds on to her father's hand as we walk down the hill (so well I remember the hill with my mother's neat vegetable garden stretching down the enclave) onto the meadow. The grass has not been cut yet, and bright field flowers color and intermingle with the green of the grass. Eline, Ruta and I pick the blues, the whites, the reds, and the yellows, and soon our hands are holding a rainbow bouquet of flowers. We walk to the river. Our swimming hole is still there, however, the river is overgrown with reeds. "Up the stream a dam has been erected," says Rihards, "that is the reason for the low water. But the water is much cleaner now, even crayfish have returned!" Yes, crayfish!

As I listen to Rihards and watch the river, my memories lead me into a path, long not visited. I remember the warm summer evenings when I accompanied my dad on his crayfish catching expeditions. He stepped into the water near the shore, long rubber boots covering his legs, his hands seeking crayfish hiding holes in the riverbank. What an excitement it was when one was pulled out! And I look at little Elinite, field flowers in her hand, her light hair in two obedient braids, her blue eyes looking around, attentively listening to her father's words, and suddenly a bright light floods into my silent heart. In Eline, I can see myself many years ago, age five, happy and carefree on my farm, among my animals, my apple trees, lying blissfully in my meadow, watching the lark in the blue summer sky bringing its happy song to heaven. And I know, Plikeni will give Eline what once, a long time ago, it so generously gave me: a happy childhood.

Our tour continues. We meet the two cows that provide the family with milk, and the chickens. We walk through my father's apple orchard. Many of the trees have died, many others are old and bent. "They still bear an abundance of fruit," Rihards tells us. He is in charge and interested. "Every morning", he says, "I come out and look for projects. What can I do today?" Rihards' face is always lit up in a smile, and we enjoy listening as we follow him around.

Our next stop is the harvest barn. We walk inside the large, almost empty building. Its cool semidarkness and familiar smells meet me. Here, years melt away. I have come home! It is here where I used to help dad stack the harvest of wheat and rye as it was brought home from the fields. It was an important task, and I was proud that father had chosen me to help. The barn was the place of much activity. Here one could feel the change of seasons, the fertility of the earth, see the fruit of one's labor.

Today, the barn shows the passage of time. It is old now; its roof bent, but there is so much history here. This is the soul of Plikeni. I think of my father. He was only forty-four years old when the communist invasion forced him to leave the farm, to leave his work half-done, plans not realized. How much I wish we could restore and preserve Plikeni as a legacy to him.

SERGEJS

"Who would like to adopt a godchild from Latvia?" is a question asked during one of our Parish meetings. It is early 1990. Life in Latvia has become more free and open. This new freedom has also opened doors to places that, up to now, have been shielded from the world's view. The restricted traveling has ended, and movement through Latvia is now allowed, which has led to new discoveries, among them the existence of orphanages. There are many of them scattered all over Latvia. Here live children whose parents have either died or who have been removed from an abusive home environment. After visiting some of these institutions, a young woman from Canada has made it her mission to connect orphan children with a caring person in the West. A "godparents program" is born.

"Yes, I would," I respond immediately to the question of adopting a godchild. There is no doubt in my mind. I clearly know that bringing warmth and love to a lonely child would be something I would like to do. It is my hope that I could bring joy into one little person's life, that my caring would make a difference. I do not have to wait long. A letter comes from Ingrid Mazute in Canada introducing me to a 6-year-old boy named Sergejs. A photograph is enclosed. The letter explains that, at the age of four, Sergejs had been removed from his alcoholic parents' abusive and neglectful care. The family had three other children, and Sergejs's little brother is also living at the orphanage. Nothing is said about the other two. I examine the photograph. On a small child-size wooden chair sits a little boy, a slight smile on his lips. A pair of dark eyes looks seriously at me. He has a pretty face topped by a crown of dark hair. He sits straight as a soldier, feet together, hands resting on his knees. Such a nice boy! So innocent, so vulnerable. My heart fills with sad tenderness. This little boy is my adopted godchild and I am going to show him that I love him. I want him to know that he is special to me, that he is important.

I begin our relationship by writing short letters and sending small gifts to Sergejs. In response, he sometimes sends me pictures he has drawn. I also correspond with the administrator of the orphanage to emphasize my caring and interest. I want to know more about Sergejs, his personality, his daily activities. I learn that Sergejs is an active child who likes to work and help out in the orphanage.

In the following year, during my visit to Latvia, I meet Sergejs for the first time. I am very nervous. "How is he going to react to me? Will he like me?" are the questions that I ask myself. I buy gifts and sweets not only for Sergejs but also for the other orphan children. My sister, Ruta, our friend, Maija, and our ten-year-old relative, Karlis, join me in this visit. Since it is July, the children are living in their summer home on the lake of Baltezers. The camp had originally been built for boy scouts during Latvia's independent years. We board the bus in Riga and travel to Baltezers. The bus driver lets us know where to get off, and we follow the road sign to the camp. A path through the woods leads us to a group of buildings, and with some help, we find the house where Sergejs lives. A group of children come to meet us and we are embraced by small hands; little voices ask and tell, all together, in joyous ramble.

"Where is Sergejs?" I ask the counselor. She points to a boy who stands apart from the group, looking shyly at us, expectantly. I walk over to him, give him a hug and say, "Hello, Sergej! I am your godmother." His body feels stiff against my embrace. It takes time for him to soften up, to relax, and to talk. Eventually, he begins to open up, and allows himself to show some caring and recognition.

After a few hours, our visit has to end, and we have to say goodbye. A strange thing happens. Without a word, before I can say goodbye, Sergejs turns and walks quickly away. He does not look back. I am surprised and taken aback. Soon, I realize what has happened and why. The boy has been hurt many times by the people who have been important to him, whom he has loved. Now another person has arrived who says that she cares and loves him. And she also leaves. He is angry and hurt. "I understand, Sergej. I understand!" I am sad as I watch his small frame disappear among the buildings. I wish I could give more, leave something more permanent with him, not just a short visit. Time and distance are Sergejs' enemies and mine. It is so very difficult to break the barrier of mistrust and hurt, especially over long distance.

Sergejs continues to be an important part of my life. My visits to Latvia are also visits with Sergejs. I try to show him that my love for him is permanent and real, even though we are separated by distance. Have I succeeded? It's hard to tell.

In June of 1993, we have a family reunion and midsummer's night festivities at Plikeni. We have regained ownership of our homestead, and to celebrate this event we have invited all our relatives to join us there. They come from all corners of Latvia. Close to eighty people arrive, and Sergejs is among them. He seems to enjoy himself. He makes friends with other children and looks relaxed and happy. Having Sergejs in my childhood home is especially meaningful to me.

It is June 23rd, the shortest night and the longest day of the year. The night brings hardly any darkness, and any darkness there is is lit up by a huge bonfire. We have come together to celebrate our newfound togetherness. The joy is almost tangible; it vibrates through our beings; it touches our souls. We dance, we sing, we drink our "Janu alus," a beer especially brewed for this event, and eat the special "Janu" cheese, our cousin's contribution. In the morning, I see Sergejs browning hot dogs over the still smoldering bonfire. He looks relaxed and happy. He does belong with us! The thought makes me happy.

Many institutions in the newborn Latvia are undergoing changes to rectify the Soviet system's endemic corruption and dishonesty. Life in orphanages is also changing as the old system undergoes reconstruction. Sergejs has a new counselor, Alma. I write to her, and in time we develop a close and friendly relationship. She understands that my interest in Sergejs' well-being and future is not a passing fancy. She has taken a special interest in Sergejs. A very important and upsetting change in Sergejs's life has been his transfer to another children's home/boarding school in a remote area of Latvia, Rauda. This is a special school for children with some intellectual or physical impairment.

"Why was Sergejs transferred?", I ask the director of the orphanage, when I meet her on my next visit to Riga. Her answer is: "Sergejs could not follow the public school's program and had some disciplinary problems. He needed to be removed." When I continue my questioning, she finally says, "Well, some children just have to be sacrificed." "Children, sacrificed?" I ask in dismay. I look at her in total disbelief. "How can you sacrifice a human being?" She has no answer. My questions make her uncomfortable. I leave her office with a splitting headache. A migraine, that I very seldom experience, has attacked me.

I visit Sergejs in his new home in Rauda. It is a remote backwoods area in the Latgale's region of Latvia. It is very peaceful and beautiful there. The children are taught minimal intellectual skills but are introduced to various practical skills. The school seems to be very well run, the staff pleasant, and Sergejs happy. He proudly shows me the garden that he helps to plant and maintain, the animals the children care for, and the woods where they go berry and mushroom picking. We go down to the river where he fishes during warm weather and skates in winter. A healthy environment for children to grow up in. That is how life in Rauda seems to me.

"But what will they do when they graduate?" I ask one of the teachers. "Well, we mostly prepare manual laborers or household help. The brighter children can attend a trade school," she answers. That will be Sergejs's future. Not too bright a prospect. "Was Sergejs's transfer to this boarding school justified?" is a question that continues to bother me.

Alma continues to be my immediate contact with Sergejs. She is taking a special interest in him. She also knows that I care. In the spring of 2000, Sergejs graduates from the Rauda's Specschool by completing nine years of education offered by the school. My husband, Frank, Sister Ruta and I, together with Alma, attend the graduation ceremonies. Alma has arranged a bus to take us to Rauda. This is Sergejs and Frank's first meeting. The graduation exercises are very impressive, with lots of pomp and circumstance. Sergejs receives many awards. He looks proud and handsome in his black and white uniform. The small shy boy I first met nine years ago has developed into a nice young man; still a bit shy and quiet, and seemingly not too sure of himself. He has had many stumbling blocks to climb over, many adjustments to make. His young life has been filled with hurts, losses, and disappointments.

After graduation, Sergejs moves back to his original home in Riga, Imanta, where he lived before his transfer to Rauda. Alma is still working there and has promised to watch over him. Alma has been a guardian angel to Sergejs. With her help, he is admitted to a trade school in Riga where he studies woodworking. Sergejs loves the practical workshops and excels there, but has difficulty with the studies like math and science. Rauda's curriculum had given him very little background in these areas. With some extra help and hard work, Sergejs successfully completes the trade school program. Alma and I have continuously encouraged him: Alma with her direct presence, and I, long distance, through letters and regular visits.

Over the years, I have tried to be a positive force in Sergejs's life, and my sincere hope is that I have made a difference. My wish for him is that he recognizes his self-worth, is proud of his accomplishments, and has the wisdom to make the right decisions when he is presented with important, life changing choices. Sergejs is part of my family, and I wish him a good and successful life.

LOST IN THE WOODS OF LATVIA - 1997

Today is May 30, 1997. It is Saturday morning, bright and sunny, and I am on my way to visit my adopted godchild Sergejs at his school in Rauda. The school is located in the Latgale region of Latvia, about four hours drive east of Riga. To get there, one needs a car and a driver. Alma, Sergejs's teacher and benefactor, is joining me on this trip and has arranged with her daughter's boyfriend, Janis, to drive us to Rauda.Janis has a new car, a bright red sports model Huyndai; a nice car to sit back in and relax. The small village of Rauda is approx. 15 km south from the main highway, and the roads to Rauda are mostly gravel and not well marked. At times, Janis stops and looks at his map to try to figure out which direction to go. That happens mostly at cross roads. The countryside we travel through is picturesque, with fields and small farms scattered along the way.

It is lunchtime when we reach Rauda. The School is located on a narrow country road. Sergejs and many of his friends are outside waiting for us. It is a big event in this remote area to have visitors from the outside world. Since I am from America, it adds to the importance of the event. The children who live and attend the school here are mostly orphans, or are wards of state, who have been removed from their parents' care because of abuse and neglect, mostly due to alcoholism. Sergejs belongs to the second group. Tragically, Latvia has a great number of these children.

The school's personnel warmly greet us. After the first "halo's" and general introductions, we are invited to a richly clad lunch table. Sergejs and couple of his closest friends are also invited to share the meal with us.

After lunch, the School's principal takes us around the property. The buildings and workshops are old but well maintained; not state of the art facilities and equipment. But is that always necessary to teach and have satisfactory performance? I wonder. The curriculum emphasizes practical learning and trades, such as sawing, woodworking, gardening, cooking. Intellectual development is limited to basics. A great number of children who attend the school have learning disabilities or are psychologically troubled. Considering the background of many of them, it is not hard to understand why their souls and minds bear these deep scars.

Sergejs and several of his friends accompany us on our tour. I can feel the children's longing to be close to us, to hold our hands, to be noticed. The need for recognition, the need for affection is plainly visible in their young faces. "Will you also be my godmother", a blond girls asks me. "Can you find someone who will write to me?", asks another child. I hug them, and for a moment hold them close to me. I wish that I were a Fairy Godmother and my magic wand would give these children all that their young hearts wish for, especially, to erase the damage and the scars of their past experiences. Instead, I leave only a promise: "Yes, I'll find a friend for you". It is not much. It is almost nothing. The sunny day is leaving big shadows in my heart, shadows of the children's neediness and pain. And my inability to lessen those.

It is late afternoon when we leave Rauda. Sergejs is coming with us to Riga to spend the summer months at a camp there. The children and the teachers have come out to wave us good-bye. We wave back. "Good-bye! Good-bye! See you again!" Janis's red sports car takes the right turn on the narrow gravel road, and soon they disappear from our view. He drives fast. Our car is followed by a cloud of dust, pebbles, and small stones fly around us. "Bang". Something hits the bottom of our red Huyndai and it stops dead in its tracks.

"Hey, what was that?", we ask in one voice. Our chauffeur gets out of the car, lifts up its hood and looks. No damage can be seen. Again and again, he tries to revive the engine but it stubbornly does not budge. What now? We are deep in the woods of Latgale. Where can we get help? We'd passed a small house some minutes ago. There might be help, and Janis walks back to investigate. After awhile, he returns without success. We wait. We take short walks up and down the road to ease the waiting. This certainly is a "road less traveled" as Robert Frost would say in a much more poetic sense. It just could not be that no one would ever come this way. It just could not be! We listen to the birds that merrily chirp in the otherwise silent woods, and try to be optimistic "Ku-ku, Ku-ku", a cuckoo's call sounds through the trees. What a happy surprise! A bird that I have never heard in the United States is greeting us here. A magical sound from my distant childhood.

We wait. Then, finally, what now seems like a miracle, a sound of a motor is heard, and soon an old jeep stops by our side. Three young men jump out and ask in Russian: "Can we help you?" Janis knows the language well. In Latvia, during the Soviet regime, everybody had to learn the language. He explains our dilemma. The men look at the car, lift its hood and shake their heads. "Net, net", Russian for "No, no". It is a foreign car and they have no idea what could be wrong with it. Were it a Russian made one, they might possibly help us. But there could be a silver lining. In their village, Pašuliene, is a mechanic who knows about foreign cars. They will go and fetch him, that is, if he is not drunk and is able to function. The village is about an hour's drive from where we are and they should be back in about two hours. That is a promise. The three men jump back into their rusty jeep and leave us alone in the silence of the woods.

"Will they be back?", we look at each other and wonder. What other choice do we have, but to wait? Luckily, summer days are long in Latvia. The sun sets around 11 o'clock, so we still have plenty of daylight left. It is almost two hours to the point when we hear a car's engine and the familiar jeep come into our view and stops. They have come! What a relief! What joy!

"The car needs to be towed to their village to be "looked

at", the men explain to Janis. They have brought along a rope. Soon our new disabled red car is attached to the old but strong jeep, and we are on our way to get help. After several mishaps with the breaking of the rope, we finally reach the village of Pasuliene.

As we arrive, we are greeted by most of the village men, who now try to diagnose the problem, without much success. A Russian made car would be no problem, but who knows how to fix an import? Nobody in the village Pasuliene, not even the mechanic who claimed to be an expert. We need to get back to Riga. On his cell phone, Janis finally reaches a friend in Riga who agrees to come to pick us up. He will use his car to tow us back to the city.

By now, it is dark. A young woman from a nearby apartment building invites us to wait in her house. She is a Latvian girl married to a White Russian. She and her two children are the only Latvian speaking people in this village. We are offered tea and encouraged to rest and relax after our ordeal. "Feel at home. You are welcome to stay as long as necessary", she says. As hours drag on, and our waiting time extends late after midnight, Jolanta, our kind hostess, brings in soup and other goodies. We are strangers imposing on her time, depriving her of good night's sleep, and she is welcoming us as long time friends or relatives. Something to think about and to remember!

It is close to daylight when Janis's friend arrives. He is clad in a black tuxedo, having come straight from a party. How much is a friend ready to do for a friend? Here, one can find a good example. Finally, with our crippled car in tow, we are ready to leave the hospitality of Jolanta and her family. "Thank you, thank you!"

It is late morning when we arrive in Riga. I am dead tired, but happy to be back. The experience has taught me a valuable lesson about generosity and kindness of total strangers. A lesson I will never forget. Good Samaritans live among us, often unnoticed, but very visible when opportunity calls them to service.

VISIT TO LATVIA IN 2002

Present meets Past

Our plane lands at the Riga Airport in the early afternoon of May 29, 2002. The airport has changed its face from my visit two years ago. It is now clean and modern; the Soviet-time shabbiness is gone. Ruta and I go through customs easily, and are greeted outside with flowers from our little five-year-old relative, Eduards. Latvians love flowers; they are a sign of welcome.

In the evening, the whole family gathers at one of Riga's most popular eating places on the banks of River Daugava, called Lido. It is a huge cafeteria-style restaurant where one can find a great variety of mainly ethnic dishes. The highlight of this evening, for me, is the arrival of Sergejs, my adopted godchild. He has changed and matured, and has just finished the second year of the three-year trade school course. He is proud and happy. I share his pride and happiness, and we talk more openly than ever before.

The next day, we visit our cousin's father-in-law, Gava, who is fighting cancer at the Oncology Center in Riga. He is very ill, but recognizes us, and smiles. Our past meetings have been at his hospitable house in the seashore town of Jurmala, where he invariably had been a charming, jovial, and welcoming host. He is a professional writer, and his house had always been filled with guests from around the world. It is sad to see Gava so very ill and weak. His wife, Ļaļa, is always by his side. She tells us that she knows that Gava is going to get well again. Let's hope so. My heart is heavy as we leave. I do not have Ļaļa's faith.

My sister Ruta and I take a walk through the old city of Riga. Riga was founded in the year of 1201, and walking through the ancient narrow cobblestone streets, viewing the old buildings, breathing in the city's long past, one can almost touch its colorful, often tragic and changing history. In the Middle Ages, Riga belonged to the Hanzan Trading partners and was one of several European cities united by mutual commercial interests. Many of the old buildings date back to this period, and many of the streets bear the names of the artisans and tradesmen who worked and lived there. I love the Old Riga! It would be a privilege to live where one can feel the touch of times past, in some sense, walk among, and with, the many generations preceding mine. For me, however, it is only a dream. Real estate in the old part of Riga is very, very expensive, and there is almost none available. Ruta and I go into some of the gift shops, look around, and buy a few souvenirs.

Riga is famous for its Jugendstyle architecture. Among the many grand and beautiful buildings, most notable are the magnificent churches. Many of the churches were closed during the Soviet times; a few were used as concert halls, and some as storage areas or for other secular purposes. Very few were places of worship, since religion was strongly discouraged if not totally forbidden. Now they are open again for religious services.

On our way back home to a small rented apartment, a short walk from the center, we go by the Freedom Monument (Brivibas Piemineklis), built from donated funds in the early 1930's during the era of free Latvia. It was designed by a famous Latvian sculptor, Karlis Zale. The Monument towers over the city plaza, and is the symbol of Latvia's freedom and national pride. The Monument's base has several panels depicting significant moments of Latvia's history. On this base, towering to the sky, stands a young woman holding, in her outstretched arms, three golden stars that symbolize the regions of Latvia and the nation's sovereignty. People place flowers here in honor and respect. We do too. An Honor Guard stands on each side of the Monument and is changed every hour. The changing of these guards is very solemn and dignified.

Another landmark of Riga is its beautiful opera house, called the White House. It is now completely renovated and looks like a Greek temple with its white columns and magnificent façade. Standing on its steps, one can see the profile of the Freedom Museum against the changing sky, a sight that never fails to touch my soul. Ruta has ordered tickets for a couple of events at the Opera, and we stop by the box office to pick these up. That concludes our activities for the afternoon, and we head back home to rest and relax.

Our days in Latvia are filled with activities. Each day has an agenda. In the morning, we look at the day's schedule, place and receive telephone calls. Is this a vacation? We wonder. It would be wonderful to just relax and sightsee. That is never possible during our short visits to Latvia, however. Too many obligations crowd our vacation time.

Ruta and I serve as messengers from our Church in Boston to the organizations and people our parish supports. That means that some of our time has to be given to these obligations. On Sunday, we attend a service at the Anglican Church. This church serves the non-Latvian speaking population of greater Riga and the services are conducted in English. Revered Juris Calitis, a Latvian from Canada, serves here as its pastor. He is also a pastor of our parish's sister church in Riga, and we are here to deliver a contribution to help finance the children's summer camp.

We arrive an hour early. Not by choice, but by not knowing the starting time of the service. We are welcomed by a tall, smiling man who introduces himself as the caretaker and supervisor of the church. He tells us that during the Soviet times, the church was used as a grain storage area; the altar had been covered over by paint, and the interior furnishings removed and destroyed. The building itself, an impressive stone structure, dates back to the early eighteen hundreds.

Now, the Church has come back to life, physically, as well as spiritually. He is proud of his part in the church's rebirth.

"Please sit down and enjoy the beauty and peace here", he invites. We do that. Soon, a middle-aged man approaches us. "Could you help me with a couple of Lats (a Latvian currency)? I have some problems with my mother's will," he says, and shows us some papers he has pulled out from his shirt's pocket "Don't believe to him", whispers the church's supervisor in passing. Apparently, beggars are regular Sunday visitors, and pick mostly on people who look like tourists. As the service starts, our beggar friend also sits down. It is sort of comforting to see that he has not come here only to beg. As in Jesus' time, when beggars were common outside the Temple door, in today's Latvia, they also stand outside the churches with extended, begging hands.

In the afternoon, we visit our cousin's wife, Banga. Banga is a remarkable woman, a real warrior. She developed diabetes in her young years, did not receive proper treatment, and eventually lost her sight. Now she is totally blind and lives with her elderly, disabled mother in a small three-room apartment in a suburb of Riga. They share the toilet with a neighbor. The tiny windowless kitchen is also used as their wash-up facility. The apartment has no shower or bathtub. They manage, however. Banga is a meticulous housekeeper; that is the only way to be. Everything in her small apartment has its place. If anything is moved, the order and familiarity in her dark world collapses. To cope with life, she has developed a rigid self-discipline, her tool to a relatively normal existence. Radio connects Banga to the world outside; it is a source of information and entertainment. She loves music and knows it very well. She has won many prizes in listeners' call-in competitions. Last year, she won a trip to Italy for two, and her daughter, Anna, and a friend were the lucky travelers.

Banga is expecting us, and welcomes us with a smile. Her dark eyes look searchingly at us, as they always do. When Banga looks at me, I have a feeling that she sees more than my physical person. I believe that Banga has developed a deeper vision; that the loss of her physical sight has been replaced by a keen spiritual insight. Tatina, Banga's mother, has her own small room. I go in to say "hallo". She sits on her bed, a tender smile lights up her kind face in response. She does not talk much. Just a couple of words and one does not really know how much she understands. Tatina seems to live in her own private world. Banga and Tatina need each other for company, as well as for survival. In case of a crisis, each one is there for the other.

After a short visit, picture taking, and ice cream, we say good-bye. It is a perfect, warm, and sunny spring afternoon, and we enjoy the short walk to the local streetcar stop. The streetcars come at frequent intervals and are a convenient and inexpensive public transportation. I find a seat at the window and watch the passing landscape.

We go by the Arcadia Garden, a park, where, as a child, I played during the summer months, sledded in the winter snow, and walked hand in hand with my special friend, Irene. Many wonderful memories come back into focus. The park looks well maintained. I see families on their Sunday outings, just as it was years ago when I was part of this landscape: children playing, laughing, and running among the green trees.

Beyond Arcadia is Tornkalna Railroad Station. A tragic landmark. It contrasts heavily with my happy memories. It leads me back to the night of June 14, 1941 when hundreds of innocent families were gathered here, crowded into cattle cars to be transported to Russian Siberia. I look at the passing building. I remember Aijina, my lovely, gentle friend, who was one of the tragic victims of that night. She and I had sat next to each other in school, played together in the Park. How can one understand the darkness and evil of man's soul, the inhumanity it is capable of? How can one reconcile it to the goodness and light that has been, and still is, a part of this day?

The next day, our rented Opal Astra arrives, and my sister Ruta, cousin Aivars, and I are ready for our adventures outside Riga. Today's plans include a visit to Sigulda, a small town east of Riga. It used to be a resort and vacation place. Now, as most anything in Latvia, it has a different face, marked by the Soviet era of neglect. It is a friendly and colorful face, however, and the town is gradually coming back to life. Many gardens, greenery, and flowers are very much a part of today's Sigulda.

We have come here to visit cousin Aina, who lives in a small apartment on the fourth floor of a Soviet built apartment house. The house that belonged to her family before the Russian occupation is being renovated. It was nationalized by the Soviets in 1940. The Communist system did not recognize private property; everything belonged to the State. It had taken Aina considerable time and effort to eventually get the property back. The scars of fifty-years of neglect and abuse, however, has made the building uninhabitable. Much needs to be done.

Aina and her family had been among the many Latvians who were deported to Siberia in 1949. They spent a number of years in the Soviet Gulag in extreme hardship. Eventually, the family was allowed to return home, without the father, though. While working in the Siberian forest, a falling tree had killed him. Life had taught Aina many lessons: survival and endurance among others. But the years in deportation had damaged her health. She is an invalid now and can hardly walk because of severe arthritis. The first things one notices in Aina, however, are her smiling clear blue eyes and ever-present cheerful disposition. She is welcoming us in her tiny apartment with a warm: "Come on in! Sit down, please!" We arrange chairs around her small dining table, sit down, and partake in the delicious meal she has prepared for us. We enjoy a couple of hours visiting and reminiscing.

Our next stop is the city of Cesis, a short distance from Sigulda. It is an old and beautiful city, now trying to come back from many years of neglect. It was founded in the late 13th century but hardly anything has survived from those ancient times. The medieval castle ruins are still there and are used as a background for open-air summer concerts.

Aivars' cousin, Augusts, and his family live in Cesis, and we are here to pay them a visit. Augusts and his wife Aina share a lovely small house with their daughter, Olita, and her two sons. Again, we are warmly welcomed. Latvians are very hospitable and they love to eat. A table is set for us and we are invited to sit down and partake. So, we sit down and eat again. The food is delicious, and it is enjoyable to be part of the family and see their warm and caring relationship. Augusts' health is poor, and his wife, being a nurse, watches over him with loving concern.

The house is surrounded by a lovely garden. It is a true plant lover's delight. As we take a tour through the rows of flowers, vegetable beds, berry bushes, and fruit trees, we can see the attention each growing thing is receiving. The plants look healthy and happy. Gardens in Latvia are not planted only for beauty. They also supplement the families' food supply. Most Latvians live on a relatively small income, therefore, it is almost a necessity to plant a backyard garden to make meals healthier, and make ends meet.

Later in the afternoon, we check into a small guesthouse for a night's stay, take a walk around the palace garden, and watch ducks swimming in the pond. I notice a tiny duckling, all alone, swimming vigorously in the water. "Where are his brothers and sisters?" I wonder.

The day has been perfectly sunny and warm, an added blessing to our vacation joy. We have invited Augusts' family to join us for dinner at our guesthouse. The food is exceptional and by American standards, very inexpensive. We talk about their life, our life, how they differ, and what is good or bad in each. It is a wonderful evening with a great family. Tomorrow, we will visit Augusts' brother who lives on the family's old homestead, a farm where all of them grew up. This visit is especially important for cousin Aivars. It is his father's childhood home.

Broks's family reunion

The high point of our visit to Latvia is the reunion of our mother's family, the descendants of our great-grandparents, Karlis and Marija Broks, who were blessed with nine children, seven sons, and two daughters. Their farm had been located in the northern region of Latvia. I remember my visit to the old homestead. I was about five or six years old when our mother brought us children back to her grandparent's house. The place had impressed me greatly. It was spacious. Sprawling gardens of trees and flowerbeds enclosed the many farm buildings that probably dated back to the early 1800's. To my child's eye, they had looked ancient. Everything blended together in one mystical unit. In the courtyard, there was a swing with four chairs attached by heavy ropes to a long central pole. It impressed me greatly, and was, for me, the focal point of our visit. That day I had met Vija for the very first time, the cousin who organized the family reunion. "Sauliesi", as the farm was called, had been her family's home. During the Soviet Regime, the farm was nationalized, and the buildings were destroyed by fire and neglect.

What are the beginnings of our large family? What kind of life did our great-grandparents have? What I gather from the bits of information available is that they had a busy and a good life. They were successful, hard working farmers and good parents to their nine children. Then tragedy struck. Karlis, the head of the household, died at the age of forty-five, leaving Marija alone to manage the farm and take care of their numerous children, the youngest of them not even a year old. It must have been extraordinarily hard for one person to bear all that responsibility. Apparently, she was an able and strong woman, took care of the farm, and brought up her children to become successful adults. Three of them remained in the area and became farmers, among them my mother's dad. Others moved away, continued their education, and apparently worked hard in their chosen fields. Today the descendents of Karlis and Marija have come together to celebrate our beginnings and to enjoy a day of togetherness.

The sun shines bright on this Saturday in June when we meet at Riga's main railroad station. A double-decker bus is waiting for us. Cousin Vija is the main organizer of this event. On her list she checks off each arrival, and when everybody is accounted for, we board the bus and take our seats. I have met most of the relatives on previous reunions, but some are new to me. There are also children who have joined the ranks of our large family. When all heads are counted, we board the bus.

I take a seat next to my mother's cousin, Biruta. She and her two sisters are the oldest members of the family. Biruta is frail. My memories of her date back many years. I remember a young, elegant and pretty woman. I admired Biruta and was a bit intimidated by her. She came from a world of refinement, and I was just a plain country girl. Many years have gone by since then. We both have walked a long road to the present moment. Much has happened in our lives. We have lived continents apart and life styles apart. My years were lived in the free world, mostly United States, hers in Latvia under Soviet dictatorship. The years of separation are not important now, however. I feel very close to Biruta. We share our experiences. My family escaped from Latvia when the Soviet army moved in; Biruta remained and lived under the Russian occupation, experiencing the repressions and hardships of that regime. Later on in life, she married a war veteran who spent many years in prison camps, which severely damaged his health.

I met Alfreds, her husband, on some of my previous visits. He was a refined, elegant human being. Now Biruta is a widow. She tells me about the ill health of her two older sisters, Marta and Mirdza, and also her own, and how difficult it is to manage their small house in the town of Valka. Her mother, Alvine, was one of the two daughters born to Karlis and Marija, her great-grandparents, and mine. The sister's home is going to be the last stopping place on our reunion day.

On our way to Valka, we stop to pick up other members of our large family; the final count is 85, ranging from age two months to the mid-nineties. Here, we also have a short rest and a picnic on the shores of the picturesque River Gauja. We need to stretch our legs. We take this time to walk around, get acquainted again, chat, relax, have a beer, cheese, and our traditional snack, piragi. "Time to go", we hear Vija's voice. We board the bus to continue our journey.

The next stop is a visit to a school where one of our forefathers received his teacher's training. The school, Teachers' Training Seminary, was administered by a Latvian educator, Janis Cimze, from 1839 until his death in 1881. It was the only such school in northern Latvia where young Latvians and Estonians would receive education in music and teaching. The German nobility, the feudal landowners, had a strong influence in the government and it was in their interest to discourage the intellectual and the cultural development of the local people. Enlightenment was a danger to their political power. However, the seed was planted. Many graduates of this Seminary later became outstanding educators, musicians and conductors of choral groups, and were instrumental in awakening and developing the national spirit and cultural interests in the Latvian and Estonian populations.

We visit the school and the adjoining museum, and listen to the curator explaining the history, the importance of this Institution and professor Cimze's influence on the cultural development of the Latvian people. We see the diploma and photograph of our great uncle, Janis, on the wall in one of the rooms. I am impressed! He was the second oldest of the nine children and had a career as a teacher and organist. We walk around the grounds, take pictures, and continue getting to know each other.

The next step is a visit to the cemetery where most of our family's deceased members have found their final rest. It is a beautiful place, like a park, with groomed walks, impressive monuments and well-attended gravesites. The Latvians like to keep their loved one's resting places beautiful, with greenery and planted flowers around them. We place candles at each grave and have a moment of silence. It feels right to give this respect to the departed, to the ones who came before us and, in a way, brought us together this day. We also visit the gravesite of the educator Janis Cimze, whose spirit, intellectual curiosity and determination encouraged the young Latvians to pursue education and develop their national identity.

The day has stretched into the afternoon. Vija has made reservations for us at the local, and the only, restaurant for lunch. Again, back to the bus!

The restaurant is in the middle of the town of Valka. The main dining room and the terrace are set up for our group.

There is plenty of food, and plenty of noise, as we all try to make conversation with one another. The atmosphere is festive. Someone starts a song and others join in. Latvians love to sing. I believe that it was the song that kept our ancestors' spirits alive and hopeful during the many hundred's years of serfdom under the feudal lords.

Vija reminds us that time has come to get on the bus again and depart for our next stop. The bus takes us to a nearby concert esplanade where there is plenty of space for the children to run and play and the adults to sit on the rows of benches to rest and converse. I sit next to a cousin whom I have met before but really do not know well. Her name is Areta. We talk. I learn that she had spent many years in a Soviet Gulag, together with her parents and a sister. Her father had been an officer in the Latvian military, and it was a good reason for the family to be deported. Her parents have long been dead, but her sister is here with us. Also, her children and grandchildren are present. A bridge of closeness is being built between us, and it feels good.

I also have a conversation with cousin Aina's son, Ivars, and his wife, Lucija. I hear another tragic story. The night when Aina and her infant daughter were deported (I have mentioned this event previously while telling about our visit to Aina), her four-year-old son (Ivars) was spending a few days with relatives in the country. Thus, he escaped deportation but felt abandoned and alone. This was a tragic time for the little boy. In order not to be discovered by the authorities and placed into a Russian orphanage (which was the rule for parentless children), he was frequently moved from one relative's house to another.

For several years, Ivars' life had no permanence, until the day when he went to live with a kindly uncle. Here, he finally found a real home, love, and security. It was only many years later when he discovered that "the kind uncle" was really his father who had, for security reasons, changed his identity, and was afraid to reveal the truth even to his son. During the years of separation, Ivars had become estranged from his mother, and when she eventually returned from Siberia, real closeness never developed between the two of them. Many unresolved issues stood in the way. As I talked with Ivars, the pain of his past still resonated in his voice, was visible in his face. His tragic story touched me deeply. If I only could help him somehow!

"Ivar", I suggest, "why don't you write your life's story? Tell the paper what you feel, what the four-year-old boy felt when he found that his mother had left without him; how he felt when he was taken from house to house, without good explanation, good reason; how he felt when he found out that his uncle was really his father." "You know", I continued, "I have written my story and it has helped me a great deal. I see my life in a clearer perspective. It has given me peace."

I hope that Ivars takes my suggestion to heart. Telling his story would give him a release from his internal emotional turmoil. I strongly believe that.

The sun has moved far to the West. In June, the daylight in Latvia diminishes around 11 o'clock. The days are long, the nights short. However long our reunion day has been, however enjoyable for the family to linger longer, we need to move on to our final destination, to our final "goodbye". Our "director" Vija calls: "Time to board the bus".

We move back to the town of Valka and to the house of the most senior members of our family, the three Kalnins' sisters. We all gather in their garden, rich in fruit trees, vegetables, and flowerbeds. "How can they keep their garden so beautiful?", I ask. "They have help", somebody answers.

I remember that my mother had stayed in this house while attending school. It makes my visit more personal. I can look back in time and see a young girl, my mother, walking through the garden, picking an apple, tasting a berry, and possibly helping out at times.

We linger for a while. The sisters offer us coffee and refreshments. Ivars, who has a beautiful tenor voice, starts a song. The sound of "Put, vejini!" (Blow wind, blow) resonates in the evening air. Many of us join in. This is our last farewell. The bus is waiting to take us back to Riga.

Kurzeme

Kurzeme is one of the four regions of Latvia: Zemgale, Latgale, and Vidzeme being the other three. It is situated in the most western part of Latvia, and eventually joins the Baltic Sea. Kurzeme has a significant place in Latvia's history. In the middle ages, it was one of the most prosperous regions in Latvia. Its ruler, Hercog Jekab, built merchant ships, traded with other countries, and also acquired colonies in the Caribbean: Tobago and Trinidad. On these islands, even today, one can find landmarks from that distant time such as Latvian place names. Some important events mark Kurzme's most recent history. At the end of the Second WW, when the Soviet forces were overrunning Latvia, many refugees boarded small fishing boats and set out over the Baltic Sea to Sweden. Kurzeme was the last fortress of the Latvian military forces. They desperately tried to resist the invading Russian army. As they were overpowered, many retreated into the forests and continued fighting the enemy as partisans. The local farmers supported these men by providing food, and at times, shelter. However, this effort was ended in 1949 when most of the farmers were deported to Siberia. Thus, the dream and hope to save Latvia from the Soviet grip was buried, the freedom fighters were found, and most of them tortured to death. (When I write this, I have to think of the Chechens and their desperate struggle for freedom from Russia.)

It is Monday now. The sun shines brightly as we leave Riga and head west. Our plan is to visit our friends, the Veides, who live in the village of Valdemarpils. Mika and Brigita Veides are old and good friends of ours. When the Soviet Regime collapsed in the early 1990's, they left the United States to work in Latvia.

Mika is a chemist and is teaching at the Technical University in Riga. Brigita used to teach English at the local school high school but has given up this effort. "The children just are not interested in studying", Brigita says. She is very discouraged with life in Latvia and soon hopes to return back to the USA. I recall how important the Latvian culture and language are to her. For years, she worked at the Latvian Saturday School in Boston. Her mission was to teach children about Latvia. She was a dedicated teacher. When Latvia regained her independence, Brigita felt obligated to go back to her native country and work there. She said to me: "I would be a hypocrite if, after all these years of telling the children to love the land of their parents and to be faithful to their heritage, I would not practice what I had preached". She went back. However, Latvia was a disappointment. I have a feeling that to Brigita, Latvia was a shining star, to be reached, held, and cherished. Latvia was a dream, a perfect place. Reality showed her an impoverished country, suffering from the results of fifty-year communist rule. A rude awakening.

On our way to Valdemarpils, we stop at a supermarket. We want to buy some pastry to bring along to Brigita, and some fruit and snacks for the children of Rukītis, the orphanage that we are planning to visit tomorrow on our way back to Riga. Our church supports Rūkītis, and we would like to see how the children are doing. The store is huge and the selection immense. I do not believe that anywhere in the US one can find such a variety of food and drink items as we see in this Superstore in Latvia.

Brigita and Mika live in sort of a fruit-tree dreamland. Some years ago, they purchased this property: an old barn amidst an old orchard. Mika's greatest joy in life is to fish. This property abutts a lake, a perfect place for a fisherman! Soon, however, they found out that the lake was barren of fish. Early each spring, the local people came to the lake with their nets and all the fish went home with them. It was a great disappointment for Mika. Yet, the place was beautiful and peaceful. They remodeled one end of the barn to live in. Brigita planted a garden, and it was a good place to be.

We arrive in the early afternoon. Brigita is expecting us, and has prepared a delicious lunch. The pictures of their three children and three grandchildren cover all the walls of their small living/dining room. The family takes a central point in Veide's life, and they miss having them close by. "Next fall we plan to return to U.S. for good", says Brigita. After lunch, I walk through the orchard, take some photographs, and listen to the birds. The sun is bright, and the air seems to shimmer in the summer's heat.

VIZBULITE

I visit Latvia again, with an important objective: to meet some of the people whom I had come to know through my Church aid work. Several times a year, The Aid to Latvia Committee members, of which I am one, package and send a variety of useful items to needy families in Latvia. We receive letters of appreciation and thanks, and over the years, many of us have tied close knots of friendship with the people we help. I have several pen friends in Latvia whom I have never met in person. For me, the time had come to change this. Before I left Boston, I wrote to four of my distant friends about my visit to Riga and my wish to meet them. Vizbulite, a woman who loves to write, and weekly has written me long and descriptive letters about her life and family, sent me a note even before I had left home. She wanted to meet me. Definitely!

On my arrival in Riga, cousin Paul met me at the airport, and when I mentioned to him my wish to meet some of my pen friends, he immediately offered to drive me where, and when, I wanted to go. Vizbulite's home was in an isolated area in eastern Latvia, about a three-hour drive from Riga. Paul said that he would get his car (an aged Saab) serviced and be ready to go within a couple of days. I called Vizbulite about our planned visit. The joy that I heard in her voice was my best reward. I was excited.

On the day of our trip, Paul picked me up early in the morning. The day was sunny and relatively warm. To avoid the rush-hour traffic, Paul chose to drive on narrow country roads. This gave me a chance to see Latvia's countryside.

Another unexpected surprise was a visit to an old farm that his son, Ilmars, had just purchased. As the car stopped in front of the main house, a gray-brown wooden building, I had a strange feeling that the people who used to live here many years ago still lingered around, holding witness to their life of hard work, prosperity, happiness and eventual tragedy. The past was still here in the overgrown gardens, the ancient barn that was disintegrating without its roof and proper care, the old well with its broken lid. I remembered how most of Latvia's farmers had been deported to Siberia in 1949, to force the farms into state owned communes and, at the same time, to end the continuing partisan resistance to the Soviet regime. At the end of the Second World War, many Latvian soldiers did not give up their arms, but withdrew into the forests to continue their opposition to the occupiers. These young men received their food and other help from the local farmers. The deportation broke the backbone of the resistance movement and destroyed private farms in Latvia. As I slowly walked around the property, looking at the abandoned, neglected and injured buildings, I experienced, with overwhelming intensity, the history of this ancient place and its people.

After this brief visit, we continued our journey, at times on unpaved and rough country roads, consulting our map and Vizbulite's directions on how to find her house in the small village of Lubana. On reaching the village, I called Vizbulite on my cell telephone. She gave me the final directions and said that she and her grandson, Nauritis, would walk out to the main road and wait for us there. Both would be wearing red coats. Five more kilometers through the woods and we would be there.

As we approached the 5 km mark, I noticed two figures in red standing on the roadside. Paul stopped his car as I got out to greet and hug Vizbulite and Nauritis. Vizbulite was all smiles: her blue eyes, her kind face, her whole body was filled with a welcoming joy. We got back into the car, and on Vizbulite's directives, Paul turned his car onto an unpaved narrow road. "Please drive slowly so you don't miss my drive-way", Vizbulite said. "This is it!"

On our right, there was a path, not a road, into the woods. Paul guided his car carefully through the trees, and soon we came to an opening and a small wooden building hugged by an old apple tree. We had reached Vizbulite's home. "A little house in the woods"! I thought. Like the dwelling place of the three bears that Goldilocks visited. This was a different kind of a world, seemingly far removed, distant from the twenty-first century's turmoil and loudness. "There is Ursulina", Vizbulite remarked, hearing a loud barking from the house. As soon as the door came open, out ran a spirited little dachshund. It jumped and whirled all around us in totally unrestrained exuberance. Vizbulite invited us into her home. On entering, a wood burning stove with a friendly fire welcomed us. This small room, apparently, was Vizbulite's kitchen. From there, we were led into the adjoining living/dining/bed room and invited to take off our coats, sit down, and feel at home.

Vizbulite was all hospitality and kindness. She had prepared a feast for a king. The table was beautifully set and displayed with what surely had been hours of preparation, baking and cooking. I was overwhelmed. She sat me down on the sofa, took out her family album, and page by page, introduced me to her much loved family. I had already met them from her letters, but now I was meeting them face to face through these photographs. I looked at the pictures of her two sons, her daughter, and several grandchildren. Her oldest son, Nauritis' father, had been in a very serious car accident and was an invalid who could work only part time. Her second son was in his second marriage, but it was a good marriage, Vizbulite noted. Her daughter had had serious health problems, had been hospitalized with a brain tumor, and while she was in the hospital receiving treatment, her husband had found a new girlfriend. Now she was divorced and lived with her three children in a neighboring town. I had heard these stories before, through the many letters, but now they acquired intimacy and presence.

Vizbulite's life had never been easy. She told me that many

years ago her husband had been murdered while she was pregnant with her last child. She had to raise the children alone. At that time, she had worked as a nurse, but also continued her education at night and eventually received a law degree. As an attorney, she had worked with prisoners, a difficult and interesting experience. Vizbulite shared her life's story with me, openly and unreservedly. It seemed to me that she needed to confess, to unburden her soul from the past and present hurts and difficulties. I was a perfect listener: a stranger and a friend in one person. Also, she wanted me to know that her life under the Soviet regime had been easier than the present one under the government of independent Latvia. In the old times, she did not need to worry about much. She was taken care of by the state. Now, she had to struggle and worry about everything. Her pension was minimal, she had no health insurance. Her meager income hardly covered her daily needs. I listened and understood.

The evidence of the hardships of Vizbulite's life was all around me. At the same time, I tried to tell her how limited her life had been under the Russian dictatorship, how she had lacked freedom of speech, freedom of choice, freedom of press, freedom to see the world outside the Soviet Empire. I was telling her that even though this present moment her life was hard, her twelve year old grandchild, Nauritis, would have a better future with many options and possibilities. Vizbulite just listened. Did she believe me? She lived in a house with no running water, the outside well was contaminated, and clean water had to be brought in from the village, there was no inside toilet, and the outhouse that she used was across a long courtyard. The new freedoms had not eased her way of life or raised her living standards.

Time came to depart, to say good-bye to my new friends, Vizbulite and Nauritis. As we drove off, I looked back and waved to the two people standing by the little house in the woods. This had been an unusually rich and enlightening day; a day to remember and reflect on.

WHEN OLD FRIENDS MEET AGAIN:
HIGH SCHOOL REUNION IN ESSLINGEN (2006)

It is summer in Latvia, August of 2006, the first day of our Esslingen, Germany High-school reunion. The day is filled with lightness and sunshine, truly reflecting our excitement and joy of meeting after years of separation. Being together again is a special event for each of us. A charming country inn, Turaidas Ziedi (in translation: "The Blossoms of Turaida"), arranged ahead by our classmate Andris Priede, will be our home for the next four days. We have come together here from many corners of the world. My friend, Ruta, and her husband, Ilgars, have traveled from Melbourne, Australia. For them, it has been a 22-hour journey. Most of us, however, come from United States, mainly from the western part of the country. Only my sister, Ruta, and I are from the Atlantic coast, Boston.

The town of Turaida, where the inn is located, and the neighboring town of Sigulda, are two of the most scenic places in Latvia. Rolling hills, covered by lush green forests, meadows with a scattering of old farm houses, and the river Gauja, which snakes through this scenic countryside, captures one's soul with its tender beauty and leaves one with a sense of wonder and respect.

Turaidas Ziedi is a compound of several buildings next to a forest, and is clearly visible from the main road. We each arrive at different times of the day, and the early arrivals meet the later ones with cheerful greetings and warm hugs. "How wonderful to see you again!" is a greeting repeated many a time throughout the day. True is our joy and no words can adequately express what our hearts feel. It seems that we have taken over the small inn. No other guests are checking in. It is good to see only familiar faces around us; it gives us the feeling of being at home with family.

We toast our first afternoon together with a happy hour in the inn's luxury suite, occupied by Andris and his wife Ievina. Andris' ancestral home, a farm, is in the nearby town of Sigulda. He has acquired part of the land back, excluding the buildings, and is now building a summerhouse for his family. Andris has invited us to his homestead for a picnic tomorrow.

This is an afternoon of sharing wine and our mutual memories. Some of them are quite amusing ones, such as when we decided not to do a written exam in the History of Art class, and passed in blank papers to the teacher, or how Andris had acquired the text of the next day's English exam and, in the evening, we all gathered in his room to memorize it. A few days after the exam, we were met by a shocking surprise, when our teacher, before returning our exam papers to us says: "I am so very disappointed in all of you!" Apparently, she had changed the text, and our answers did not fit the questions. I still remember the shame I felt then. Miss Priedite was a great teacher, and I respected and loved her. To disappoint her was the very last thing I had wanted. A good lesson on the value of being honest.

The day ends with a gala dinner at the inn with more celebration, talking and laughing. After the afternoon of sharing and reacquainting, we are more relaxed and at ease with each other. Years of separation have vanished, and we are back in our youth. It is sort of strange and unusual that we can feel so very close, as if time and space does not really exist. What matters is our friendship, a bridge that closes the gap of many years.

The next morning after breakfast, we drive to Turaida. It is a place of much history and beauty. The Turaida castle, an impressive structure towering over the countryside, is undergoing reconstruction. The original castle was built in

1214 by the invading crusaders, after they burned down the wood fortress of the endemic people and eventually conquered their land. This is a place that attracts many tourists, and we are among them. Before going to the castle, we visit the near-by sculpture garden (Dainu kalns), a very picturesque park with stone carvings featuring Latvian mythology and culture. We take pictures of the beautiful country that unfolds before our eyes. The day is a perfect day in all respects: the clear blue sky, the various greens of the trees and grass, the changing light on the sculptured stones, and our being there together has a very special magic. We all feel it. There are moments in life that need to be treasured as a very rare gift, to be sheltered and saved. Some of us climb down the sharp incline through the woods to the castle hill. My friends Ruta, Dzems, and I are the adventurers; the others take the paved road. After the visit to the castle, it is time to return to the inn and get ready for our picnic at Andris' place.

Andris and Ievina are perfect hosts, and the setting for our afternoon gathering is another place of beauty. The tables are set among a birch growth. Birches are Latvia's signature trees, and their white/green slender shapes always bring me back to my childhood and the birch trees in Plikeni. Andris' land slopes down to the river Gauja, regarded as the most scenic river in Latvia. Painters have painted it, poets have immortalized it in romantic stanzas, and lovers have walked its shores. We decide to walk down to the river before starting our meal. The short path through the woods takes us to a clearing where the breathtaking view of Gauja enfolds before our eyes. We proceed down to the shoreline, and for a while we just stand there looking at Gauja's flow and allowing ourselves to absorb the peace, silence, and magnificent beauty of God's creation. This is another moment to be treasured and remembered; a moment of mutual sharing.

The afternoon continues in happy conversations and laughter as we enjoy the delicious meal. There isn't a cloud in the sky, and no cloud obstructs our mutual time together. As a Latvian proverb says: "Happy people don't count hours". Our hours pass by quickly, and the time does come when we have to thank our hosts and return to our home away from home. Andris and Ievina chauffeur us back to the inn and continue to be our hosts for an evening sing-along and some wine. As I sit there among my friends and sing with them, I ask myself: "when was the last time I enjoyed such an evening of singing"? Hard to remember when. In times past, almost every get-together was marked by singing. Latvians have many folksongs and love music. This evening is a return journey to those musical gatherings of our young days; another pearl to be added to our memory string.

The last full day of our reunion has a very special plan: we are going to visit a home, Zvannieki, which houses abused and neglected children. The children come from alcoholic or otherwise troubled homes. The shelter is run by a Latvian minister, Reverent Calitis, who is originally from Canada but now lives in Latvia. He also serves as the pastor of two parishes in Riga. My sister, Ruta, and I have become acquainted with Zvannieki through our Church's aid work.

We all have agreed that to visit the children would be a good way to end our reunion. Our days have been blessed with so much joy that to bring some of it to the young occupants of Zvannieki would be a mutually shared blessing. Soon, after breakfast, equipped with detailed maps, we start our journey; on the way stopping at a local grocery store to buy fruit and other goodies for the kids. Our journey is quite complicated because, for the most part, the roads are not paved or well marked. At times, it is true guess work of which direction to go. It is an adventure! Finally, after a three hour drive, we see a big green sign, ZVANNIEKI. We have arrived! Finally! As we disembark from our cars, we are greeted by smiling faces and loving hugs. Small hands take our hands in theirs, lead us around the place, and proudly show us their home. It is a touching and heart warming experience for everyone. As we say goodbye, we know that at some time, in some way, we will have to return again.

On the last evening, we share a dinner in Sigulda, at a restaurant overlooking the magnificent view of the valley of the Gauja river. As we watch the spectacular sunset from our balcony table, as we join our hands and hearts together in a parting song, we know that we are taking leave of a very special time and very special people. We all recognize the immense blessing of being part of this circle of true friends.

A STORY OF NEW FRIENDSHIP
AND LATVIA'S REBIRTH

It is early in June when Daina and Andris, a young couple from my native Latvia, arrive in Boston. Daina needs medical help, and my sister Ruta and I meet the couple at Massachusetts General Hospital to be of assistance, if there is a need. We meet, complete strangers, and at the very first glance, a bridge of warmth and knowing seem to join us. Andris is tall, slim and handsome; a friendly smile lights his face, and there is a glow of great warmth in his eyes. Daina stands next to him, a dark haired, beautiful woman, a bit shy. Andris gives me a warm hug, as if we have always been friends and now meet again after some time of separation.

From this day of our first meeting, Ruta and I are always there to help our new friends. Daina is very ill and needs extensive surgery. By a miracle (which would be Andris' interpretation), or a mere coincidence, Daina's surgeon is my former boss, Dr. Fuller. I know Dr. Fuller well, and it makes the treatment period much easier and more personal. Daina gets the best of care from a world-renowned surgeon. It is difficult time for both of them. To be ill, always in pain, and to face major surgery and an uncertain future is difficult under any circumstance. Daina and Andris are in a foreign land, among strangers. All the people they love and who would be their support are in Latvia. It is a frightening situation. Ruta and I represent the only home, the only security they have. We are their family. In the few weeks that Andris and Daina spend here a truly deep friendship develops between us. It is not just simply friendship, we become relatives. When we say good-bye as they leave for home, we know that it is just a temporary separation.

In the beginning of July, Ruta and I travel to Latvia again to spend some time with our friends and relatives and see the country. On the first morning after our arrival, the telephone rings. It is Andris' friendly voice that says "Labrit", and it marks a beginning of an unbelievable extension of hospitality, generosity and love.

Now, as I write this and reflect on their very difficult and also frightening time in Boston, I can understand their appreciation of what we gave them. It did not seem much to do; it was just being helpful to people in need. But for them, it must have seemed a great gift, a home and family away from their loved ones.

Andris is a very spiritual person. He allows God to guide him and depends completely on this guidance. While in Boston, we had many talks, and Andris discussed his life's remarkable journey. He had finished medical school during Soviet time. At that time, it was a requirement to pass a course in the Communist Party's history before graduation. Andris did not pass it and never became a physician. He went into business. He has been very successful in it, and now is one of the wealthiest businessman in Latvia.

The first week of our vacation in Latvia starts in a chauffer driven limousine, compliments of our friends. It is a real luxury, and we enjoy seeing historic and beautiful areas that we had never visited before. It is a real treat. When Daina returns from her chemo treatment in Oslo, Norway (here I must mention that Daina is getting the same chemo drugs that I received, and I can be helpful to her by telling my experience), we are invited to their country farm to spend a weekend. This is their Shangri-La, a beautiful, almost unreal place in the middle of woods, meadows, lakes and fields. It is a fairyland created by Andris and Daina.

Some years ago, the couple had bought two old, totally

neglected farms (the previous owners very likely had either been deported to Siberia or had left their place before the Soviet occupation and escaped West). The couple had cleaned the land and the lakes, reconstructed the main farm house that was still standing, and built some additional buildings. Daina had planted beautiful gardens around the property. "Here, we come to relax and to unwind. Here, we sit in silence and let the outside world disappear," says Andris. We feel this peace and silence as soon as we enter the homestead after a long drive through a state forest. Yes, it is very secluded and remote, as Andris already has mentioned. Here, the farm, as it was in the free Latvia before the second World War, has been reborn. I think: "If there only were more people like Andris, Latvia would soon grow into a prosperous country!" It is sad to realize that Andris is one of the very few, and Latvia is still undergoing a very difficult and slow rebirth.

Our days in Azkalni, as the farm is named, are charmed. We walk through the woods, stop to marvel at the beauty of the many ponds and lakes, the stillness of the water ,and the unbelievably clear reflections of the trees and the sky in their clarity. We relax, we eat, we think, we read and we talk. To be together with Daina and Andris is a gift we are very fortunate to receive. Andris would have a definite explanation, he would know why our paths crossed, why we came together at a certain point in time, why our destinies intertwined and enriched us: it is God's way, and He knows our life story.

Part Five:
As the Years Pass...

"In my early life, as I was growing, developing and learning, several questions pursued me. Why am I here? What is the meaning of my life? How can I be useful? What can I do to make a difference? At that time, I believed that something grand had to be accomplished by me to make my life worthwhile. I am much humbler now. If I can be of a small usefulness to my family, my friends and neighbors, that is almost enough to justify my contribution: my life. I try to keep in mind Jesus' words: "What you do to the smallest one of them, you do to me."

Astrida

MY YEARS AT MGH

Sentimental Journey to the Past

"Charles/MGH. Massachusetts General Hospital", the loudspeaker announces. The train stops, and the doors open to let the early morning commuters get off. Today, I feel like one of the commuters and follow them down the steps to proceed to the Hospital to start my workday there. It is very rare now that I make this commute. But since my retirement, I am occasionally invited to help out, and I welcome this opportunity to connect with some of my old friends. These return visits are sentimental journeys into the past. The place has changed considerably, and a great number of my coworkers have departed the scene. We belong to history. As I walk through the familiar buildings, I try to recollect the many years of my affiliation with MGH. Much has changed!

I enter the old Clinics building, where the medical records department was when I started to work there in 1957. The department is still there, but the physical environment has changed considerably. Progress has marched through the place. A wall has replaced the door that had once led to my small windowless office.

I had worked for Mary Converse, the Department's director, whose office, an even smaller room, had been directly behind mine. The only access to that office had been by my desk, but there had been a window in it, which added some spaciousness and light to her surroundings.

I had been Mary's right hand, her Girl Friday, and had been responsible for running her office smoothly. We'd worked well together. She was a capable director, a thoughtful and fair boss and, above all, a good and kind person. Mr. White, the Hospital's administrator directly responsible for our Department, had been a frequent visitor here. He was of a medium build, always wore gray suits and a smile on his face. He and Mary Converse were more than colleagues; they were friends. His sudden death from a massive heart attack had been a great shock to all of us. We missed Mr. White.

Directly across the corridor from our offices had been the so-called "doctors reading room", where the physicians came to review records and write research papers. My friend Hilda had been in charge, sitting behind a large mahogany desk, always fashionably dressed, always professional. Today the reading room is gone, and Hilda has departed, not only from MGH, but also from this world. She died in 1992 after a short struggle with a malignant brain tumor. We shared happy times. Mary Converse held us all together. Many close, long lasting friendships were formed. As I stand here reflecting, my long time friends walk out of the shadows of the past. One by one. I hear Hilda's quick steps behind me, but I look back into an empty space.

After six years, I had left MGH and the Medical Records Department to raise my two children, Peter and Kristina. Ten years later I returned, first as a part time employee working for Hilda, cataloguing medical records. It had been a challenging job, and I learned a lot. Very soon, I'd found out that it was difficult to work for a friend. Hilda's and my friendship was in jeopardy. "Why?" It is hard to say why, hard to pinpoint the exact reasons. I had to move on to save our relationship, so I applied for a full time position in the Department of Gynecology. The opening was for a research analyst and a postgraduate course coordinator. The work in the medical records department had given me administrative experience and some knowledge in medical research. So I encouraged myself: "What can I lose?"

My first interview had been with the Chief of the Service,

Dr. James Nelson, a distinguished looking gentleman who briefly outlined the responsibilities of the position. My next interviewer was Dr. Francis Ingersol, who was in charge of the department's postgraduate education. He had obviously been very busy seeing patients, and our meeting had been short and matter of fact. He did not ask me if I ever had organized a course or had any experience in this particular area. I had just listened to him and tried not to show my ignorance. At the end of our short interview he'd said: "I am sure you can do the job!" I recall him shaking my hand, his eyes smiling behind the thick horn-rimmed glasses, and knowing that, as far as Dr. Ingersoll was concerned, the job was mine.

The third person who had interviewed me was Dr. George Richardson. He was in charge of the research part of the position. Dr. Richardson came from a long line of distinguished physicians and belonged to the, so-called Boston blue bloods. In beautifully phrased English, he had asked me questions about my experience and education. He was impressed by my high grades at Northeastern University, where I was completing my education in medical records administration. My lack of experience was outweighed by my scholarly success. I got the job and it changed my life.

In the medical records department, the employees were closely supervised, and I was used to that sort of work environment. In the department of gynecology, the atmosphere had been totally different. Employees were considered responsible and trustworthy professionals. This freedom was new to me and most enjoyable. It was great to be able to move around without reporting every step I took.

"How will I manage? Wasn't it totally crazy of me to assume responsibilities I knew nothing about?", were the first questions I had asked myself. I'd felt overwhelmed and, at times, intimidated by the challenge. It did not take me very long to learn the ropes of my new job, however, and my co-workers were helpful and encouraging. Because I had worked with medical records, my past experience in this area was very useful. I did surprisingly well and gained trust and respect from my superiors. Dr. Nelson was especially supportive. His kindness and understanding was a great help to me during my husband's illness and eventual death. Arvids had become ill soon after I'd started my new job. The support of Dr. Nelson and others helped me through this difficult period. In addition to being a generous and kind person, Dr. Nelson was a superb gynecologic oncologist and surgeon. His administrative style was relaxed and hands-off, which had a positive psychological value. He expected employee responsibility and good job performance, and I believe that in most cases these expectations were met.

I had had two main responsibilities. First, I was in charge of the department's tumor registry, including assisting in research projects. Second, I organized postgraduate courses. I liked my two hats and was rarely bored. My job gave me almost total independence. No one was looking over my shoulder to check how and what I was doing. To do the job well was my responsibility and obligation. I tried to do my best and generally succeeded.

The Gynecology Department offered annual postgraduate courses that were attended by professionals, not only from the U.S. and Canada, but other countries as well. To organize these courses required considerable time and effort. Timely planning and attention to details were essential. October was usually the month when the courses were held, and during their presentation, I had to make sure that all went smoothly, assist the professors, and respond to the requests and needs of the students. I became an expert trouble shooter. It also gave me an opportunity to meet interesting and eminent professionals. The courses provided me an opportunity to learn. Whenever possible I listened to the lectures.

The most fun for me was the course directed by Dr. David Nichols, held at the Ritz Carlton in Boston. Because I stayed at the hotel and enjoyed its elegance and service, I considered this time a mini vacation, a chance to combine work with pleasure. Frank usually joined me there for an overnight stay. After an elegant dinner at the Hotel, hand in hand, we would wander along the Back Bay streets, window-shopping and people watching. We had felt like a couple of tourists enjoying the atmosphere of Boston at night.

In 1996, Dr. Nichols offered his postgraduate course on a cruise ship to Alaska. I went along to help with administrative duties and Frank was invited as a guest. It was a dream vacation for both of us. The Inner Passage along Alaska's shores is indescribably beautiful. We cruised by stately glaciers that grew out of the dark waters as magic castles. We stopped to observe the giant whales as they turned somersaults near our ship.

Because MGH is a world-renowned hospital, physicians from all parts of the world came to visit and learn. They stayed for longer or shorter periods to observe, study or do research.

Dr. Marco Filicori came from Padua, Italy. He was a gynecologist who specialized in reproductive endocrinology and did his fellowship at our department. Part of his work involved research on in-vitro fertilization(IVF). This was in the early 1980's when the procedure was in its infancy. I remember one of his lectures. He was telling about the work he was doing in the laboratory and illustrated it with a film that showed how a fertilized ovum from a single cell divides into two and at an almost incredible speed continues this duplicating process. It was fascinating! This early research, in a way, laid groundwork to today's controversy of harvesting stem cells from unused embryos.

Dr. Shilang Wang was a visitor from China who spent six months at MGH. His main interest was gynecologic surgery. Dr. Wang was a professor of the West China University of Medical Science in Chengdu, Sichuan and was the director of the University Hospital's Department of Obstetrics and Gynecology. He was well trusted by his government. Otherwise, he would not be visiting the U.S.A.! Since my office had an extra desk, we shared a lot of time together. We became good friends, and he will always have a special place in my heart. At the end of his stay with us, he said: "Astrida, I think that your form of government is the best." It was a surprising statement from a true believer in the Communist system. It is my opinion that Dr. Wang went back to China a changed man. He learned, here, more than just new approaches to gynecology. I often think of him. He was a kind and compassionate person with great intelligence. From Dr Wang, I learned about the two aspects of Chinese medicine: treatments based on science and treatments based on folk medicine. They were both equally recognized and practiced there. Through him, China grew a human face for me, and my hope was to follow Dr. Wang's invitation to visit him and his country.

MGH attracted professionals from many countries. As I look back now, I realize how fortunate I was to come in contact with so many great people, and for a short moment in time, to be a part of their learning process and learn from them.

Solveiga, a young Latvian woman was admitted to the Gynecology Service under Dr. Nelson's care. I was told that she was seriously ill with a widely spread cervical cancer, and decided to visit her. On my way to her room, I met Maureen Nelson, Dr. Nelson's wife who was doing her residency at MGH. She had just seen Solveiga and I asked how she was doing. "She is dead as a door nail", said Maureen. I had never heard that expression. It shocked me.

I walked into Solveiga's room, introduced myself, sat down on her bed, and took her thin hand into mine. She had lost all her hair as a reaction to chemotherapy; her body was skin and bones; a tragic figure with immense blue eyes that held me in their grip. "Astrida, I want to live!" she said. "Will I get better?" "Dr. Nelson is a superb doctor. This is a very good hospital. They will do everything to help you." I stroked her hand. In my ears still sounded Maureen's words: "She is dead as a door nail". This young woman was here, so very ill, because of her family doctor's negligence. He had ignored her symptoms. It is hard, often impossible, to fight cancer once it has gone out of the primary site. It spreads through blood vessels and lymph nodes to other parts of the body. Cancerous cells deprive normal cells of food, they develop their own blood supply on which they feed and grow. Cancer is a parasite. My new friend died the same week.

It was very seldom that I came in contact with patients. My job was a desk job. I kept records on oncology patients, provided information to GYN oncology fellows for their research, prepared case histories for presentation at Tumor Board conferences, but mostly patients remained only names to me. Only in rare cases, did I ever become personally involved; only when someone I knew came for treatment.

I once asked Dr. Goodman, a GYN oncologist (and a good friend who had trained at MGH and was on the Hospital's staff), how she could bear to take care of those patients where no real help or cure was possible. "You know, I never think about my patients in these terms. I help them. I make their life easier. I am with them, always for them." I know, if I ever need treatment for a GYN cancer, Dr. A.K. Goodman will be the person I will turn to.

The years have brought considerable changes to MGH. It is a new place now, and the old lives only in memory. Many of the people who were my colleagues have departed. Dr. Nelson left the Hospital in 1986, soon after his wife completed her residency. He is retired now. For a while, Dr. Richardson served as acting Chief of Service. GSR, as he was affectionately called, now enjoys his retirement, his family, and continues to travel. The new Chief of Gynecology is Dr. Isaac Schiff, a wonderfully gifted administrator. Under his stewardship, the Gynecology Department has grown in prominence and size. Dr. Ingersoll, the person who first interviewed me, retired many years ago, and tragically, soon after, developed Alzheimer's disease and died. I truly believe that, for him, medicine was his very soul, his life's sustenance. It was painful to see the downward course, the changes in the personality of this brilliant surgeon and kind man. My very good friend and mentor, Dr. David Nichols, died very suddenly, in July of 1998, from a major heart attack. It was a tragic and shocking loss to his family, especially his wife, and also to the medical profession. He was a rare personality and a brilliant surgeon.

I retired in 1997. I had worked at the Massachusetts General Hospital for almost 31 years. My years there were rich in relationships, growth and learning. They were good years for me. I have been very lucky.

Dr. David H. Nichols

It is a Thursday morning in July. The telephone rings. It is my friend Janice from work. "Dr. Nichols died yesterday", I hear her say. "Dr. Nichols died?" I voice in disbelief. "Yes, he collapsed while seeing a patient in consultation".

I hang up the telephone, still trying to grasp the reality of what I had just heard. Dr. Nichols, my friend, my mentor, this great human being: how can he possibly leave this world so suddenly, so unexpectedly? I can almost touch the empty place where he stood. My heart fills with pain.

Flashbacks, memories of the years of my association with Dr. Nichols, fill the day. I feel his presence around me; it is powerful and alive.

I first met Dr. Nichols when he joined the staff of the Gynecology Department at the MGH to establish a Pelvic Reconstructive Surgery Division. I was introduced to a distinguished looking, white-haired gentleman. The most immediately noticeable feature about him were his deep blue, kind eyes. His smile and his soft voice were instant bridge builders.

As Dr. Nichols presented and directed a postgraduate course in Pelvic Surgery, my job was to help him with the administrative and organizational work. At the very beginning, I suspect he had some doubts about my performance. Could he trust me to do the job responsibly? Very soon, however, a wonderful working relationship and also a close friendship developed between us

As I grew to know Dr. Nichols as a professional and as a human being, my admiration and respect for him grew. Dr. Nichols was a world-renowned surgeon; he refined old and introduced new procedures. He was the author and editor of many medical publications, and a sought-after lecturer. During his courses, I had the opportunity to listen to his lectures. Often, I only half understood what was said, but the manner of his presentation was powerful and interesting. He was a wonderful teacher, always willing to listen to questions, and to share his experiences and expertise. His courses were always filled to capacity. One year we even had to post a policeman at the door to ward away declined applicants!

His course was an annual event, lasting three days, and was always held at the Ritz in Boston. It was a fun time for me, a short vacation. Mrs. Nichols always joined her husband there, and so very apparent was their close and warm relationship. How devastated and lonely she must feel now!

Above all, Dr. Nichols was a warm, kind, and caring human being. There are many incidences I remember where he went out of his way to help his patients or his associates. Just to mention one: when our daughter's HMO would not pay for her office visits with Dr. Nichols, he examined and treated her as a "professional courtesy". He had a golden heart and a brilliant mind. This world is a much poorer place without him.

The following quote from Bessie Anderson Stanley was included in Dr. Nichols's memorial program: "He has achieved success who has lived well, laughed often, and loved much; who has enjoyed the trust of pure women, the respect of intelligent men and the love of little children; who has filled his niche and accomplished his task; who has left the world better than he found it, whether by an improved poppy, a perfect poem, or a rescued soul; who has always looked for the best in others and given them the best he had; whose life was an inspiration; whose memory a benediction". This describes Dr. Nichols. It was an honor to know him.

RETIREMENT

What will I do with the rest of my life? It is an important question, a question that needs a careful answer, an answer that needs to be pondered and reflected on.

I am retired now, and have more time to spend, or waste. Work-life had a certain routine; there was a plan to each day. Retirement has taken away this planned lifestyle. To some extent, one loses one's sense of usefulness and is deprived of an easy way to contribute. Most of the job related contacts and friendships tend to evaporate, or at least diminish. That is a real loss. I also have to learn to discipline myself, to develop a daily routine, otherwise time just runs away with nothing or little accomplished.

Frank and I love nature. We have done quite a lot of hiking and plan to continue this in our future years. As time and finances allow, our agenda also includes some traveling, which we very much enjoy. Presently, however, we have responsibility over Frank's ill and aging mother. She needs us on a daily basis, therefore, long absences are not possible at the present time. But in the future, we are planning to take a car trip in the U.S. to visit the places we have not seen yet. We'd also like to go to Europe, visit my native country Latvia, return to Alaska, or maybe visit Australia. I would just love to see the world! That has always been my dream. Maybe, some day...

I need to be useful in a giving way, to help those less fortunate, especially children. Through my church, I am already involved in this kind of work. That will be a very important part of my activities in the future.

Now, my plans very definitely include writing the story of my life. When I mentioned this to my daughter, Kris, she said: "Yes, mom, it is so very important to have your grandchildren read about your life!" I was pleased to hear her reaction. I have always doubted the importance of my experiences to my children.

Well, that is, in a nutshell, a view of my future plans. Certainly, nothing is cast in a stone. Nothing is totally predictable. However, it is important to plan, to see one's way somewhat clearly.

THE GIFT OF A NEW PURSUIT

I have a new fascination, and my life has become rich in color and form: watercolor, and the forms and pictures that I can create with its help. There are hidden riches that gradually unfold through the way I look at my surroundings. It is remarkable how more acute my vision has become. I look at the trees, the sky, and the world around me. My eyes are especially focused on the trees: the way light shines through the leaves and branches, how shadows play with the forms, how delightful and alive everything appears. The richness of the visual world has increased remarkably since I became interested in watercolor painting, mixing colors and putting them on the paper. It feels like a miracle.

Never did I think that I would have the slightest talent in painting. I have never been especially good at drawing, though never really bad either. I enjoyed art classes in school, and did relatively well, but not exceptionally well. My closest encounter with any form of creative arts was the crewel embroidery that I did many years ago. There, I learned about color, their relationship to each other, and about the elements of design. I enjoyed painting with needle and thread, which is how this form of needlework was called. For several years, crewel embroidery dominated my free time, I felt very creative and happy in it.

How did I start my pursuit in watercolor painting? Almost by accident. For years I have enjoyed photography. When the

Needham Adult Education Program offered classes in photography, I signed up. There were very few of us who were interested in learning the skill of taking good pictures, however, and the class was cancelled. On leafing through the brochure, I noticed that a class was being offered in watercolor for beginners. "Why not?", I asked myself. Nothing ventured, nothing gained. I signed up. Each class was two hours long, and my first two hours flew by and seemed like two minutes. The teacher gave each student a palate of six colors and a list of instructions how to mix them. The result was an almost unbelievable variety of colors. It was the most fascinating task. After several sessions of experimenting with color mixing, the next assignment was to bring in an object to paint. An apple was my first attempt. Again, my whole attention was focused on the subject in front of me. The rest of the world did not exist, except the teacher who came by with suggestions and help. The most surprising thing to me was that I could paint that apple. And quite a good looking apple at that. I was hooked!

After the first semester, I signed up for the next, and then the next! One spring, an outdoor class was offered. "Hmmm...Can I do it?", I asked myself. I decided to attend the first class to see what would happen. What happened was that a brand new painting enthusiast was born. One of my winter classmates, Mary Gillis, became my painting friend and partner, and we continued to meet after the formal classes ended. Each week we met at some scenic spot and painted. It was fun and exciting. In addition to sharing many creative hours together in fresh air and sun, Mary and I also shared our life experiences and have become good friends.

I paint often now, and find great joy and relaxation in doing so. My knowledge and sensitivity have improved. I will never be a Monet or Renoir, but as our teacher has said: "Anyone can paint." I completely agree. The same as in writing. One develops the skills of expression, be it in color, form or words. As one goes on and does not give up, one's proficiency improves, and the enjoyment increases. Often, new and untried pursuits bring pleasant surprises and joys previously not imagined. Writing, as well as painting, have added much pleasure to my life, have enriched my days and, also, have enriched myself. I am very thankful for these gifts that so very unexpectedly have come my way.

THE JOY OF GRANDCHILDREN

Erin

I hold in my hand a small packet of cards and letters, carefully compiled and secured by a ribbon. These are mementos that I have received from my granddaughter, Erin, and have saved over the years. They each hold a treasured memory. Never has a special occasion in my life gone by without Erin remembering it, or an acknowledgment missed for something that she had received from me. Many a gift and small treasure has come my way from Erin. On my bed sits a white bear wearing a chef's turban and an apron saying: "Grandma cooks with love." Yes, cooking has been one of the many activities we have enjoyed together.

Erin is the first of my grandchildren to join our family. We first met at the Leonard Morse Hospital in Natick when she was just one day old. Erin was born on November 9, 1983. I was greeted by a petite, blond, beautiful baby. "So very fragile and vulnerable! So tiny! And such a big and complicated world!", I thought.

As Erin evolved from a tiny baby and grew into a lovely teenager, our relationship also evolved and grew – always loving, always very special. Erin has added a lot of joy, fun, love and laughter to my life. I have many wonderful and treasured memories of our special times together. I do hope that these memories will remain with Erin as something positive and enlightening, that our shared experiences have helped her to see the world in a broader perspective. Erin is a beautiful young lady, mature and continuously growing in wisdom. She is a joy and I love her!

Larissa

As I write this, Larissa will be fifteen on June 30, 2001. Already fifteen! I remember the tiny little bundle that was brought home from Leonard Morse Hospital. A picture of that first day shows her safely lying in her mother's arms, looking trustingly up at her. Life was just beginning, like the garden outside the glass door behind them, ready to bloom, to become.

I recall how much I enjoyed our visits over the years and the way she would greet me, running up to me and jumping into my arms for a big hug. We had a special bonding, a warmth, a closeness that held us together. Taking walks, going to the playground, Thanksgivings at Astra and Tom's, the animal farm with Erin, and our summer visits to the East Hill Farm are just a few of the treasured memories of our times together. There are so many more memories, but one of the most memorable and touching moment was when she and I went down to help Omi, Frank's mother, to prepare for bed. Later, as I was tucking her into bed and gave her a goodnight kiss, she looked at me and said: "Grammy, when you get old I will take care of you just as you are taking care of Omi." She couldn't have given me a greater gift! Her words touched me deeply and I will never forget them and always treasure them.

A grandchild is truly one of the greatest joys in this world and I love Larissa with all my heart.

Tara

The phone rings. It is early morning on July 21, 1991. "It is for you, Astrida", my cousin Maija announces. I am in Riga on my regular visit to Latvia and staying with my relatives. "Who could it be?", I wonder, as I pick up the receiver. It is my daughter, Kris. "Hi, ma, I have a baby girl. She was born early this morning. You should see Tara. She is beautiful. Such a perfect little person!" Kris's voice sounds tired but jubilant. "Frank brought me a bouquet of flowers," she adds. "How considerate of Frank", I think to myself.

A flood of bright light brakes through the dark walls, enters my soul and stays there. Such happy news! A child was born a few hours ago, my granddaughter. It calls for celebration! We have a bottle of champagne in the house. Maija's son, Karlis, is going to get pizza, a special treat in Riga. The city is gradually waking up from the years of Soviet poverty and now many things are available from the West. Soon we have a joyous feast in honor of Tara's arrival on our Planet Earth.

When I arrive home, Kris and her girls, Larisa and Tara, are waiting for me in Needham. After the first hallo and hugs, I reach over to take the tiny Tara in my arms and hold her tenderly. She seems to be so very fragile, open to injuries and hurts. She needs to be protected and guarded! "Will she be?", is my silent question. My heart wraps Tara in an invisible protective shield as I hand her over to Kris before they leave for their home in Maine. "Take special care of her, please!"

Tara grows into a pretty blond girl with blue eyes and a sunny personality. She loves to smile and dance, and "OK!" is the favorite answer when asked to do something. Tara is fun to be with. I look forward to her visits and our times together are always enjoyable. We play in the yard, read, go shopping, visit museums and, at times, go to the movies.

A very special annual event is our vacation at the East Hill Farm. On our first stay at the farm, Tara is only two years old and she needs supervision. The two of us spend a lot of time together.

I am so grateful for the many wonderful memories and special times with Tara over the years. I love her very much.

EAST HILL FARM VACATIONS

June has arrived, and my three granddaughters and I, are ready for our annual vacation at the East Hill Farm. This is a very special place for us: our special time together, a chance to get acquainted again, and to renew our closeness.

The Farm, located in Troy, New Hampshire, is a very popular family vacation spot. The same groups of people return annually during the same weeks of the year, and thus, good friendships have developed over the years. The children, especially, look forward to seeing their friends again. Happy "hallos" and warm hugs mark our arrival.

This year, Erin, Larisa, and Tara spend the night before our vacation at my house, to make the next day's departure less complicated. I pack the trunk of my small VW Fox with our vacation luggage on Saturday evening. Sunday morning arrives bright and sunny, and after a pancake breakfast, we start off for Troy.

"I am so very happy, Grammy!" says Erin, "I cannot wait until we get there." Erin has come with me on this vacation almost from the very beginning, nine years ago, and has always enjoyed her time there.

On this particular trip, our spirits are high, our hearts are happy. In the car, we chat and snack on grapes, and strawberries. Erin reads the directions to me, just in case I have forgotten how to get there. Larisa, who for several years had not come with us on these vacations, is a bit quiet. Tara, who is only six, the youngest of the three, is her usual happy self. She will be my roommate and has accepted this fact without much complaint.

We arrive at the Farm around lunchtime. After a quick check-in, we stop for a buffet picnic lunch, which is served in the back of the main house overlooking scenic Mt. Monadnock. The meal is very generous: all sorts of choices to pick from, from soup and salad, to hamburgers and hotdogs. We find an empty table, and soon are joined by the Kauffs and the Powers, our longtime vacation friends. The usual, "hello, hello! So nice to see you again! How have you been?" is heard all around. Our vacation has started.

After lunch, we visit the farm animals. East Hill is a working farm. All the guests are invited to take part in the activities of the farm, to get acquainted with the animals, and are encouraged to partake in their care. It is a fun place. Tara loves the bunnies. I love the little piglets that wander around the courtyard. Erin and Larisa have disappeared. We see each other again at five o'clock for the "cocktail hour." The adults are served cocktails, and the children enjoy pony rides and soft drinks. Tara joins the pony ride crowd, and I, with a glass of punch in my hand, find my old friends to enjoy a relaxed, lighthearted chat. At six o'clock, we all gather in the huge dining room and find a seat at our table, which has grown in length over the years. This summer, there are five families at this table; twenty-one heads, all counted. It sort of reminds me of the summer days on my father's farm.

After supper, we all play BINGO. Tara and I are partners. There's no luck as far as winning goes, but that is not of great importance. We have fun. Tara has found two friends, Melanie and Camilla. Over the five days we spend at the farm, this friendship grows into a real togetherness. The happy triplets!

The next day is spent mostly in the swimming pool. The most popular of the three pools is the indoor one. It is always warm, not too deep, and the kids (and also parents) can feel safe (not that safety is an issue for the children!) Tara, who is not a good swimmer, loves to jump in at the deep end of the pool, and my heart at the same time jumps in horror for her safety. But with time, my little grandchild changes into a real mermaid and swims under the water like a regular fish.

In the evening, after supper, we wander into the horse barn, precisely at the time when the blacksmith is changing a horseshoe on one of the horses. He explains to us what he does and why he does it. It is fascinating! The man seems to have come out of the pages of a book about the past. We notice his rugged, unkempt appearance and shoulder length hair, as he answers our questions with kindness and patience.

The next day arrives. It is cloudy, and a fog covers Mt. Monadnock. After breakfast, Tara gets her first riding lesson. Larisa, Erin, and I look on. It seems that the two girls have had a run-in and are not on speaking terms. All will blow over, I am sure. The cloudy morning changes into a rainy day. Tara and I play Candyland and do picture puzzles. We have lots of company. The indoor swimming pool is a very popular place today and also a very crowded place. I sit by the pool and read or talk with the other adults. Today, June 30th, is Larisa's twelfth birthday. I have ordered a cake from the kitchen. At supper, the cake is brought in. We all sing "Happy Birthday!"

In the evening, the tables are pushed aside to make room for square dancing. Young and old, short and tall, follow the caller's directives to the best of their abilities. The evening ends with the chicken dance and musical chairs. Another full day has come to a close. The rain really did not dampen the fun.

The sun returns on the following day. After breakfast, Erin and Larisa go horseback riding. It is one of the activities that is a very enjoyable part of the life on the farm. Tara, her friend Darci, and I, go for a walk up the hill to the cow pasture. Two donkeys share the space with the cows and come to the fence looking for handouts. We offer them clover, and they accept it with greedy pleasure. Tara and Darci pick field flowers to bring back to their mothers. Two colorful bouquets are the end result.

Erin does not feel well. She has a migraine headache. Poor girl! Since that is something I suffer from at times, I understand how poorly one can feel. Larisa has found new friends, and seems to really enjoy herself. Swimming is the favorite activity. I find her often in the pool with the other children. Larisa swims well, and it is fun to watch her dive in and do all kinds of tricks under the water. To see the children enjoy our short vacation is what makes it perfect for me.

In the afternoon, we all take off for Silver Lake, where the Farm has a waterfront space, a motorboat, canoe, rowboat, and water-skis. All that is there to enjoy and use. Tara decides to swim with the other children to the float, anchored in the lake a distance from the shore. I freeze! All I can think of is that she cannot swim. She makes it across, though, to my great relief and surprise. Tara can swim quite well now, I realize. I relax.

The last full day of our vacation is here. Tomorrow we say goodbye in the hope of returning next year. I reserve our space as I pay our bill.

The day of our departure is perfect! Mt. Monadnock glimmers in the bright sun, it's bald summit clearly chiseled against the blue cloudless sky. Why does the mountain have a completely treeless top? The story goes, that at the time when the surrounding area was farming country, the farmers set fire to the forest on the mountaintop in order to get rid of the wolves that had overrun the land and threatened their livestock. The trees never grew back.

After the usual generous breakfast, we say goodbye to all our friends, pack our belongings into the car, and take off for our journey home. So long! We shall return!

MY DEAR SISTER, SKAIDRITE
Eulogy-1993

How can one define a person, describe the essence or life of someone? It is not easy. Especially today, when Skaidrite's sudden passing has so deeply affected us, her immediate family, and all who love her. But I will try.

I think back to our childhood years on our family's farm, Plikeni. There, we all lived protected by our parent's love and caring, surrounded by nature and animals. Skaidrite, being the oldest of us three sisters, had a special place in our family, and she watched over Ruta and me almost like a substitute mother. She was kind and considerate and never excluded us from her activities. It was good and safe to be around Skaidrite. She exhibited strength of character and a natural caring for others that were the hallmark of her life.

From very early on, Skaidrite knew that her goal in life was to be on stage. She wanted to be an actress. She had a natural gift for acting. She participated in school plays and was usually chosen to recite poetry at formal functions. After we left Latvia and were living in Esslingen, Germany, Skaidrite joined the Latvian theatre group there and studied acting under Karlis Veics, a famous actor and stage director from Riga. In Boston, she joined a Theatre Studio established by Karlis Veics and took part in the stage presentations of several plays. The members of this group continue their friendship, and once a year meet to commemorate the Studio's founder, Mr. Veics. The celebration had often been held at Skaidrites house.

Our parents' wish for Skaidrite, however, was that she would become a professional gardener, and that is the path she eventually took. She graduated from Bulduru Darzkopibas vidusskola, a school that trained landscape design architects. (Here I wish to mention that Skaidrite's friends from this school meet every year on her birthday in Riga, Latvia, to remember her and celebrate her birthday and their friendship.) I believe that Skaidrite's love for gardening started to blossom in Bulduri. Beside acting and poetry, gardening gave her the greatest joy. Those of us who have visited the Anderson's house in Sherborn have seen the lovely, artistically unique garden that Skaidrite created there. Over the years, her garden became a true thing of beauty to be enjoyed by her family and all of us who came to visit. A great help in this work was her son Paul, or Paulitis. I can still see him pushing wheelbarrows and diligently helping his mother to dig and plant. When Annele joined the family, she also was assigned garden duties.

With Skaidrite's failing health, the garden has lost its sparkle, but even now, one can see and enjoy its original charm. Now it is a jewel in the rough. Lately, when Skaidrite could leave her house, only on rare occasions, she often remarked how she enjoyed sitting in her chair and looking through the window at her garden, watching the birds in the feeders, the trees moving with the wind, the sky, and an occasional deer walking across their land. "I am happy," she said. I often wondered about her true feelings. It was not easy for her. Her mobility was very impaired. Skaidrite never complained.

Skaidrite had several other talents. I remember that during our refugee years in Esslingen, I had located a dress, hot pink in color, in a pile of garments that were sent to us from United States. Under Skaidrite's creative fingers that dress became my best party dress. She also made my Confirmation dress out of parachute fabric that our mother had acquired somewhere. I thought that it was the most beautiful dress, and only recently parted from it.

How can one define Skaidrite? First of all, she was a totally positive person. The glass was not only half full, it was almost always ful for her. In a way, she created her own reality that excluded all that would disturb or disrupt the harmony of her world. She was a person who loved life and loved people. Her house and her heart were always open to receive and to give. So many of us have enjoyed Skaidrite and Juris's hospitality and have been part of the happy gatherings: the food, the singing, the dancing, and the enjoyment of being among friends.

To me, being with Skaidrite was being at home. And I know it was also the same for Ruta. We are very close to each other, and losing Skaidrite is like losing a part of us. All I can say on this day of parting is: "Thank you, Skaidrite, for being my friend, for being with me in good and bad times, and for always wishing me well!"

A HOUSE REVISITED

I have come to Sherborn for the very last time to visit the house that had been home to Skaidrite and Juris for more than forty years. During the past year, both Skaidrite and Juris departed for their eternal home, dying within a few short months of each other. The house has been sold now and is waiting for its new owners.

I enter the building through the front door and walk into the living room. The room is cold and barren. Nothing welcomes me here. I find myself in an empty space and look around at bare walls. I feel overwhelmed by this emptiness. It is difficult to accept that all that was is gone, that a family's life can abruptly disappear, vanish from a place that held so many years of living. But is it really gone? Sights and sounds come back: the many family gatherings, the laughter, the joy, the tears. All is still here, captured in the soul of this house. The past slowly emerges from its hiding.

I remember the Halloween evening in 1961 when we visited my sister's family. They had just moved in, and it was their first evening in the new home. The house still needed some finishing, and the smell of newness and the excitement of a fresh beginning surrounded us. Skaidrite, Juris, my husband Arvids, our mother and I sat on the sofa in this same room where I am standing now. Little Paul, the family's six year old son, my godson, was happily running around exploring his new domain. The house, which they had planned and built had been theirs to live in and to enjoy.

Many years of fruitful and busy living lay ahead. The family grew. Little Paul (Paulitis) was joined by his sister Anne (Annele). They enjoyed a carefree and happy childhood here. Skaidrite worked at her garden and, with great love and patience and some help from her children, landscaped the originally wild and untamed land into an object of beauty. The garden not only gave joy to the family, but also to the many visitors who enjoyed and admired the changing loveliness of Skaidrite's garden. I look now through the glass door into the garden. In its silent beauty I see peace and permanence.

The house witnessed many happy gatherings. It was a hospitable house, always welcoming friends and relatives, always being open to good times. How many a time have I sat in this living room? I wonder. Too many to be counted, too many to be recalled in detail. But they all are still here, still lingering, almost palpable. The traditional family Christmas comes to mind when we all gathered around the tall Christmas tree, warmed by the lively fire burning in the grand fireplace; Juris watching over it, adding logs, as needed. We sang Christmas carols and listened to our children reciting poems of the season. Skaidrite's voice still sounds somewhere, reciting one of her favorite poems about Christmas.

I walk from room to room. The long dining room table is gone. An empty space looks at me. But I know that the many festive meals we had enjoyed here are still somewhere buried in the closed corners, the silent walls. The house stands in guard of them, and memories will forever remain as faithful witnesses of the happy times. I walk into the kitchen. The counters are all empty. My sister's knick-knacks are gone. The big photo frame of the family pictures that captured the weddings, the christenings, the grandchildren and the important events is gone from the familiar place on the wall. An empty space looks at me, but I sense Skaidrite's presence here. I see her standing at the stove preparing food, getting a meal ready for her family. Skaidrite was a very hospitable person and a wonderful hostess. Just like our mother, she welcomed everybody with a treat, was ready to serve each and everyone who stepped over the threshold of her home. Those moments, I am sure, are still written into the fabric of this house. They are permanent.

I walk into Juris's study. Years ago, this room used to be Paul's room before he left for college and his independent life. Now it is empty and quiet, just walls and windows. Is everything what this room saw and experienced gone? As in the rest of the house, I also see the hidden memories of years past: Juris's desk, his computer, his drawing board, and papers. Juris was a very good engineer and numerous hours of work were done here. All is saved and remains a part of silent history. Also, Paul's many years of growing, developing, and learning are part of the hidden memories this room holds in its heart.

I continue my journey into Anne's room. The past is safely preserved here, also. If its empty space could talk, the room would tell much about Anne, Annele's, dreams, her beautiful talents, her plans, her struggles, and longings.

I walk back through the house, deeply experiencing the hurt of its empty spaces. The walls are barren of the beautiful paintings, the paintings that told of the magic and mystery of the artist Visvaldis Reinholds' soul. His magnificent art had been displayed in every room here. But though they are all gone from this house, they have not vanished. Paul and Anne continue to enjoy these treasures in their own homes.

The last room I visit is Skaidrite and Juris's bedroom. Here, the emptiness hits me with great force. It hurts. The books, the many family photographs, all the very personal and intimate items that once held the very essence of this room are absent. Nothing of their lives remains here anymore. This room seems to cry out, it seems to say to me: "we are still here, we wish to be remembered. Keep us in your hearts, be witnesses to our lives." It is difficult to be in this soul-touching, painful emptiness. I say good-bye. I feel, though, that my good-bye is a very temporary act. Something eternal and permanent remains here. The house holds in its soul (and I believe that every house has a soul), the very essence of the lives that it has protected and nourished. It holds in its memory, the joys, the pains, the consummate existence of the people it sheltered. All is ingrained in its very essence and will remain there forever.

ANNELE

A spark of new life. Fragile, vulnerable, to be protected, to be loved. These words come to mind as I now reflect back on the day my niece Annele, (Anne), was born. Skaidrite's daughter, Annele, has been a very special person in my life.

From the beginning, the center of Annele's life was my mother, her omi. Annele was a new life force for my mother, a new reason to live and look forward to the future. Annele's dark eyes and shiny black hair were in deep contrast to her light, almost transparent, complexion and gave her an ethereal look. She was a delicate child, and her thin body was her grandmother's ever-present concern. Annele needed a lot of "fattening up", according to her omi, and she took good care of her grandchild; tender care, protective care.

Then Omite became seriously ill. She had injured her back while raking the ever-falling leaves from the multitude of trees that grew in their property. The injury developed into a growth, and when it was finally diagnosed as a type of bone cancer, sarcoma, prospects for a cure were dim. Omite underwent extensive surgery at Mass General Hospital, and then radiation therapy. Those were difficult times for everybody, and certainly for Annele.

Omite was able to come home for a short while until the disease came back, but eventually returned to the hospital to die. How much does Annele remember of this very painful period? She was only four, a small girl with a big loss. How much did this loss affect her at the time? How much did she miss her Omite?

Over the years, Annele and my daughter Kristine became good friends. Our families spent a lot of time together. From ballet lessons, drives to stores, shopping, eating out at restaurants, horse back riding to sleepovers, these events filled many happy days for the children. I recall the time when Kris and I took our big trip to Latvia. Annele had come to the airport with an album for Kris and to say good-bye to her very best friend. She had placed her own photograph on the front page and written beautiful sayings about friendship, love, and meaning of their special relationship. Arvids had not allowed Kris to take the album along. It might have jeopardized our entry into the Soviet world. It might have. Annele had been very disappointed and hurt. I felt badly for her. And also for Kristine.

There are many other memories, many happy, some sad. A very tragic one is connected with the trip to Canada to take part in the Latvian Scout and Guide World Jamboree. Annele, Kris, Peter and many other Latvian scouts and guides from all over the world attended this Jamboree. Annele had signed up, but when the time came, she did not want to go. Her mother thought that a last minute change of mind was not a thing to do so Annele went on the trip. I had volunteered to help in the kitchen, but was delayed in order to attend a social event in New York City. When I arrived a few days later, I found Annele, seriously ill with a flu, and dangerously dehydrated.

Annele was then hospitalized, and I visited her every day. She had more than just a flu, however. Annele was homesick to the point of desperation. This event started a stream of events that deeply affected her health and cast a shadow on her young life, at least for a while. A different Annele returned home from Canada. Her soul had suffered an injury that took many years, many downhill and uphill emotional journeys to eventually reach a plateau of spiritual calmness.

It was during this troubling period that we had many discussions and many heart to heart talks. Annele and I had similiar natures. In my childhood I was a dreamer, a searcher, a questioner. My world was filled with fantasy, much like Annele's was. I understood Annele and wanted to help her, to calm the storms that her young heart was experiencing.

Annele's dream had been to become a ballerina. Her God given gifts in writing, music and art came naturally and effortlessly, and she loved dancing. To make this dream come closer to reality, her parents enrolled her at the Walnut Hill School in Natick, a private school for aspiring dancers. But Annele had a very traumatic experience there. The school did not treat all students equally; excelling some, neglecting others. Anne was among the unfortunate ones, left the school after a year, and never danced again. The disappointment was very deep.

But life molds, blends, forms our personalities. All experiences eventually, hopefully, lead us to a more perfect being, to clarity of mind and spirit. We all go through a process of growth. I believe that the hard times for Annele eventually led her into the sunshine of clarity and wisdom. She eventually graduated from Mt. Holyoke College in liberal arts earning a master's degree in Museum administration/education. Art is Annele's main interest, as well as teaching. She also loves to work with children. She understands them.

When Anne met her future husband Jerome at a wedding of a mutual friend, they were seated next to each other at a dinner table and fell in love. Across a continent, two souls came together and found their mate. Was it destiny? They married on September 8, 1990.

All was well with the world as these two people joined their lives into one. We celebrated with them in the house where Annele grew up in, where she had experienced much joy and much heartache, and where she had done a lot of growing, overcoming, and becoming. "Some things are just meant to be", as Annele strongly believes. "We are here for a purpose. We have to find where we fit in, where we belong, where we can do the most good."

A philosopher and a mystic, Anne writes beautiful poetry and introspective essays. Her whole being is like a musical instrument that plays in response to the vibrations within herself and the world that touches her. Anne is unique, a very special person. In Jerome, she has found a perfect soul mate, a perfect partner. Jerome's gentle soul, his unselfish and kind person is a twin to Annele's.

A new miracle eventually enters their lives. Twin babies are born to them on January 26, 2001: Piper and Ethan, two precious, beautiful human beings. "They are not ours", Anne says in her gentle, soft voice. "They have been put into our care for the time being to help them to grow. I hope that we do no harm, that we are kind to them!" Such tenderness and caring flows from the two young parents. I say: "How fortunate are your babies to have been born into such love!"

WE ARE GATHERED HERE…

It is December 16, 1999. Our Omi, Frank's mother, departed from this world on the 12th of December at the German Altenheim, where she had spent the last year of her life. Today, we have come to St. Bartholomew's Church in Needham to pay our last respects, to say our last goodbyes to her.

The church is filled with mourners. Omi's four children are here. They have come from California and New Mexico. Most of her grandchildren and great-grandchildren are also present, as well as the family's friends and relatives. It is a sad and solemn occasion. Her grandson, Deacon Joseph Ramrath, opens the memorial service: "We have gathered here to remember our Omi, to give thanks for her life." He continues by remembering specific incidences by which she has touched his life in particular and the family's life in general. He lovingly walks through the 94 years of her life: briefly touching her beginnings and youth in Germany, her marriage to Joseph, the very difficult first years in the United States; raising two children, Frank and Eleanor, during the depression time, and the family's fateful return to Germany in the late 1930s and the tragic experiences in the Second World War. During these very trying times while in Berlin, her two younger children, Thomas and Elizabeth, were born. He spoke of the family's arrival back to the States in the late 1940s, and the challenges they faced as they resettled here, after the many years of absence. Omi's life had not been easy, but her will and spirit had always been strong. Her spirit and love, her intelligence and strength of character, have been the guiding light, the beacon to the family.

After Joseph's thoughtful and reflective memorial address, Eleanor and Frank read from the scriptures and add a personal goodbye message. Joe's girls are the altar servers, and it is touching and fitting to see them take part in this final tribute to their grandmother and great-grandmother.

I look at the white-clad coffin that holds Omi's body. It holds the mystery of death and the mystery of life. Her body lies in a permanent stillness, forever physically removed from us, the people who have loved her and whom she had loved. But has she really left us? What does the word "death" really mean? I remember from my physics lessons, the law of transformation: nothing is ever lost, it only changes its form. I look around and see and feel Omi's spirit in the many faces of her family. She lives through Frank, through Eleanor, through Tom, through Elizabeth. She gave them life, guided their first unsure steps, nurtured, instructed, and protected them. Now, her four children will carry with them, preserve, and protect what she has given. In departing, she has left "footprints in the sands of time."

Next to me sits Frank, his face is closed in sadness. Frank is his mother's firstborn. This made for a special bonding between the two of them. Frank tells me that his mother was the very source of wisdom for him; he considered her almost a sage. He often consulted Omi and relied on her advice. I believe that the reason why it was so very heartbreaking for Frank to accept his mother's progressively waning mental health, her inability to rationalize and communicate, was directly related to this special role she played in his life, that of an advisor. The last years of Omi's life were very stressful for Frank and to a lesser degree for me. When he was just a boy, Frank had promised to always take care of his mother, and he faithfully and dutifully kept this promise. Frank's strong sense of responsibility, his rational and thoughtful approach to life, his thoroughness in both practical as well as intellectual pursuits, are characteristics he, to some degree, inherited from his mother. During the last period of their life, Omi and Opa lived with us, had found a safe haven in Frank's house. Here, they could live in relative peace and comfort. Frank took care of all their needs. The family came for visits and life was good for Omi and Opa. And also for Frank and me. We enjoyed having the "old folks", as Frank often referred to his parents, downstairs. Seeing Omi in her spotless apron and fine jewelry attending to her household duties was touching and reassuring. She was always perfectly groomed, her silver hair cut short, intensifying the watchful expression in her brown, all- observing eyes. Nothing much passed Omi's attention. She was keenly interested in her family here in the United States and the one living in Germany.

Omi did not believe in an open show of affection. It was not her style. Her caring was shown in more indirect ways. When Frank or I were sick in bed, often there was a quiet knock on the door and Omi's concerned question: "Are you all right"? These were the only times when Omi broke the "rule of privacy." She was careful not to intrude in Frank's and my life, and almost never gave unsolicited advice. The definition of a lady was well represented in Omi. She had my deepest love and respect.

During the warm summer afternoons, we found Mathilde and Joseph on the porch: Omi in a recliner with her ever-present book in hand, Opa in a chair next to her with a cigar in his fingers, observing the birds and neighborhood activities. Opa died in March of 1993, at the age of 90. In the last couple of years of his life, Opa suffered several small strokes and became semi-invalid, more mentally than physically. His wife was his nurse and caretaker.

Omi's daughter, Eleanor, and her husband, Lou, sit in the pew behind us. Eleanor is Omi's second child. Eleanor deeply loved her mother and always looked for her mother's approval. She wrote beautiful, heartwarming letters to her mother expressing her love and admiration. For Omi's 80th birthday, Eleanor compiled and edited a book, a story of her mother's life: Mathilde, A Woman for All Seasons. It is a touching tribute to a woman she held a sincere affection for and truly admired. I wonder if Eleanor ever felt that she received the recognition she so very much desired from her mother, and also in every respect deserved? I wonder. Eleanor is sensitive and creative, a deep thinker. Eleanor's personality sparkles. In this, she differed greatly from her mother. According to Frank, Omi had never been a very happy person. She had said: "I was born to be unhappy." Could it be that this significant difference in their personalities was the reason that the two women found it difficult to achieve real closeness? Eleanor is, however, much like her mother in her search for truth, for answers to fundamental questions. Eleanor found Carl Jung during her search, and much of her beliefs and philosophy are grounded in the Jungian thought. Where did Omi find her peace, her answers? Eleanor is a recognized author and painter. She is a daughter that every mother could be proud of. I believe that, in a silent way, her mother was.

I look at Tom, Omi's youngest son. He and his wife, Jeri, have come from Albuquerque to be here today. Omi's visits with Tom were very special times for her. Tom's lighthearted personality, charm, and genuine caring could win over the most stubborn stranger. Omi's unconditional love was his! For a couple of years, Tom had regular job-related visits to Boston, combining business with pleasure, and was a monthly guest in our house. These visits were a special treat for Omi. Frank and I also looked forward to Tom's knock on the door and his friendly hug. Now, as I write this, I feel nostalgic for these very special times. Many an evening we spent in captivating conversations. Tom had retired from his Airforce career as a major and now worked in the private sector. His years in the military had exposed him to adventures that a regular earthling could only dream about. Often during these visits, Omi was treated to one of Frank's superb martinis, while her two sons enjoyed "Cactus juice" drinks, margaritas. My taste for both of these "heavenly potions" improved with time. Tom was often here when Omi's health started to go downhill. He was a support to his mother and also to us. Here, his caring and devotion were most obvious. Omi's intellectual curiosity lives on in Tom. Her love for books, and for knowledge, are so very much a part of Tom's personality.

The youngest of her children, Elizabeth, has come from San Diego to say good-bye to her mother. Her brown eyes, which are so much like her mother's, are sad. It seems to me that of all the children, Elizabeth had the most distant relationship with her mother. At least in the years when I had become part of the family I observed no special closeness between the two women. However, Elizabeth has told me that she and her mother had been very close in the past, and had often shared laughter and intellectual discussions. Frank tells me that Omi thought of Elizabeth as the brightest of her children and that she admired her intellect. I think Elizabeth is most like Omi in her looks, and to some degree, her personality. I see Elizabeth as a quiet person, somewhat subdued, introspective. Of all Omi's children, I know her the least because there has not been too much of an opportunity for us to be together and become close. I understand that Elizabeth reads a lot, and her house displays a beautiful selection of paintings; especially those of her nephew Tom's. Tom is Eleanor's son, a talented painter who has spent most of his adult life in Italy. Elizabeth took Tom in when he was a teenager, after he had developed serious conflicts with his father. As I listen to the stories of Elizabeth's generosity and kindness to young people who for some reason or another had gone the wrong way and were now trying to turn their lives around and walk the straight and narrow, my admiration and respect for her grow immensely.

Another person who had a very special kinship with Omi is her grandson, Eleanor's son, Jimmy. Jimmy and Omi's relationship had a special flavor of intellectual dialogues. Omi came from a different world, a different generation, and, Jimmy, who loves to explore, to investigate, was fascinated by her keen insights, her intellectual acuity and curiosity. He lives in California but found many opportunities to visit the east and Omi.

I could go on and on, mentioning all the people whom Omi touched in meaningful ways, like Frank's children, Karen, Joseph, Robert, and their families. Each of them received Omi's attention, love, and words of wisdom. Each of them, in full measure, returned their affection and caring to her. Especially of note is the time during Omi's illness when they never forgot to visit her or offer their support to us. They are all here in the church, remembering, honoring, and saying their personal goodbyes.

I glance at Berta and Herb Pflanz, Mathilde and Joseph's very special friends. The Pflanzes never forgot the kindness that the older Ramrath extended to them, when, as a young couple, they arrived in Boston from Germany. Omi and Opa "adopted" the young folks into their family and made them feel welcome and at home.

When I called Berta and Herb from the Altenheim on the night when Omi died, they came immediately. They wanted to be with their friend and to say the last goodbye to her. So very often, they had come for visits during Omi's stay in the Altenheim. They, as is their love, are very special.

The service has ended. The ushers line up around Omi's coffin. At that moment my heart cries out: "Don't take her!" All of a sudden everything seems to be so final. The end. We follow her from the church and watch as the black limousine pulls away under the grey sky. We wave goodbye. I remember the psalmist's words: "Surely goodness and love will follow me all the days of my life, and I will dwell in the house of the Lord forever." I am sure Omi's soul lives with the Lord. Life does not end.

THOSE WHO HAVE TAUGHT ME IMPORTANT LIFE LESSONS

Today I wish to remember some of the people, outside my family, who taught me an important lesson or whose guidance directed my path into a new direction. There are those who challenged my capabilities, recognized some hidden talent, opened, until then, a closed door to my own self, or helped me to understand myself. A number of people come to mind. As I walk back through the years, they stop and beckon to me. "Do you remember?" they ask. Yes, yes, I do! And here they are. I will call them by name, acknowledge and thank them.

Irene Abols

She was my closest friend in grammar school. Actually, she was my very first important friend. The most meaningful lesson she taught me was the significance of getting along with others, the wisdom of peaceful coexistence. It was a summer's afternoon on our farm during school vacation. We were standing in the garden. "It is silly and wasteful to quarrel. It does not lead to anything", Irene asserted as we discussed the value of arguments. Irene's voice, her sunlit person facing me, etched a permanent lesson into my book of wisdom. I never have forgotten either the day or my friend's statement. We are still friends today, have always kept in touch and shared life's most important events.

Ruta Karklins

I walk on. I am in Esslingen, Germany and say "hallo" to Ruta Karklins, my very best high school friend. We dream together, walk hand in hand along the Neckar River, and share our hopes. The future, for us, held many unknowns, since we were in Esslingen only temporarily; we were refugees, and would have to find permanent homes somewhere soon. Very likely, our paths would lead in different directions. And they do. Ruta's family emigrated to Australia and mine came to United States. In the meantime, however, we enjoyed being young and relatively carefree. We studied together in our small rooms or, in the summer months, wandered over to the hills that surround the ancient town of Esslingen, sit on the soft grass under the shade of an apple tree and read. Beautiful days! At times, we debated serious issues: the value of life, human destiny, our importance in all of this. The recent past had been traumatic. Leaving home and war had left permanent imprints in us, and had given us wisdom beyond our age. At times, I felt very old and could share it with Ruta. Ruta and I were very connected, like sisters. When she came to visit me a couple of years ago from Australia, she told me that I had been the sister she never had. In many respects, in Ruta, I found my third sister. I was godmother to her son, Martin, who was tragically killed in a motorcycle accident. Ruta left Esslingen before I did. The morning I'd said "good-bye" to her at the railroad station, the world had darkened. Esslingen was never the same again.

Irma Cebere

Another person during my years in Esslingen, whom I wish to recognize, is my literature teacher, Irma Cebere. She opened a new world for me. I had always liked to read. Books were my friends from early childhood on, but Miss Cebere showed me how to read beyond the words, how to understand and interpret what the author says and means. I became an enlightened reader. She recognized my soul and encouraged me to develop self-confidence. At that time, I was painfully insecure and shy. She forced me to accept tasks that I felt were beyond my abilities. It was a surprise to me that I did well!

Now I wish that I had acknowledged to her the significance of her guidance in my development and had said "thank you". She died many years ago, and my gratitude remained hidden in my heart, unsaid.

Hilda Sequeira

Hilda was my first and foremost friend in the U.S. In the fall of 1949, our family crossed the Atlantic and after a short stay in Virginia, settled in Boston. It was after my father's sudden death in Virginia's hot summer, the first year of our arrival in the United States.

I met Hilda when I started work in the Medical Records Department at Mass General Hospital. Hilda was also a new employee. Mary Converse, the director of the department, had hired us both. It was only natural that we shared coffee breaks and lunches. We did not immediately connect. The reasons were several. The most important one was our contrasting views on faith. She was a devout, conservative Catholic, raised in a strict Portuguese home. I was a Lutheran with considerably more liberal views. At the beginning of our friendship, we often had deep discussions, almost arguments, about religious issues, and it seemed "that never the twain shall meet". She did not convince me, nor did I convince Hilda. Over time, our disagreements mellowed and grew less important and did not stand in the way of our ever-deepening friendship. Hilda became my soul mate and I hers. Our mutual trust was total. We held each other's confidences in the locked safe of our hearts. I knew that Hilda would never betray my trust, nor I hers.

Hilda died very unexpectedly of a very malignant brain cancer. On her trip to Florida to visit her son, she developed slight facial paralysis. An initial x-ray showed a brain lesion. She came back home to be further evaluated and eventually treated. On the morning of her surgery, I went up to the hospital room to be with her. It was very early, and the room was semi dark. I sat on Hilda's bed to be close, held her hand and we prayed together. It was a special, holy moment. Our souls blended into one voice asking God to make her well. We did not have a crystal ball. We could not look into the future, and we did not know that God had other plans. Hilda never completely recovered and died within nine months. Our friendship had been unique. There were no walls of distrust between us, and to know that one human being can safely trust another one completely and without prejudice is very special. We were blessed.

Mary Converse

Mary was instrumental in my professional development and an eventual career change. She guided me to discover my dormant potentials. Under my calm exterior, had lived a timid country girl. Mary helped this girl to come out of her shell. She'd hired me to be her office assistant and secretary. That was the job description of the position I was to fill. It was a newly created position and not very well defined. Therefore, my responsibilities could change and did change greatly over the six years I worked for Mary Converse. My duties expanded, and my workload grew. I administered Mary's office and she trusted me completely. I was always learning, developing new skills and assuming new responsibilities.

At that time, Mass General was affiliated with Colby College in Maine, and the students who were in Medical Records Administration Program spent their senior year in our Department. They gained practical "hands-on" experience by working in the Department and in addition, underwent formal classroom instruction in medical science and learned about diseases and their treatment and other health related subjects. It was my good fortune that Mary allowed me to attend classes with the students. As a result, I became interested in the medical records field that eventually lead me into becoming a certified tumor registrar, the position I held in the Department of Gynecology after my return to MGH several years later. In addition to being my benefactor, she was also my friend. On my recent visit to Chicago, where Mary now lives, I called her. She was in ill health but was happy to hear from me.

Edith Jones

I met Edith in the first months of becoming a full time mother. Edi lived a short walk from me in South Natick, and we met regularly to allow our two little boys, Peter and Christopher, to play together. During these visits, we had long conversations on a variety of topics, and we shared recipes and philosophies. Edi was very intuitive, very objective, and had a clear perception of the world around her, especially, political situations. My knowledge of politics was very limited. I had lived under a variety of political systems, never truly analyzing them, generally accepting the way things were. Edi was very much interested in politics, having been a Political Science major in college. I listened to her and gained a new insight and perception, especially, of the American form of representative government. Through Edi, I learned to think critically, and most importantly, not to accept press presentations as gospel truth. I distinctly remember one telephone conversation when we discussed something that I had just read in a newspaper. Whatever I said brought out the following comment from Edi: "Astrid, do you really take that as the only truth there is?" Her tone of voice, and the little laugh that followed her comment, hit me like a bullet and made a fundamental change in my perception of the printed word. It was a contribution from my friend Edi that has truly made a difference in my life. Now, I read and listen to what the press has to say with a grain of salt and a healthy skepticism.

My friendship with Edi was intellectually stimulating and never boring. Edi was very straightforward, very down to earth, and had very few inhibitions. She did not look kindly on pretentiousness and doing things "just for show". She was a wonderful role model to follow. We are friends today and keep in touch.

Lee Shull

I met Lee at the YWCA program, "Holiday from Apron Strings", and intimately got to know her during the reflective "Understanding Yourself" discussion and self-analyses group meetings that the program was sponsoring. There were six women in the group of all ages from all walks of life, talking about our innermost feelings, trying to come to terms with our past experiences that shaped our personalities. The goal was to understand ourselves better in order to live more effective lives today.

Lee had spent her childhood on a farm in Utah; I had grown up on a farm far away in Latvia. Our physical beginnings were on the opposite sides of the globe, however, emotionally, we seemed to be connected by common experiences. As Lee talked about her early life on the farm, her family relationships, especially about conflicts with her mother, I saw myself reflected in her memories. My early years came dramatically into focus. I was overwhelmed with feelings from my past; I swam in the often-murky waters of my childhood happenings. After each session, I came home troubled, forced to relive, to bring back and to face buried and forgotten hurts. Lee, unknowingly, helped me to heal the wounds of my soul, the wounds that I never even knew existed. By reliving her past, by opening her doors of recognition, she enabled me to open mine, to meet Astrida, the child, to talk about her, recognize her, and begin to understand her. It was the beginning of a journey of knowing and understanding myself. Lee and I became close friends and we still are.

*   *   *   *   *

I wish to end this essay by quoting Celia Thaxter: "As you say, we don't need soft skies to make friendship a joy to us.

What a heavenly thing it is; "World without end", truly. I grow warm thinking of it, and should glow at the thought if all the glaciers of the Alps were heaped over me! Such friends God has given me in this little life of mine!"

NEWS – NOT SO GOOD

The day before we are to leave for our trip to Europe to introduce our grandson, Timothy, to the countries of his grandparents' birth, Germany and Latvia, the telephone rings as I am going over the last minute details of our trip. It is Dr. Treadway from MGH. "I just want to let you know that the CT scan you had on Wednesday shows enlarged lymph nodes. It may be due to several things. Since you have the gluten allergy, it may indicate a lymphoma. I talked to my colleague, a specialist in lymphatic cancers. He felt that even if it were a lymphoma, it very possibly is the low malignancy type, and it would be safe for you to go on the trip! I will schedule a biopsy of your nodes the day after your return."

My heart stops beating when Dr. Treadway mentions lymphoma. Does it mean that our trip will have to be cancelled? So much planning has gone into it. We are all packed and ready for a liftoff. I would hate to be the cause of such a disappointment, so it is a relief to hear that we could go on as planned.

(Now, when I look back to the feelings I had on first hearing the news of a possible malignancy, I remember two: concern and relief. Concern that I may really be seriously ill, and relief that our trip can go on as planned. At that moment, the relief was dominant and left the cancer fear in the background.)

Throughout the trip, though, I feel a nagging concern, but I try to act normally and not bother my travel companions much about my feelings. When I feel physically low, I go to my room to rest. At this point, my main concern is the allergy to gluten. Certainly, I did not want to get a reaction in a foreign country, therefore, before each meal I check on flour-free foods. It seems that, in Europe, this type of allergy is much more common, and I am almost always lucky to have a good meal without gluten, without much effort. I carry my rice patties along for breakfasts and become thoroughly sick of them!

Our trip was close to perfect! In Denmark, we visit Lego Land (Timothy's very favorite place) and the Viking Museum. In Latvia, the main attractions are the old fortresses (very close to what Harry Potter called home and school) and the Old Riga street vendors, where eventually Timothy found an almost perfect reproduction of an ancient clay dinosaur. In Germany, we visited cousins, ancient churches and a "Wasser Burg", a fortress surrounded by a moat, a canal protecting the Burg from invaders with draw bridges to let friends in and out. Days are filled with excitement and mostly fun!

Our trip ends in the German city of Frankfurt with a delicious dinner served in the garden of the hotel, where we spend our last night.

On our arrival home, we are greeted by four voicemail messages from the Hospital reminding me that a lymph node biopsy has been scheduled for the next morning and that I need to come in NOW for pre-op blood tests. Down from the dream world, back to reality. My wonderful sister Ruta takes me to MGH for the test. It is a sweet reminder that I'm not alone in this. Many caring people surround me with their support and love. Like Angels from heaven, they descend upon me and cover me with their loving wings.

The biopsy results come back in about a week. Dr. Treadway calls: "I would like you and your husband to come in tomorrow to discuss the biopsy results. There is some concern about the findings." I had worked in a hospital long enough to understand such an invitation. The news would not be good! As I hung up, the phone rang again. It was my niece, Anne, my caring and loving "soul sister". "Annelit, Dr Treadway just called me" and I started to cry. "I can come right over". "No, no.

It is not necessary. I'll be fine!" Anne lives almost two hours away from me and has 2-year-old twins to take care of! But she hadn't hesitated to offer me her help. An Angel, for sure!

The next day, Frank and I meet Dr. Treadway and hear the news. I have metastatic adenocarcinoma in the abdominal lymph nodes. She has already contacted Dr. David Ryan, a GI oncologist. He will take over my care and schedule tests to locate the primary source of the cancer.

The following Monday, Frank and I meet Dr. Ryan in one of the several exam rooms of Mass General Hospital's Cox Cancer Center. It is a thoroughly impersonal room, with an exam table in the middle of it, a computer desk next to it to check patients' history, lab results, and whatever other information was needed. Nothing in the room made it inviting or personal. As Dr. Ryan enters, he introduces himself. "Too bad that we have to meet under these circumstances", he said, and proceeds to explain my diagnosis and what kinds of tests he will need to schedule. One of the most interesting sounding of them is called PET Scan (Positron Emission Tomography). It is a relatively new scan that can identify many diseases, cancer being one of them. In the case of cancer, the patient is infused with a radioactive substance that is mixed with sugar. Cancer cells love sweets and absorb sugar more readily than normal cells. Thus, cancer cells will light up during the exam and pinpoint malignancies. In my case, there were hardly any new findings, except for the thyroid gland that unexpectedly lit up.

In the days that follow, I undergo many tests. I have good and not so good days, try with all my spiritual strength to keep a positive attitude and to rely on God's help, which comes to me through my loving family and friends, and my faith.

At the time of my diagnosis, the only treatment for a "cancer of unknown primary" is chemotherapy; the two most effective agents are carboplatin and taxol. The plan is to give me a five-hour infusion of these two drugs every third week. My friend, Ieva Broks, who is a chemo nurse and works for Dr. Ryan, would supervise my treatment. That again, was a blessing.

I ask Dr. Ryan about my prognosis. "Will I be cured?" "You

will not be cured", he says. "If you respond to treatment, you will have five to six years to live. If you do not respond, you will be dead in six months". "Dead in six month?" That sounds unreal and totally impossible! "Why did he say that?" How can anyone know, how does he know?

On Tuesday afternoon, I participate at a cancer support group meeting. There are people who have had this disease for years, some with fresh recurrences, with no hair, terminal. I am one of them. How can it be that I fit in with all these ill people? I have always been so healthy. What has happened? I am shaken! Suddenly I realize that I have a long road ahead of me. A road of many unknowns, many compromises, many acceptances. A difficult road, a lonely road, for sure.

It is Wednesday, as I make this final entry. Today I had a thyroid ultrasound at MGH that showed a seriously abnormal gland. Tomorrow I will have a thyroid biopsy. This may be the missing link, and the end of the long search for the primary site. Thyroid may be where it all began. I hope so! It will make the treatment so much easier and more effective.

TO BE OR NOT TO BE

When life suddenly takes an unexpected turn, and the future is not as clearly cut out and predictable as before, one is forced to stop and evaluate one's priorities. The scale of measuring the importance of events and things in general, what is valuable, and what is trivial, radically changes. One climbs into a different climate, a new reality, feels outside the regular flow of time. Moments of separateness from the rest of the world and loneliness become more frequent.

This is the place where I am at, now, as I write. It is 2003, and the cancer that has sneaked in and invaded my body has, to some degree, also invaded my soul. It has changed the perimeters of my existence. The closure of my time in the world, death, has become more of a reality. It is not somewhere in the distant future (as one usually thinks), but may be just around the corner. It is here to shake my hand and remind me about the speed of time, specifically my time, but, in general, anyone's time. I reflect on the events of my life more frequently now; how very short life seems to have been. Even the more difficult parts now appear to be only short intervals. More than ever, I realize that life is a unique gift and treasure. It has taught me many lessons, allowed me to grow through joy and pain; has made me into the person I am today. I often think of Robert Frost's words: "I have promises to keep and miles to go before I sleep". For me, there are so many unfinished tasks that are waiting to be completed (like my life's story), many places to visit, family and friends I still like to enjoy, be close to, and to share time with.

How much time do I still have left? That I do not know. I do know, however, that each day is a gift God is giving me to grow, to enjoy, to work.

"To be or not to be": that is a question I now ponder upon, reflect on. We know for sure that "to be" in this life is a certain present reality. What happens when we depart, when death cuts into the flow of life? Do we enter a no man's land where "to be" changes into "not to be", into nothingness? These questions we all can answer only on a very personal level.

From early on in my life, I have been guided into the Christian faith, and Christ has always been my Master, my Teacher, my Support. His Resurrection is a precedent and a hope for me to believe; to accept the surety of survival of the soul and a continuation of life hereafter. In many instances, I have deeply felt, more on a metaphysical level, that death does not have the final word, that life continues on. Those moments have often been when someone dear to me has died. As Apostle Paul says in his First letter to Corinthians: "Now we see through a glass, darkly; but then face-to-face: now I know in part; but then shall I know even as also I am known". Death is a curtain that separates our present realities from future possibilities.

I live my days with optimism and look to my future with hope. Certainly, I wish I were healthy and the dark cloud of uncertainty would be lifted from my soul. But, I am trying to accept what is not in my power to change, and do the best I can with what is mine to bear. Faith in God is my rock of strength. This strength I have received through many avenues: my husband Frank's daily concern, the support of my loving family, my friends, my neighbors, and people in general whom I have met along life's way. People's generosity and love have touched me deeply, and this outpouring of support has taught me a valuable lesson about the basic goodness of human hearts.

Part Six:
Coming to Terms...

"...My own life is moving into the last part of its journey. All I wish is that the people I love continue to be with me in this journey, and that I can bring light, not darkness, into their lives. I have no great ambitions or grand resolutions. I just wish for peaceful days, more time to read, walks in the woods with Frank, and to be grateful for the small things. Today, my life is good. Tomorrow it is in God's hands. Nothing is ever totally perfect, totally predictable. My wish is that I continue to learn, to grow, to be a giver, and to accept with patience, grace, and wisdom the gifts of living."

Astrida

A SEARCH FOR ANSWERS

Seldom does morning light bring light into my waking soul. I am not a morning person. I do not feel invigorated, energized, ready to take on the world.

Usually I wake up too early. I look at the illuminated face of the small alarm clock on my bedside table, and my first thought is, "time for more sleep". Retirement has given me the luxury of leisure. There is plenty of time for the "get up and go". I close my eyes and hope for more sleep. But as the seconds and minutes tick on, they do not bring more sleep; with regular intensity and persistence, thought after thought fill my chest with heavy restlessness. I understand, very well, the expression "heartache". It really is an ache that settles in the area where my heart is beating. All the possible negatives visit me; the promises I have not kept, the tasks that have been left undone, the multitude of obligations that wait for my action. Since I tend to procrastinate, this list is too long! The friends who have not called me, or whom I have not called, drift through my receptive consciousness, and with it comes regret, guilt, isolation, and eventually, a deep feeling of aloneness.

"Why do these demons visit me? Where do they come from?" Mornings should fill one's soul with happy expectations, with positive energy. I ask my husband Frank, "How do you feel when you wake up in the morning?" "OK", he says. So, it is only me who is struggling with the waking hour darkness. It is a puzzle I would like to unravel. Is there an answer? Could understanding bring me peace and release? Possibly.

Where to begin my search? Childhood would be the logical time to start. That is when I began my journey, when first impressions and first influences entered my receptive soul. I was a very sensitive child. Like a sponge, I absorbed the outside world, the people in this world. Are there any painful, troubling experiences? My little sister's sudden death when I was three. How deeply did I hurt, how long did I hold onto that loss? No clear memory remains. My godfather's death I remember very well. That hurt deeply. I had just turned six. Godfather was very special to me. I well remember the telephone call. I remember it was Sunday morning and the words: "Augusts drowned." Drowning was such a horrible thing. To be under water, not to be able to come up and to breath! Death under water! There was a hushed talk that he had committed suicide. He knew his rivers, lakes and forests.

The funeral had been on my grandfather's farm. Everything was gray, and I felt lost. I walked around the courtyard and then went into the building where he was. I had to see my godfather. The room was in semidarkness. It was empty, except for a coffin in the middle of the room. I walked over. I looked at him and could not recognize my godfather in the silent body. His face was bluish, very still, very cold, very distant. He was gone. My very special person had deserted me, his special girl. I felt deeply abandoned and betrayed. I am sure that day, and the loss, have never left me. I wear his ring that was given to me on my Confirmation Day. It links me to Augusts Dreimanis, my godfather. It is hard to tell if any permanent subconscious imprints have remained in my soul to rise with the rising sun.

In general, however I remember the early years of my life as a happy and lighthearted time. I loved to dance, to play imaginary games, to create my own perfect world in which I lived out the stories that so playfully and effortlessly came into my fantasy. There is no reason to believe that the mornings of that carefree girl were marked by some kind of pain and darkness. I lived in the security of my dad and mother's love. My sisters were there to share my days and evenings, if I so desired. There was no serious lack in my early childhood days. There were fields and meadows and animals to be with, and Plikeni to feel safe and secure in.

The beginning of school time marked the beginning of life away from home. I was taken to Riga to live with my godmother's family and attend school. I was terribly homesick. Evenings were especially difficult. For several days after my parents' departure, I cried myself to sleep. There was one especially lonely night. The longing to be back in Plikeni and with my parents was overwhelming. Sleep just would not come. My heart ached. My aching heart pleaded with God. "Please take away this pain! Please, please!" Then a miracle happened! The pain vanished and peace replaced it. The relief I felt was magical. God's hand had touched me.

Then came the year of Communist terror. The cruelty of that year is forever embedded - in my memory. People disappeared. What happened to them? Aija Ziedins, my dear school friend, gentle and kind, was among the victims. In the darkness of night, a truck came for her and her family. They, and thousands of other totally innocent, bewildered people, were placed into cattle cars that night, and deported to the distant, desolate Siberia. As we know now, most of them died. Aija died. She had suffered polio as a small child. Her health was fragile. I still cherish her gift, a white ceramic piglet, that she gave me when we said good-bye before starting our summer vacation. I have a feeling that Aijina knew that this was our very last meeting. Three years later the small figurine was one of the very few treasures that I took along on leaving Plikeni.

Could it be that leaving my home, Plikeni, at night, and facing this loss and many uncertainties in the morning, would taint all my mornings from then on? That night cut my life apart. Nothing has ever been the same. What followed was the unpredictable journey of a refugee. Saying good-bye to Latvia fused together with the departure from Plikeni in one single inconceivable loss. It was like walking in a bad dream and wishing for morning's light and awakening.

I remember the sadness of the mornings in the refugee

camps in Germany. We lived in uncertain times, filled with both hope and despair: hope for a miracle of a free Latvia and a road back home, and despair, because of the eventual realization that the miracle will never happen. As Winston Churchill said: "An Iron curtain has descended between the free world of the West and the communist dictatorship in the East". These years of uncertainty affected me deeply. It could just be… that my present is so much a part of yesterday… that the events of this distant past still throw shadows on my life today. It could be.

Accumulation of experiences molds and forms one's psyche. What we are born with and what route our living takes, are most often decided by factors outside us. Many a time, what seems to be predictable and certain, blows away like a feather in the wind. What is one to do? Adjust, accept, regroup, and continue on. That is what living is all about.

As I reflect now, one common denominator comes into focus. There is one common thread that weaves throughout my life; a difficulty detaching myself from places, from people, and from events, and the need to hold on and to remain in touch…but with the painful realization that it can never be possible, that the separations and the losses in my life are irreversible and permanent. Does each new morning remind me of this unalterable truth?

After a fruitless struggle to fall asleep, I get out of bed and the cloud soon lifts. The demons depart. The heavy burden of the waking hours fall off my shoulders, my heart lightens up. I start the new day.

THE ROAD I TRAVELED
My Faith and Philosophy over the years

It takes a great deal of reflecting and analyzing to look back at one's life and its beginnings, to retrace the steps of what makes you who you are today. Life is a journey of learning, growing, and developing, as we walk the road of "cause and effect" that lead to our present beliefs and philosophies.

I was born into a Lutheran family and have always belonged to this Church. My mother was a highly ethical, religious, and generous person, almost puritanical in her beliefs. She always impressed on her children the Christian values of humility, charity, and love of one's neighbor. We were taught to share and give the bigger half to the other person. My father taught me the value of fairness and the respect for each individual person. Both of my parents believed in hard work. Both of my parents, in their own way, gave me the foundation on which I could continue to build and develop my own faith and philosophy of life. One thing never changed: from early on I have tried to follow Christ's example and teachings. The Christian values were the cornerstone of my life, the source of strength in times of trials, and the path to follow in times of indecision and confusion.

What has my faith meant to me? I can truly say that, without the belief in a Higher Power, in a loving and caring God, the trials, the pain, and the losses that I have had to face in my life would have been, I believe, too heavy to bear. My faith has always carried me through. I have been strong because, behind me, was God's love and support.

Because of my faith, I have seldom felt really alone. Here, I would like to mention an incident that clearly showed to me God's grace and caring.

In my forties, I went through a very traumatic and painful period. There was so much darkness and hurt in my heart that each day felt like a burden too hard to carry. One day, while looking at rows of paperbacks on a store shelf, I noticed a small volume, Beyond Ourselves, written by Catherine Marshall. The title of the book seemed to say something to me. I bought the book and started to read it almost immediately. Here, Catherine Marshall was telling her own story about a very desperate period in her life. She related an incident when, through a miracle of God's love, she became a believer and was lifted out of her misery. There was a chapter in the book where she outlined a way how, through prayer and total submission to God's will, one can find His grace. It was a Sunday afternoon when I read this. I was home alone, sitting at the dining room window overlooking our garden in its summer colors and beauty. I prayed. My whole being was crying out to the Lord: "Please, God, please, remove the darkness from my heart!"

A miracle happened. An overwhelming light and joy entered my soul. From the dark pain, I stepped into a brilliant sunlight. God's presence was with me...so very real, so very true that I could almost touch it. For years from that moment on, I walked in light, always knowing that He was with me. The Presence is still with me, not in such intensity as in the period directly following the experience of light, but very real and very true. I know that God is and God loves.

Did I ever strongly question God's existence? Not really. There certainly have been times of not understanding the reasons for the horrible events that the world experiences, and the almost unbearable suffering of the human family; why God does not intervene. There is really no good answer. However, my belief is that we are God's messengers, God's instruments on this earth. It is up to us to change, to make the world a better place, a more loving place. God gave us a free will. We cannot hold God responsible for man's inhumanity to man. I also believe that God does intervene in our lives and helps us to solve problems. "Ask and it will be given to you". We have to listen and follow. In my life, the most serious mistakes have been made when I did not listen to the "small voice" inside me. An example I can mention is my first marriage. When Arvid and I were making plans for our wedding, my heart was not filled with joyful expectations and lightness. It was heavy and sad. I never listened to what "the small voice" was telling me. We both lived many years in an unhappy relationship. It could have been avoided, for both of us.

What is my philosophy? What conclusions have I made through my travels on earth? I believe that man is a spiritual being, that this spirit is not a part of matter, and is not an accident of earthly evolution. I am inclined to think that the spirit of man is an extension of a Universal spirit, a universal consciousness, and has its origin in God. We have been given the thirst for spiritual and intellectual growth.

In my early life, as I was growing, developing, and learning, several questions pursued me. Why am I here? What is the meaning of my life? How can I be useful? What can I do to make a difference? At that time, I believed that something grand had to be accomplished by me to make my life worthwhile. I am much humbler now. If I can be even just a little bit useful to my family, my friends and neighbors, that is almost enough to justify my contribution, my life. I try to keep in mind Jesus words: "What you do to the smallest one of them, you do to me".

My life has gone through many phases, many periods of growth and regression. It is like climbing a mountain: one has to go through some very difficult terrain, slide back and rest for a while, but then one resumes the journey, and finally reaches the summit. One has to keep on learning and growing, keep on climbing. This is our responsibility. Life has taught me many good lessons. I have grown in wisdom in my own way. At least, I have tried to follow the road that, in my view, was the right one for me.

THE GROWING EDGE

When I retired, I attended an "Empowerment Workshop" that encouraged self-analyses, and was lead through a path to finding one's own truth, one's personal "power mandala". The process was to become, to evolve, to recognize the "growing edge" of one's being. It acknowledged that to "know thyself" was central to a content life, and the workshop's goals were to lead us to this self awareness.

As in nature, a tree or any other growing, living thing develops a tender, sensitive area at the edge where the next growth will develop; so does a person feel a particular sensitivity, a vague or more marked dissatisfaction about an area in one's personality or life where a change needs to be made. This is one's "growing edge". It is important to respect this often vague invitation, to look at those feelings closely, and to follow their lead.

Everybody's life is rich in challenges and opportunities. It is disappointing, and at times tragic, to neglect our body's or our soul's call for change. In my own life, at times, I have experienced the nagging feeling that all is not right. To find the true cause for this call to change has needed reflection and introspection; to look within and ask "what", "why" and to search for my "growing edge". It has not always been easy, and I did not always want to change. My nature is to procrastinate, and I find it easy "to think about it tomorrow".

Through the course of this workshop, we looked at seven

areas of growth our "power mandala": love, commitment, creative mind development, discipline, lightness, inner guidance, and support systems. To look at, and analyze each of these areas, leads to one's own inner truth. A person can grow in many areas at the same time: expand, change, and evolve.

The most important "growing edges" for me have been my inner development, my relationships with other people, friendships, and my relationship with God.

Much has depended on taking inventory, an inner "soil test" to find out my fundamental attitudes towards life. To follow the call of some inner urge for change, is often very hard work. But it is also difficult to walk around with a dark center and a troubled mind. I sit down with myself, ask questions, and listen. It takes time and discipline to allow the growing edge to grow.

Life is a classroom. Experience is such a marvelous teacher if we care to listen and absorb the lesson. I seem to learn a lot by osmosis. The learned lesson comes to light when I am tested at some future time. To remember and not to repeat past mistakes is a challenge. Always a challenge! There is always room for growth here: to have a vision, to be sensitive to one's self and to one's environment, and understand the relationship between the two.

To believe in my own self, to be strong and intact in my inner being, is forever a tested ground. Often, I feel very vulnerable and fragile. If my strength is tested in some way by circumstances or people, I question my self-worth and my power to overcome and persevere, another growing edge, another tender area in my evolvement and growth. I do realize, though, that I have a strong and basically sound inner center. It needs to surface at these times of testing.

The foremost, the most important source of strength in my life, is my fundamental trust in God. It is my sincere belief that each person is God's instrument on this earth, that through us He does His work. It is a great responsibility to do God's work the best I can. That is, and always will be, my most important "growing edge".

FAITH, HOPE, AND LOVE

Lately, my thoughts often turn and return to the meaning and value of these three basic and very important human emotions - what they really are, and what the significance of each of them are in our lives.

I have been faced with situations where faith and hope have been an encore that has sustained me. When I heard my internist say: "Your pathology report came back as positive for cancer", the world seemed to close around me. It took time to comprehend, adjust, and raise my heart up to light again. Faith was what I held on to: faith in my ability to overcome the disease, faith in the prayers of my family and friends, and my own faith in God's love and support.

FAITH is a guiding light in our human existence. Most fundamentally and importantly, we need to have faith in ourselves, our ability to perform, to be of value, to have the wisdom that leads us through life. One can have faith in many things, positive as well as negative, I suppose: faith in God or other Supreme Being, an orderly Universe, the value of life, ones destiny, faith in the final victory of good over evil. I wonder if the terrorists who wage destruction on innocent human lives, as yesterday in Madrid, Spain, are guided by some strange version of faith. I wonder. Faith, as I would like to define it, should lead one to something positive, and support positive actions, and goals.

HOPE is another human emotion that is tremendously

important to a healthy and positive living. Again, I can refer to my own experiences in the past year. I look back to how I felt about my cancer (I say "my" even though I rather not claim it as belonging to me) and recall my immediate reaction to the oncologist's statement: "You can be dead in six months". "You are joking", I wished to say, but said nothing. I did not believe him, but the seed of concern and doubt was placed in my heart. I responded to the chemo treatment very well, started to feel healthy again, but I never could shake off the threatening cloud of cancer lurking around the corner in wait to get hold of me again. What was seriously injured in me was my sense of hope- the hope that I would be well again. I realize now, in a most profound way, that hope is what a person needs to live a healthy and free life. Hope is what gives us strength to face tomorrow with a smile and sense of promise. Hope is another encore so very essential to our happiness. It is like the awakening of spring in nature, filled with expectation of the greening of our universe, the renewal of life in all its glorious colors. When hope is injured, one looks to tomorrow with doubt, always questioning and always wondering.

LOVE, the third emotion I wish to talk about, is, in my view, the very soil that our tree of life is rooted in. Love gives us light, strength, support, and the very essence of our will to live. Human life cannot develop properly and adequately without love's nourishment. Here, I do not want to talk about scientific proof of the importance of being loved. Every day we see and hear about wayward souls, children and adults who have wilted without love's support and nurturing. In my personal life, I have been abundantly blessed with loving and caring people. Especially, again, I have to relate back to my experience during the past year. Love is what has sustained me and given me strength to go on when the going got rough. It was the light that I could hold onto and gave me the reason and will to survive. If there were no love and no one who cared, would there be any value in living?

It is difficult to say which of the three emotions, faith, hope, and love, are the most vital in a healthy, happy, and fulfilled life. All are essential, all are important and necessary.

CIRCLING THOUGHTS

Thoughts come and go, persistently, and not in good order or even logically. They visit like uninvited guests, linger for a bit, and leave.

This morning I was busy organizing my day. As I was doing it, I suddenly felt the precursor to the very unwelcome visitor, migraine, come on. It invariably disrupts and changes my day. The rescue is fiurinol, the medicine I always carry along, just in case. I swallowed a pill and lay down to relax. Fiurinol helps my headache, but it also gives me sort of an unreal, euphorical feeling. As I was lying on the sofa, trying to relax, a deluge of thoughts, the circling kind, danced behind my closed eyes.

A note about "circling thought" - Years ago I attended a workshop called "Practical Philosophy". It was a very interesting experience, and "circling thoughts" was a term used to describe undisciplined, uncontrolled thinking.

There I was, trying to relax, while at the same time, visited by unexpected insights into experiences, feelings. I could not control my brain; it worked outside my will, opening many avenues for events, sights, and feelings to come in and go. It felt like I was apart from myself, being fed information from an outside source. I was looking at my past, my childhood on the farm. I felt the warm security of the evenings around our dining room table, the family together, the games, and the talks, the smells of spring and summer, the apple orchard in bloom, and the fragrance of new cut grass. Then the picture changed. The peaceful scene faded away. The warmth of family gatherings, summer smells and colors are replaced by the pain of leaving Plikeni, the subsequent good-bye to Latvia, and by the darkness of foreign occupation, war, and refugee camps. I walked in and out of events, as in a dream. For a moment, the faces of Lenin, Stalin and Hitler step into the flow of images. My soul is captured by the evil of these men; the trail of suffering, damage, and death that follow in their footsteps; the seemingly permanent effects of their actions; the seeds planted by their depraved minds, by their hearts of darkness. Then bin Laden comes out of the shadows and walks the road of evil of his predecessors. Another time, another century, but strangely still the same. Trapped. The world of today, the war in Afghanistan, the bombs, the suffering humanity, New York on September 11th, the flaming twin towers loomed before me. In a short span of time, my mind had taken long leaps, traveled great distances, and experienced a whole scale of emotions.

As the effects of fiurinol wore off, I climbed out of my dream state and returned to reality and my aching head. Some fundamental, hard questions remain, though: where are we, as a people, going? What are the reasons for our insane evil acts? Where and what are the solutions that will take us out of the hell we often live in? Where hides our goodness, our salvation, the wisdom of ages?

Thoughts persist; the mind looks for reasons; the soul longs for peace. I think of the great minds, the prophets, the wise, and the good who have lived on our earth. There is light and power of the positive. I want and need to believe that, in the end, it will overcome the dark forces that sometimes enter the human spirit. Among the great and the holy, there is the sitting, introspective Buddha, whose images were destroyed by the ruling Taliban in Afghanistan, and Mohamed, whose teachings guide the Muslims, including BinLaden, however misguided he seems to be. There is Christ, the Son of God, who came to earth to teach men to be brothers, and to love one's neighbor as one's self. Certainly there is goodness. It does not really hide. It is among us, walks beside us, is in us. It is the responsibility of each and every one of us to unravel the secret wisdom and let it take root and find the lost Paradise.

SEASONS OF LIFE

Seasons. They come in regular progression. Nothing changes their sequence or their predictability. We know that spring is the very beginning, when life begins. It opens, rises out of the earth, and greets the sun and air, full of hope, full of growth, and full of its future. Such a happy, joyous season!

Summer follows. Life force develops into full fruition, growing, and completing itself. Summer. One can say it with a smile on one's face, and a song in one's heart. Summer is a happy season, a season when it is good to be alive, to be part of the rhythm of nature.

Comes autumn. The sound of autumn is a melancholy sound. It resonates in a minor key. It is sadly beautiful, a golden peace; a bright light before silence and death, like a light bulb that flares before it burns out. I walk through autumn as through a wake. Soon, very soon a "good-bye" will be said to all that spring nurtured and summer developed. Autumn rings cemetery bells -the Saturday evening bells from my childhood that were rung in the small country cemetery where my two sisters and my godfather were buried. It was a beautiful and peaceful place. One could sit there silently and reflect on what once was, and now, is gone. Air filled with sadness. That is the sound of fall to me. That sounds fall to me.

Winter. So white, so cold, so lifeless. The season when all visible life goes under a deep sleep. I want to hold my breath, close my eyes and just wait. Yes, wait. Somewhere, beyond all the stillness and lifelessness there is a hidden spring of life. To wait for another beginning. To know that spring will come again is the only way to survive winter.

Man's life cycles parallel those of nature. The seasons of our existence are a predictable journey. Childhood and youth is our spring. Our summer reflects the years of productivity and accomplishments, our personal maturity. From there, we drift, almost unnoticed, into the autumn of our lifetime, when the energy and zest for new beginnings start to ebb, when our steps grow slower and time runs on faster. This is the time when one wants more than ever to hold on to the moment, wants to resist the ebb of time. The clock ticks on. Winter comes. Suddenly we look into the sunset and have to come to terms with the finality of our existence and be able to say good-bye. Our life is a one-way street. There is no turning back, no possibility of retrieving lost or wasted moments, no way to relive happy, blissful ones.

I write this now as I am facing the autumn of my life, and somehow have to find the wisdom and strength to accept my age and my finality graciously. For me, it is a difficult task. As a child, I felt that my life was a never-ending process and would continue into eternity. The horizons were wide, the possibilities limitless. The end was unimaginable. It did not exist. People around me were of all ages. Some were young; some were old. Were they ever children like me? Would I ever arrive at their point in life? I remember an incidence when, for the first time, I did think of the possibility of growing old. I was about fourteen years old and was coming home for a school vacation. On the train, an old woman sat directly across from me. I looked at her, observed her wrinkled face, the strands of grey hair visible from under her kerchief, the knobby hands resting on her lap, her bent shoulders. Everything about this woman was old and grey. "Will I ever be this old?", I had wondered. "No, no! Never!" I immediately answered my own silent question. 'Me' and 'old' were not reconcilable.

That was a long time ago. Nothing stands still. My life has marched on. My childhood, the growing up years in Latvia, in Plikeni and Riga, went by quickly. They were not counted; they were like golden grain filling the almost empty basket of my lifetime. There was so much room, so much space for growing, for living, for gathering. When I wished to push time ahead, to do the things that my parents did not feel I was ready for, my mother reinforced my feeling of limitless time: "You have your whole lifetime ahead of you. You will have plenty of chances to do all this". Time was plentiful and years needed to be counted only to add some importance to my person, to become an adult and to be counted as an equal among equals.

Now, I look back with a touch of regret: "Why did I not savor more of those golden days, the carefree times when my parents covered my living with the umbrella of their caretaking?" That wisdom came much later - the wisdom to value this irreplaceable time, this ever-moving time. Spring, summer, autumn. One season followed another. I never gave much thought to the progression of time. My mother's words were sounding in my ears: "Your whole life is ahead of you." I followed that sound, and age did not effect me. It has been a blessing and also a curse. A blessing, because it allowed me to always be interested in new adventures, to learn, to grow; to expect tomorrow to bring a gift of newness; to be among people much younger than me and feel their contemporary. On the other hand, it kept me from accepting my age. Each birthday added another year to the count. I ignored the count. But somewhere, sometime, I have to come to terms with today, with this place in time; my particular time; if for no other reason than to settle my accounts with life, and to clear the path for my exit.

With a heavy heart, I realize my finiteness and the unpredictability of the final call. It can come tomorrow. I remember my father's words: "One has to live as if one will live forever, but be prepared to die tomorrow". He was a wise man and a good man. I have always tried to live by his example. I am taking his words to heart.

THE THIRD MILLENNIUM

I write this when less than thirty days are remaining in this decade, in this century. This is the time to reflect, and time to look ahead, but is it time for resolutions? I seldom make New Year's resolutions. I wonder how seriously people take these promises and how many are kept.

This essay is not going to be so much about what I'd like to do or change in my own life. It is about a dream I had a long time ago, one of a perfect world, and it will include my thoughts and reflections on the immediate and more distant past.

Sometime in my early childhood, my mother mentioned that around the year 2000, a thousand-year peace on earth would begin. Back then, the year 2000 was in the unbelievably distant future. "I may not even be around," I thought. "Oh, but how I would love to be there!" A shortcut to that time, to that future world, were my fantasies and dreams. An imaginary magic carpet took me to a world of green pastures, where lions and lambs roamed together in perfect harmony, as it was described in the Bible. People greeted each other with smiles and hugs, singing, laughing, and dancing. A golden sun spread its light from a cloudless aquamarine sky. No angry faces were seen, no harsh words heard. I lived there in a loving and peaceful community, embraced by light. It was clear to me that this world was the Paradise where Adam and Eve once lived before they were thrown out of the Garden of Eden. Now it had come back to earth to give everybody a new beginning.

Since then, much time has slipped by. The year 2000 has arrived, showing no signs of my mother's prophecies or the fulfillment of my childhood dream. We leave behind us a century of much destruction and evil. In Europe, two world wars and two bloody and ruthless regimes have left a permanent scar on the flesh of human history. Many innocent people have been killed: more than 24 million in Stalin's Russia, more than 6 million in Hitler's Germany. These numbers do not include the many who fell in the killing fields of the two world wars. Yes, this has not been the best of centuries!

But what was the world like at the end of the first Millennium? I wonder. I remove Roland Stromberg's "The History of Western Civilization" from my bookshelf and leaf through its pages. I read and learn that the world was not a kind place then. Actually, the times were very harsh and barbaric! After the death of Charlemagne in 814, the order that he had established in Europe under his reign fell apart, and a time of general demoralization of society set in. Vikings from the north attacked France and England, burning and killing, ending the political order and the Celtic-Saxon monastic life, which, at that time, held the candle of learning. From the East came the fierce Magyar horsemen, who rained much destruction on the local people, and who eventually settled in the present day Hungary. Arabs invaded from the south, choking off trade. It was a world of chaos, described in chronicles, as a world where "robbery and burglary became the custom, and everybody was a brigand." Europe experienced another Dark Age, and only slowly advanced toward civilization during the first part of the Second Millennium. For the human race, it had been a rough road to this point in its history, with many setbacks.

I must conclude, though, that human progress has certainly gone forward since the very dark beginning of the last Millennium. Another question remains to be answered, though: have we, as people, grown in goodness, in spirituality, in love, in understanding of each other? In that respect, are we any different from our brothers of long ago?

A few days ago, I had a very interesting conversation with a 90-year-old friend of mine. She is a very wise and enlightened woman, and during our long friendship has given me many insights and much food for thought. I told her that I am writing an essay about the next Millennium and, also, what I thought about the century that we are about to leave behind. She said: "Astrida, I think that this has been one of the best centuries! Disregard our own personal tragedies, like losing our home or our family members." I must mention here, that my friend had left Latvia as a refugee from Communist occupation with her six small children. Her husband had been imprisoned by the Soviets. She survived the hardships of war and homelessness, took care of her children, raised them, and educated them. "In the big picture our personal lives are not really important", she continued. "Just think of the progress that we have made! Imagine where we, as women were, in the beginning of this century, and where we are now. Look at the world of today, the science, the technology, and the medicine. Such a big leap forward! The next century, the next millennium? I do not know. In any case, it will be very different. But it will be good," she concluded. I left my friend, Ilga, with a new and different perspective.

What will this Millennium bring to the people on this planet earth? Actually, what will we, the people, bring to our planet earth? I hope that somehow, someway, we will learn to live together in peace, learn to communicate and understand each other as individuals and as nations. We have come a long way from the year one thousand. It has not been an easy road but an upward climb, nevertheless. The "thousand years of peace on earth" that my mother talked about, and I had visited in my childhood dream, is not a very realistic prospect. But, who knows? Miracles do happen!

My own life is moving into the last part of its journey. All I wish is that the people I love continue to be with me in this journey, and that I can bring light, not darkness into their lives. I have no great ambitions or grand resolutions. Just peaceful days I wish for; more time to read, walk the woods with Frank, and be grateful for the small things. Today, my life is good. Tomorrow it is in God's hands. Nothing is ever totally perfect, totally predictable. My wish is that I continue to learn, to grow, to be a giver, and to accept with patience, grace, and wisdom the gifts of living.

EPILOGUE

I have come to the end of my story. It has been a long journey, and a blessed one. The beginning of this project was not easy. I was a traveler without a specific road plan. I have to thank Sophia Nibi, my knowledgeable and sensitive teacher, who gave me guidelines to follow and basic rules for good writing. Also, my fellow writers were of great help with their critique and suggestions. My first writing exercises were on topics suggested by Mrs. Nibi: "My First Memory", "Family Gatherings", "My Favorite Holiday". Soon things started to flow more easily, memories emerged, and forgotten events came out of a hidden past. Writing my life's story turned into one of the most exciting and meaningful projects I have ever been involved with.

I believe that life is God's gift, a treasure to be valued. We come into this world totally innocent and vulnerable. We do not know what to expect, where we will go, or what this journey will be like. If I remember correctly, it was the British philosopher, Herbert Spencer, who said that a person starts ones life as a blank page, and that the page is filled, the story is written, as one journeys through ones time on earth. Much of what we experience is not of our choice. We are placed in a certain place in time, with certain travel companions. What shapes and molds us are the moments in history that we are made to face, the people we come in contact and interact with. Much depends, also, on our biological makeup, our psyche.

Each life holds an interesting story. The story has to be told to give it visibility.

I am glad that I took the time to examine and record my life experiences. It has given me an opportunity to revisit places that otherwise would have never come back to life, to meet some of the people from various periods in my life who have given me gifts of friendship, love or pain. As I revisited my past, I came upon many wonderfully sunny periods, especially from my childhood. As I remembered those, my heart often was filled with joy and lightness. I also faced experiences that had been very traumatic and painful: the very dark times when all seemed to crumble, fall into a black nothingness, the night when I left my precious Plikeni, or the gray morning when the shores of Latvia disappeared in the distance as the refugee ship took us to an unknown future, the night when my dad died. To look at those moments was very painful. But to reexamine them gave me a chance to see the lessons that I had learned through loss and suffering. The pain at the end was also a blessing. I survive, and am a wiser person. And a stronger one.

By writing my memories of these long ago times and places, and recalling the people who had been an integral part of my life during each of these periods, I have come to realize how rich and blessed my life has been. I did not choose, and would not have chosen considerable sections of my life's journey, but had I not experienced the darkness or the shadows, would I have been able to fully appreciate the light and happy times?

I would like to conclude by quoting Henry W. Beecher: "God asks no man whether he will accept life. That is not the choice. You must take it. The only choice is how."